"*Positive Couple Therapy* forges a creative, dynamic marriage: excellent scholarship and real-world tools. It offers an accessible, practical guide for helping couples reclaim their stories of togetherness. Beyond that, it inspires all of us to re-discover and share the precious crystals of personal memory that reflect our deepest love; to learn how to make the subtle but daring shift to not only being me, but being 'We.'"

—*Susan Bluck, PhD, University of Florida*

"Jefferson A. Singer and Karen Skerrett have done a great favor for couples and couples therapists. Our whole society needs a lot less focus on 'me' and a lot more emphasis on 'We.' Perhaps the best parts of the book are the stories—the authors use illustrations from their own lives in addition to tales of couples who find meaning in the relationships they create together."

—*Gene Combs, MD, Associate Clinical Professor of Psychiatry, Pritzker School of Medicine, University of Chicago. Co-author of* Narrative Therapy: The Social Construction of Preferred Realities *and* Narrative Therapy with Couples.

"Singer and Skerrett have written a wonderful book about working with less distressed couples that accentuates building and drawing on a sense of 'We.' This book artfully integrates positive psychology, narrative practice, and an often ignored thread of research that unequivocally points to the value a sense of 'We' has in couple satisfaction and individual happiness. Full of wonderful life stories and case examples, Singer and Skerrett's book points to how couples can actively cultivate and grow their We-Stories and thus their relationships."

—*Jay Lebow, PhD, ABPP, Clinical Professor, Family Institute at Northwestern University*

POSITIVE COUPLE THERAPY

Positive Couple Therapy: Using We-Stories to Enhance Resilience is a significant step forward in the couple literature. Utilizing a strengths-based approach, it teaches therapists and couples a unique method for uncovering positive potential within a relationship. The authors demonstrate how We-Stories—created, recovered, and made anew—provide essential elements of connection. With vivid imagery, these stories capture the couple's sense of We-ness, highlighting memorable moments of compassion, acceptance, and respect. A shared commitment to the "We" simultaneously builds the relationship and enables each individual in the partnership to feel a greater degree of both accountability and autonomy. Couples that can find their stories, share them with each other, and then carry them forward to family, friends, and a larger community are likely to preserve a sense of mutuality that will thrive over a lifetime of partnership.

Positive Couple Therapy provides simple and practical instruction for reclaiming positive stories that can catalyze hope in relationships that have become stressed and strained. The authors weave together cutting-edge thinking and research in attachment theory, narrative therapy, neuroscience, and adult development, as well as their own research and clinical experience to present vivid case histories, step-by-step strategies, exercises, questionnaires, and interview techniques. They cover a range of contemporary couple experiences: couples in conflict, LGBT partnerships, deployed and discharged military couples, and couples at various points across the life span. The authors' unique ME (To US) Scale, a 10-item tool that assesses the degree of mutuality a couple possesses at the start of treatment, gives therapists of any theoretical orientation the ability to put this intervention to immediate use.

Jefferson A. Singer is the Elizabeth H. Faulk Professor of Psychology at Connecticut College and a clinical psychologist in private practice.

Karen Skerrett is a staff member at the Family Institute/Center for Applied Psychological Studies at Northwestern University and Clinical Associate Professor in the Department of Psychology at Northwestern University.

POSITIVE COUPLE THERAPY

Using We-Stories to Enhance Resilience

Jefferson A. Singer and Karen Skerrett

Routledge
Taylor & Francis Group

NEW YORK AND LONDON

First published 2014
by Routledge
711 Third Avenue, New York, NY 10017

and by Routledge
27 Church Road, Hove, East Sussex BN3 2FA

*Routledge is an imprint of the Taylor & Francis Group, an informa
business*

© 2014 Taylor & Francis

The right of Jefferson A. Singer and Karen Skerrett to be identified as authors
of this work has been asserted by them in accordance with sections 77 and 78
of the Copyright, Designs and Patents Act 1988.

Library of Congress Cataloging-in-Publication Data

Singer, Jefferson A.
Positive couple therapy : using we-stories to enhance resilience / Jefferson Singer,
   Karen Skerrett.
     pages cm
 1. Couples therapy.   2. Marital psychotherapy.   I. Skerrett, Karen, 1946–
II. Title.
RC488.5.S544 2014
616.89'1562–dc23   2013040385

ISBN: 978-0-415-82446-0 (hbk)
ISBN: 978-0-415-82447-7 (pbk)
ISBN: 978-0-203-38399-5 (ebk)

Typeset in New Baskerville
by Apex CoVantage, LLC

Printed and bound in the United States of America by Sheridan Books, Inc. (a Sheridan Group Company)

From Jefferson—To my parents and Anne

From Karen—To Roger

CONTENTS

ABOUT THE AUTHORS

Jefferson A. Singer is the Elizabeth H. Faulk Professor of Psychology at Connecticut College and a clinical psychologist in private practice. He is the author of four books, *Personality and Psychotherapy: Treating the Whole Person* (New York, NY: Guilford Press); *Memories that Matter* (Oakland, CA: New Harbinger); *Message in a Bottle* (New York, NY: The Free Press); and *The Remembered Self: Emotion and Memory in Personality* (with Peter Salovey, New York, NY: The Free Press), and the co-editor of a fifth, *At Play in the Fields of Consciousness: Essays in Honor of Jerome L. Singer* (Mahwah, NJ: Erlbaum; again with Peter Salovey). He has published  more than 90 articles, chapters, and book reviews in the fields of psychotherapy, personality, and autobiographical memory. Professor Singer served as an associate editor for the journals *Contemporary Psychology* and the *Journal of Personality,* and is on the editorial boards of the *Review of General Psychology, Imagination, Personality and Cognition,* and the *Journal of Personality.* He is a Fellow of the American Psychological Association and past recipient of a Fulbright Distinguished Scholar Award, the Theodore R. Sarbin Award for Narrative Psychology, and the Henry A. Murray Award for the Study of Lives. His work on memory and psychotherapy has been featured in national and international media outlets, including *Cosmopolitan, Body and Soul, BBC Radio, Psychology Today, Bottom Line Personal, Fitness, Newsday,* and *The Hartford Courant,* among others.

Karen Skerrett is a staff member at the Family Institute/Center for Applied Psychological Studies at Northwestern University and Clinical Associate Professor in the Department of Psychology at Northwestern University. She most recently was an Associate Professor at the University of San Diego, where she designed and implemented the advanced practice program in Psychiatric Mental Health Nursing. She has taught at the University of Illinois, the Adler Institute, and has been a longtime faculty member at the Chicago Center for Family Health, an affiliate of the University of Chicago. She maintains ties to her dual training as a nurse and a clinical psychologist through a long-term clinical and consulting practice specializing in the treatment of couples and families, particularly those challenged by illness and disability. She has contributed numerous book chapters and articles to professional journals and is co-editing the upcoming *Couple Resilience Across the Lifespan: Emerging Perspectives* with Dr. Karen Fergus for Springer Press. She reviews for *Family Process* and the *Journal of Family Nursing,* among others. She presents nationally and internationally on adult development, life cycle transitions, innovative approaches to couple treatment, and the unique processes of relational resilience and growth in couples across the life span. Her work has appeared in *The Chicago Tribune, Parents* magazine, and *The San Diego Union Tribune.*

ACKNOWLEDGMENTS

Jefferson would like to make the following acknowledgments: First, I would like to acknowledge all of the many couples with whom I have worked over the last 30 years in my psychotherapy practice. Their courage and honesty in trying to work through the challenges of finding happiness and meaning through lasting relationships are a continual inspiration to me. Next, I would like to acknowledge Beata Labunko and Jenna Baddeley, two former graduate students and now good friends of mine. Their research efforts and discussions with me have played significant roles in my understanding of "We-ness" and how to measure it. Beata is a co-author of the ME (To US), an instrument for measuring mutuality in couples, and my collaborator on many We-ness projects. Jenna extended this work and conducted an innovative study of We-ness in postdeployment military couples. I would also like to acknowledge the research of Nicole Alea Albada who has studied "relationship-defining" memories and also collaborated with me in examining the importance of shared memories in couples.

For the last decade, I have taught a course on family and couple therapy for advanced undergraduates and MA students. In this seminar students interview couples from the community who have sustained lasting and successful partnerships. I purposely select couples that come from diverse backgrounds, representing a cross section of economic level, sexual orientation, age, and race/ethnicity. I am extremely grateful to all of the students and couples who have participated in this process; they have taught me invaluable lessons about the rich variety of love and commitment that partners can express. A special thank you to Tracee Reiser, Director of the Office of Volunteers for Community Service and Associate Dean of Community Learning at Connecticut College, for her assistance in identifying couples in the New London community. In West Hartford, I would like to thank Barbara Rosen, PhD, for her work with me as a co-therapist with couples and as a sounding board for many of the ideas in this book about best practices in couple therapy. I would also like to thank Larry Vogel, a close friend, fellow West Hartford resident, and Professor of Philosophy at Connecticut College, for his thoughtful discussions with me of the underlying themes of mutuality and We-ness that are at the heart of this book.

As with all my previous books, I must acknowledge the generous support of Connecticut College for providing me with sabbatical time and research funds to pursue my writing endeavors. I am also grateful to have an outstanding group of colleagues in the Psychology Department at Conn, as well as the tireless support of Nancy MacLeod, our department administrator.

Finally, I could not have written this book without all the lessons about We-ness that I have gleaned from my family—my parents who recently celebrated their 64th wedding anniversary; my brother, Jon; my brother, Bruce, and his wife, Mary; and my two daughters, Olivia and Chloe; and most of all, my wife, Anne.

*****

First, last, and always, I want to acknowledge my family: my husband, Roger, and our children, Chris and Sarah, whose steadfast love and support offered my first real experience of belonging. My daughter-in-law, Kate, and son-in-law, Chris, have enriched our foursome beyond measure. My best and favorite times are with all of you.

To my extended family, who provided my first experience of the "We" and continue to offer great humor, high energy, and nourishing webs of connection.

I have been privileged to have wonderful scholars and clinicians as teachers, many of whom have gone on to become friends. In particular, I acknowledge Mihaly Csikszentmihalyi, who first got me thinking about and examining what makes life worthwhile, who critically shaped my thinking, and whose humanity touched my heart. Expert clinicians: Bill Pinsoff, who first offered me a systematic way to think about couples and a resilient concept of my own family; Lori Teagno, who walks the talk; Bernie Liebowitz-my first supervisor in family therapy, now lifelong colleague and friend, Froma Walsh, John Rolland and other colleagues at the Chicago Center for Family Health whose strengths-based approach continues to guide my own clinical work; Judy Jordan and JBTI scholars and friends who wed the concepts of We-ness to resilience and stimulated all of what has followed. I value the countless discussions of their ideas of mutuality—its parameters and possibilities.

Jefferson and I would also like to thank Marta Moldvai for her astute editorial work, as well as Elizabeth Lotto and Denise File for their assistance in the production of this volume.

And to the last 30-plus years of couples who have graced my door; I am honored to share this journey and grateful for your willingness to teach me that if you're willing to do the work, the rewards can be great. You are a daily inspiration. Finally, acknowledgments to the couples who are part of the ongoing "Couple Projects"; the stories you tell enrich us all.

Heartfelt thanks,
Karen

PREFACE

New books are designed to fill gaps, and this volume is no exception. The positive psychology movement developed in the science of psychology because researchers recognized that the field had placed too little emphasis on the affirming aspects of human nature—joy, gratitude, compassion, and courage, among other positive emotions. In a parallel fashion, the field of couple therapy has made great strides in its empirical foundations and accompanying clinical applications, but there is still a large gap in its articulation and cultivation of the most powerful positive aspects of successful lasting relationships. Couple therapists are grappling with research evidence that suggests that simply teaching communication strategies and modifying daily behaviors is insufficient in helping couples develop new, lasting emotional habits. Hope lies in new research that is pointing to how positive interventions can increase and sustain the development of compassionate love. The purpose of this volume is to add support to this perspective by defining a critical ingredient of resilient and nurturing relationships—a couple's shared sense of the "**We**," or the degree to which they think and act with the best interest of the relationship in mind. In addition to unpacking what makes for healthy "We-ness" in couples, we offer a specific method for building stronger We-ness—the identification and telling of "**We-Stories**." When couples share vivid imagistic narratives of connection and compassion, these stories bring alive the basic love and commitment each partner feels for the other.

Although the concepts of We-ness and We-Stories may sound like lofty sentiments, this book is a down-to-earth guide for fellow couple therapists, therapists-in-training, and students. Couples can also read this book as an adjunct to their couple treatment. The chapters ahead walk the reader through a thorough discussion of exactly what we mean by We-ness and where this concept fits within the contemporary scientific and clinical literature. After describing the key elements of We-ness, we demonstrate how to use questionnaires and interview techniques to measure a couple's current sense of We-ness. Crucially, far from a term that describes merger, We-ness emphasizes the cultivation of a third entity (the relationship), one that requires two developed "I's." Throughout these pages, we repeatedly illustrate how a healthy sense of We-ness both simultaneously builds the relationship and enables each individual within the couple to feel a greater sense of self-respect and autonomy than they have previously known.

Drawing on our research in narrative psychology and our own clinical practices, we show how We-Stories are different from other kinds of shared stories that couples might tell. We then illustrate how these unique stories can be leveraged to cultivate a stronger and more resilient relationship. We offer step-by-step techniques, exercises, and lists of critical questions to move couples toward the development of We-Stories that highlight mutuality and reciprocity. We particularly show how distressed couples stuck in stories of frustration and isolation can shift their narratives toward an affirmation of what is healthy and positive in their relationships. We also devote chapters to the shifting nature of We-Stories at different developmental stages of the adult life cycle and to the sharing of We-Stories across generations and with a community beyond the immediate circle of the couple and its family members. We believe that the cultivation of "We-consciousness" can lead not only to a shift in the quality of a couple's relationship, but also to changes in how each partner interacts in the workplace, community, and larger society. Once couples place a premium on the importance of relationship, they are likely to become more expansive, compassionate, and generative in all aspects of their lives.

At an earlier point in time, couple therapy typically addressed marriages between heterosexual individuals and often did not reach across the wide span of race, ethnicity, and economic backgrounds. The current volume takes a different and far more inclusive perspective, drawing on our clinical experience with couples of different sexual orientations, cultural, and socioeconomic backgrounds. We also try to be sensitive to shifting dynamics in gender/power contexts and variations in how individuals choose to configure their partnerships. However, our emphasis in this book, and in our clinical work, is on committed, long-term partnerships.

We must emphasize that the cultivation of We-Stories is not the appropriate intervention for couples that come to therapy in certain kinds of extreme crises. In couples where there has been infidelity, domestic violence, repeated emotional abuse, substance abuse, or long-standing deceit, much more acute work is necessary before the kind of trust-based work we promote could begin. Similarly, if one partner is suffering from a significant psychological disorder, the couple is unlikely to be in a position to embark on the shared work that our approach requires. On the other hand, we have found that many couples in distress with angry or "empty" relationships, couples who are "too busy" for romance or connection, couples who question each other's commitment to the relationship, couples who experience an imbalance or lack of fairness in the relationship, or couples who simply seek to have a happier and more vital relationship, have benefited greatly from our focus on We-ness and We-Stories.

As clinical psychologists, we bring a combined nearly 70 years of therapy experience to the work we discuss in this volume. In addition to our work with couples in private practice, we are academic researchers with expertise in the study of health psychology, personality, memory, and resilience. We met each other through the happiest of means—by being excited and inspired through reading each other's research on We-ness in relationships. Despite living, respectively, in Illinois (KS) and Connecticut (JAS), we got to know each other through phone and email interaction, and slowly the idea for a collaborative work emerged. We subsequently arranged to meet, and on the basis of our face-to-face interactions, we began to carve out a shared vision of how to translate our efforts to cultivate We-ness in couples into a more systematic statement that might benefit other couple therapists. This book is a culmination of that effort, and it has indeed been a joyful experience of We-ness for both of us. We hope that readers can hear both our blended and distinct voices throughout these pages, and that our individual contributions combined make something greater than the sum of their parts. We have listed our names in alphabetical order on the front cover, but we want to emphasize that this work represents an equal contribution by both authors.

To set the scene for what lies ahead, one of us (JAS) would like to share a recent experience that typifies the essence of our We-Story enterprise. On vacation in Maine in 2010, my wife and I were riding bicycles on a small island when we passed an elderly man sitting on a beach chair in a shelter of pines by a stone gravesite. We did not stop, but I was so intrigued by this fleeting sight that I noted it in my journal and speculated about whom he might be mourning. Three years later, we took the same bicycle ride and there was the little old man again. This time we slowed down, and he greeted us with a friendly wave. With pride, he showed us the stone monument he had built for his wife of 67 years. After talking a bit more, this 90-year-old man walked us down a long dirt road to an impressive two-story brick home that he and his wife had designed and constructed themselves, finishing it over a 6-year period. He then explained that he had been too poor to go to school and that all the education that he had ever gained had come from his wife. She had taught him to read and had made a model of their future house from balsa wood for him to follow because he could not read blueprints. Showing us his beautiful home along with carved furniture and cabinets in his garage, he said bluntly, "All I am is due to her. Everything that you see is because of what we did together." And that is why twice a day, once in the morning and once at the end of the day, he sits in his striped beach chair and spends time beside her grave. Now we do not propose that all of us will be lucky enough to have marriages lasting that long, or that we will reach this pinnacle of devotion, but clearly this story points to the power that love and relationship can hold for human beings. With this in mind, we hope that you find the work that follows useful in your work with couples and perhaps in your own relationships as well.

INTRODUCTION: POSITIVE COUPLE THERAPY
Using We-Stories to Enhance Resilience

*For one human being to love another
that is perhaps the most difficult of all
tasks, the ultimate, the last test and
proof, the work for which all other work
is but preparation. . . . so we must not
forget, when we love, that we are
beginners, bunglers of life, apprentices
in love and must learn to love. . . .*
—Rainer Maria Rilke (1929/1993)

Jeanne looked at Barry at the other side of the couch in our office. She asked him if he remembered when they were first married and lived in a horrible one-bedroom apartment that barely had heat. Did he remember how each morning he would make her the worst coffee in the world, using a leaky filter and a banged-up metal pot—how he would carry it to the bedroom while she was still just waking up? Barry nodded that he remembered. Jeanne continue to search his face, "Why is it that *that coffee* tasted so good to me and now we have the most expensive coffee-making contraption that money can buy, and I have to have my coffee just right, and I don't even want you to touch the pot?"

At the heart of this exchange, Jeanne has told a We-Story—a shared story between the members of a couple that defines and guides their relationship. Jeanne has retrieved this story to remind Barry of what they have lost—of what they need to find once more if their relationship is to regain its vitality and meaning. That lost critical ingredient is what we call **We-ness**. Couples that feel this shared investment in each other possess the essential building blocks for healthy and resilient relationships. In this book we argue that positive and affirming We-Stories are powerful vehicles for experiencing and cultivating We-ness in relationships. Couples that can tell these stories, that can share them first with each other, and then with family, friends, and a larger community, are likely

1

to preserve a vision of the "We" that is sustaining and nurturing over a lifetime of partnership.

As teachers, couple therapists, and married individuals (although not to each other!), we have learned that many partners in committed relationships long to connect with their partner in meaningful ways, while struggling to make decisions in lives filled with overwhelming choices and competing priorities. Yet these couples, lacking any guidebook, race ahead, losing a sense of what they have accomplished together and the ways in which they have enriched each other's lives. Eventually, they find that habit and haste have filled the gaps in their lives with **negative** stories that often leave out the "We" or characterize the relationship in distressing imagery—repetitive complaints, tales of shortcomings, narratives of disappointment and disconnection. As an answer to these stories of frustration, we provide simple and practical therapeutic tools for reclaiming **positive** stories of connection—stories that provide a sense of hope to relationships that have become stressed and strained. We believe that keeping a vision of connection is particularly important in a society that constantly pushes us in individualistic and self-focused directions. Western culture with its emphasis on getting ahead and personal fulfillment does not take much time to teach us about the "third entity" in the room. Most individual therapists, and even many couple therapists, see their work primarily through the lens of the happiness of each individual rather than highlighting the integrity and health of **the relationship** as central to the growth and well-being of each partner.

Current research in social and clinical psychology (Bodenmann et al., 2008; Gottman, 2011; Rohrbaugh, Shoham, Skoyen, Jensen, & Mehl, 2012; Siegel, 2012; Skerrett, in press) suggests that one of the strongest predictors of marital stability and happiness is the couple's ability to build and maintain a sense of We-ness. Different aspects of We-ness have been researched under a variety of similar headings: cognitive interdependence (Agnew, Van Lange, Rusbult, & Langston, 1998), relationship awareness (Acitelli, 1988, 1993), minding of the other (Harvey & Omarzu, 1997, 1999), mutuality (Josselson, 1992; Sharpe, 2000), and the relational or connection model (Jordan, 1991; Jordan, Kaplan, Miller, Stiver, & Surrey, 1991). More recently, researchers have explicitly begun to refer to this prioritizing of the relationship as an awareness of the "We" (Kayser, Watson, & Andrade, 2007; Reid, Dalton, Laderoute, Doell, & Nguyen, 2006; Skerrett, 2010, in press, although one can find an early but overlooked "We" perspective in the writings of Sarnoff & Sarnoff, 1989). Whatever the exact nomenclature, this converging research demonstrates that couples who can articulate a sense of We-ness and experience reciprocity, compassion, gratitude, and mutual respect show greater levels of happiness, as well as better physical and mental health (Gottman, 2011; Rohrbaugh, Mehl, Shoham, Reilly, & Ewy, 2008; Simmons, Gordon, & Chambless, 2005).

In our clinical work we have found that one of the most powerful tools for building this sense of connection in couples is to help them locate stories of We-ness in their past experiences together as well as in their current lives. Once they can identify We-Stories, whether recent or remote, they have a foundation that highlights what the relationship has to offer rather than what it lacks. This simple story can then become a metaphor, an image of what works between them and can be referred to during times of stress or challenge.

Just as it is difficult for partners in our culture to think instinctively in "We" terms, stories of interdependence and mutual caretaking do not come easily to couples in Western cultures. We more easily gravitate toward highly individualistic stories based upon themes of self-reliance, achievement, and overcoming adversity (McAdams, 2013). Even though most couples have their unique success stories, too often they lose sight of them or don't know how to make use of them. Our therapeutic efforts focus on helping couples cultivate We-Stories, while simultaneously rooting out patterns that take them back to negative stories. We also help couples cope with the anticipated and unexpected challenges to their storylines, such as illness, job loss, aging, and separation, and provide them with strategies to revise their stories to achieve greater flexibility and positive change. Much of our work entails helping partners in a couple integrate individual stories of wants and needs into shared stories that align and reconcile their individual concerns.

Connecting We-ness and positive stories enhances the work of couple therapy, but we do not propose this therapeutic strategy as an alternative to more comprehensive therapeutic approaches, such as Integrated Behavioral Couple Therapy, Emotion-Focused Couple Therapy, Gottman's Sound Marital House, or Narrative Couple Therapy. Rather, we propose that our integration of We-ness and We-Stories is a valuable aid that can be linked to any of these treatment perspectives.

What does make our focus distinctive is our assertion that *We-ness is a fundamental shift in consciousness,* and that it underlies much of the couple's ability to generate the *positive emotion* that is necessary to de-escalate conflict and sustain commitment. Once couples can regularly access their We-ness through both private reflection and shared dialogue, they have an effective tool to forestall the negative relational cycles that create lasting resentment and distress. In Chapter 1 we illustrate in detail how a We-consciousness cuts across the four therapeutic perspectives mentioned and how it plays a critical role in the positive emotion that each of these therapies requires for success. We introduce seven fundamental elements (**s**ecurity, **e**mpathy, **r**espect, **a**cceptance, **p**leasure, **h**umor, and **s**hared meaning and vision—SERAPHS) that define We-ness and serve as the guiding framework for the development of We-Stories.

Chapter 2 provides background on the critical role of stories in human interaction and communication. With regard to couples, it looks at how members of the couple tell individual stories and also share **Couple Stories** that depict the interactions that define their relationship. We then introduce more formally the **We-Story** as one critical type of Couple Story that expresses in story form one or more of the seven elements of We-ness. We-Stories serve four vital positive functions for couples. They help shape the couple's mutual identity; they provide meaning and purpose in the couple's life; they serve as guides for current interaction and future growth; they are repositories of the couple's wisdom and a means of transmitting their legacy to others in their lives. A We-Story also invariably yields a memorable image, metaphor, or catchphrase that can become a couple touchstone and positive symbol of the relationship. In addition to elaborating these functions and aspects of We-Stories, we also introduce a subtype of We-Stories on which preliminary research has been conducted—relationship-defining memories (Alea & Vick, 2010)—and we elaborate the **structural features** that We-Stories require in order to be "**good enough**" (Skerrett, 2010) to serve as effective guides for the couple's ongoing efforts at maintaining We-ness. Relationship-defining memories are memories that give accounts of how couples first met or first recognized the potential for a lasting love relationship. "Good Enough" We-Stories consist of the following structural features: They consciously delineate a series of life experiences that took the couple from point A to point B. They demonstrate an internal consistency in their depiction of these events so that the overall narrative is sequential and coherent. They follow a narrative arc that acknowledges struggle and/or obstacles but ends in a redemptive manner, and finally, they link to a larger lesson or vision about the value of the couple's relationship, and often of relationships in general. Throughout this chapter we provide several examples of We-Stories that possess these "good enough" features; we also help the reader to see that these stories can come in different forms—some stories are painted with a broader brush and are collapsed across the whole relationship or a larger segment of it (what we call **macro-stories**) and some stories are about a specific incident or moment that resonates to much larger themes in the relationship (what we call **micro-stories**). Both macro- and micro-stories can be valuable resources in the couple's efforts to maintain a strong We-consciousness.

Chapter 3 turns to the first steps of a We-oriented therapy and illustrates how therapists can assess the degree of We-ness or mutuality couples possess at the start of treatment. It reviews a simple 10-item scale called the Marital Engagement–Type of Union Scale, or the ME (To US) (Singer, Labunko, Alea, & Baddeley, in press). Each item covers a critical area of the relationship, such as division of household duties, financial decisions, the couple's calendar, child rearing, physical intimacy, and relations to in-laws and extended family. We show how couples develop familiar and sometimes rigid stories about these vital concerns that block their ability to generate mutuality. To capture the most important ideas of this chapter, we provide the story of Will and Katie Owens, using their responses to the ME (To US) Scale as a way to look at their difficulties with forging a healthy We-Story. We show how many couples may share similar struggles and can use the ME (To US) as a starting point for forging a stronger We-consciousness and beginning to find We-Stories that they can put to use.

Chapter 4 zeroes in on working with couples in therapy to help them locate and leverage their We-Stories. We demonstrate how applying **Seven Steps of Good Talk** can lead to mutual development of We-Stories and can be the genesis of new We-Stories. In this chapter, we draw heavily on case examples from our work with couples (and in particular, the case of Jenn and Mark) to illustrate the strategies that are relationship-building and can lead to unifying and health-promoting We-Stories.

Chapter 5 examines the most common ways that couple's stories get stuck and/or cause hurt and distress. For example, the "ghosts" of important people from the past can dominate individual stories; unspoken resentments can lock partners into stories with plots and roles that feel stifling and repetitive. When this happens, the couple loses its focus on the relationship and misses opportunities to find valuable stories that are healing and health-promoting. Sometimes, new challenges and life transitions require the letting go of stories that have worked in the past, but are no longer effective in the present conditions. We revisit the story of Will and Katie Owens and their stand-off with regard to trust and intimacy; we detail the connections between their impasse and the emotional climates of their families of origin, and summarize the lessons they learned by moving forward from their "stuck stories." We emphasize the ways that they reframed their negative stories and mined them for positives. Moving on from the Owenses, we illustrate similar positive lessons that emerged from other couples initially trapped in negative stories, touching on diverse issues, such as unexpected illness, work stress, and multiple losses. The chapter concludes with exercises for clinicians to use with couples to break their repetitive retelling of negative stories and to move the couple in the direction of We-Stories of resilience and new possibilities. These exercises include experiential techniques, such as reverse role play, empty chair, and family sculpting.

Chapter 6 highlights the influence of life cycle development on each phase of a couple's relationship. It revisits the We-Story principles and techniques introduced earlier and matches them to the challenges presented at various points in the life cycle. Questions are posed for each major life stage along with the opportunities available for modifying one's story to fit the needs of that stage, both individually and as couples. We look at developmentally appropriate themes and stories for early adulthood (20–30 years), adulthood (31–45), midlife (46–65), late adulthood (70–80), and elderhood (81+).

Chapter 7 highlights the various effects that We-Stories of mutuality and gratitude might have on our families, work lives, and communities. We return to the stories of some of the couples we have highlighted earlier in the book and demonstrate how their application of We-consciousness in their lives, as exemplified in the We-Stories they have cultivated, has led to concrete effects for children and extended families and for others in their workplaces and communities. For example, Mark and Jenn, whose story is presented in Chapter 4, began therapy almost immobilized by the stress related to demanding jobs and the care of their four children, one of whom had severe cystic fibrosis. They described themselves as "disconnected robots" that went through each day entirely focused on what needed to be done and ended each day depleted and disempowered. As we explored and revised their stories, they slowly learned ways to tap into local and regional resources and to reach out to extended family and neighbors for assistance, and gradually transformed their relational image to one of empowerment. At the conclusion of our work, they were volunteering to parent organizations with special needs children and telling their story to motivate others. At the heart of this change was their commitment to a larger vision of connection, relationship, and mutuality.

Chapter 7 also looks more deeply at the act of story exchange between parents and offspring. Children, particularly when they begin to develop intimate relationships of their own, are naturally curious to learn more about the stories of their parents' relationship over time. Sharing the couple's We-Stories becomes not only a connecting point between parent and offspring, but assists parents in consolidating and integrating their own stories into a larger life vision. This chapter guides therapists in how to support couples who seek to share relational values, beliefs, and wider family customs and rituals so as to benefit the next generation. We emphasize oral exchanges of stories, but also talk about the use of social media as sites for storytelling in both words and images.

Telling Our Own Stories

Grasping true We-consciousness and allowing it to be a guiding force in one's life is a lot harder than it sounds. By the time most couples come to see us, they are often absorbed with personal grievances and caught up in the struggle to have their needs met; the welfare of the "We" is not necessarily on their minds at all. In the same way, many couples not in therapy have learned to make quiet compromises that placate each partner, but do little to cultivate their relationship. Reorienting two wounded and weary individuals back to a focus on the validity and value of their shared vision is often a daunting task.

The major theme of this book is that vivid personal stories are the most powerful medium to redirect couples back to a We-consciousness and to help them maintain this positive focus as they build a stronger relationship. To illustrate our commitment to this proposition, we believe that the best way to start this book is for each of us to share a We-Story that played a pivotal role in our personal lives and clinical work.

Jefferson's Story

Before I could ever cultivate the practice of teaching couples how to grow the "We" in therapy, I needed to gain my own awareness of its critical importance to loving relationships. I date this discovery to events that took place over the year 2004. Even though I was a clinical psychologist who treated couples, and even though I had been married nearly 20 years, I cannot say that I really understood or saw the "We" until that year, nor did I grasp its significance in the couples whom I treated or, for that matter, the role it played in my own life. As we have already mentioned, all of us are socialized in this culture to view the world in highly individualistic terms, and this person-by-person lens is how we make sense of our daily experience. When I finally saw the "We," it was very much like that famous illusion in psychology textbooks where you see an old woman's face in a combination of dots and shadows. Then suddenly, with a shift of glance or a blink or two, the picture completely transforms, and a young woman's face appears.

The Hibiscus

This story concerns a Hibiscus plant in my garden in August 2004, but to tell it properly I have to bring you back 16 years earlier to 1988 when my wife, Anne, and I were in the third year of our marriage. We had just arrived at Connecticut College and had recently moved from San Francisco to New London, Connecticut. This had not been an easy or graceful move for us. Not only were we leaving the cosmopolitan scene of the Bay Area for the rather small town world of southeastern Connecticut, but Anne had taken a job that required her to commute an hour each way to Hartford. With job possibilities in New York and Boston, this outcome had not been her first choice. However, she also understood how hard it was for me, a recent PhD, to land a tenure-track assistant professorship. After much discussion, we had come to agreement that I would take the job at Conn. We had also decided that we would not have a commuter marriage and live in separate residences.

There was a lot of friction at that early stage of our marriage and we even got to the point of questioning whether we should stay married. Luckily, we went into couple therapy. It helped a bit, but what helped more was the shock of realizing how close we had come to losing each other. It felt like we were starting our relationship over with a new and simple premise—our marriage, neither our work nor our ambitions, would come first. We would ask a basic question about the decisions and choices we made each day in our lives—Is this good for us or not?

Over the next decade we repeatedly used this question to guide our priorities and decisions. In a sense we were like two people in recovery, we knew the right course of action (for the addict—not to use, and for us—to put our marriage first), but we did not know a lot about how to live this new form of life. Unlike 12-step participants, we did not have a set of guidelines or a sponsor to tell us what would work. I knew that I needed to make a better balance between work and home life. Anne knew that we needed to move out of New London and that she wanted a more rewarding job with a shorter commute. Slowly, these pieces fell into place as we bought our first home in Chester, a bucolic village 30 minutes from New London and closer to Anne's new work. Our relationship seemed to solidify as we raised two daughters with strong personalities, as we endured the continued challenges of our careers, and as we faced illnesses and deaths of close family members. All of this time we were learning the nitty-gritty of what makes a marriage work—the fine details and not just the sweeping gestures. Whatever we were doing was working, and yet I am not sure we could have told you what it was.

And then it came time to move again. We had moved to Chester to shorten Anne's commuting time, but now traffic patterns had changed and her drive was stretching from 40 minutes to over an hour each way again. At the same time, our girls were getting ready for high school, and the local high school was not a good fit for their needs. The housing market was booming, and it was an ideal time to sell the 1980s Cape we had now owned for 14 years and move on to a house with a bit more style.

Our new home in the larger community of West Hartford had all the style of a house built in 1925, but not surprisingly, it also had many more complicated demands than our previous home. And, of course, with all of our years of working on being thoughtful and considerate of each other, we proceeded to fall apart and go after each other night and day. We had arguments and fights that almost equaled those early times in our marriage. It also did not help that our younger daughter was enraged with us for moving her away from the circle of friends she had known since birth and from the travel soccer team that had been her central focus for almost as long.

We were stressed with flooding basements, knob-and-tube wiring, broken window sashes, and plaster cracks. We were overwhelmed with slamming doors, our daughters' crying fits and shouting matches, and by knowing almost no one in a new place. We sat in our unhappy house during some torrential rainstorms that summer and watched the water stream across our basement floor, while the ceiling lights flickered on and off.

That first summer I planted a garden by the side of our driveway. As Anne became an accomplished painter and carpenter, I threw myself into working on the lawn and the plantings. As the summer went forward, my garden was growing, the house was improving, but our tempers still flared and our relationship frayed.

Then there was the Hibiscus. When we had lived in Chester, I had planted some Hibiscus plants and had enjoyed their large red blossoms. They are a tropical flower not native to the Northeast, and they are more likely to bloom in late summer. The flower is bell-shaped and only lasts a day or two at most. Before they bloom, they grow fairly tall with long narrow leaves and rangy stems. I planted some in our new garden along with many other flowers and shrubs, and forgot about them.

July came and went. We were supposed to be enjoying our summer, but we were still tense, unsure about the house, maybe even about the move. The Hibiscus grew larger, its reddish-green leaves spreading out on long spindly stems, but not a hint of flower. Anne turned to me in the driveway and said, "That is not the most attractive plant." I had to agree that it was not adding much beauty to our lives. Then some ants or Japanese beetles discovered it. They were munching away, making some of the leaves look like they had been attacked by a hole-puncher, leaving just the reddish veins of the stems showing through. I was out the next day with a spray, fighting the devouring hordes the best I could.

"It is getting uglier by the day," Anne was telling my older daughter, Olivia, at breakfast. I told them to hang in there—that there had been a nice flower in Chester but that it had come late. I wasn't so sure, though, given the damage the insects had done and the location where I had planted it.

"Is that some kind of weed, Dad?" my younger daughter, Chloe, asked as she waited for me to pull out from the garage to bring her to school. I told her no, but started to think that maybe I should grab the eyesore out by the roots.

August came. Anne and I were in a kind of sullen truce, but there was still little joy as the days seemed filled with work and endless repair projects. One morning, I was backing out from the garage, looking over my shoulder as I navigated our narrow driveway. And there it was. A huge red blossom, as big as a dinner plate, as big as a Frisbee. I stopped the car and ran inside.

"The Hibiscus—the Hibiscus!"

"The what?" Anne and Olivia said together.

I dragged them outside, and there, in the bright yellow morning sunshine, was the Hibiscus flower in all its scarlet glory.

Anne said, "We need a picture." Olivia ran inside and came back with the digital camera. Anne and I stood in front of the flower, framed by its massive bloom.

Back in my car, driving to my practice, I felt emotion welling up. The moment I had just shared with Anne, the laugh we had about that ugly plant that had not failed us had felt so good, so sweet, so much like many times before. I realized too that we could have missed the blossom. Walking around with our heads down, hustling with our work and to-do lists, it could have wilted or washed away by the next morning. We would have seen the wrinkled blossom and its crumbled bell, but not its triumphant arrival that thrilled us and stopped us in our tracks. There had to be a part of us ready to see it, looking for the possibility that it would appear.

Driving down the highway, I saw the Hibiscus as a metaphor for our relationship. It is always there; ready to bloom, even when weeds of discord and intemperate elements threaten to destroy it. What sustains us during the ugly, spindly moments is our trust—our faith in each other— that we will be there for the other person, that we will provide the support that is needed. Beneath all the daily efforts lies this deep red layer.

As I thought about this connection of us to the Hibiscus, I realized that I kept returning to the pronoun, "We." It dawned on me too that the flower that was symbolizing our relationship was neither of us but a third entity, something that we grew together. As odd as it might sound, the flower that emerged from those rangy stems was a manifestation of our We-ness, of Anne and me in our best moments, not when we were two people, but when we were more, when we were the literal embodiment of our commitment, a synergy beyond ourselves. It was this We-ness that had sustained us for 19 years of marriage (and now for 29 years). If we maintained our awareness of its presence inside us, we would hold our relationship together even during the most trying of times.

It seemed essential to me that I help the couples with whom I work learn how to explore the power and pleasure of the "We." Working from this new angle, they might be able to see how their relationship was much more than a reciprocal meeting of needs or an opportunity for individual gratification. To help couples, I needed to draw on the lesson I had learned from my own marriage—how faith in each partner's shared commitment to the relationship can sustain and guide a couple through all the challenges and opportunities that it will face. In the years that have followed these events, I have devoted much of my clinical and academic work to determining what might be the practical ingredients that would allow couples to grow this "We" in their relationship.

In this spirit, I have developed methods for assessing the "We" and exercises for building We-ness in the relationship. At the same time, I have been engaging in a program of research with my students at Connecticut College to examine in a scientific fashion how one might study We-ness or the dimension of mutuality in relationships. I consider all of this research in the earliest stages, but I have no question about the value and utility of promoting We-ness in my couples work. Working with Karen, I have increasingly realized that the stories that couples offer are a vital medium for uncovering a positive vision of the "We." For me, this book demonstrates how we have begun to turn our important insights about We-ness into practical steps that can help couples strengthen their relationships.

Karen's Story: Home Renovation

We met on a blind date. Were we telling this story together orally, this would be the part where Roger inserts several politically incorrect jokes about Stevie Wonder to which I laugh in response. I can't recall now if I ever thought he was truly funny or if I was responding out of some over-developed sense of the wifely role. Now I genuinely laugh—for all of the historical, repetitious absurdity of the moment.

Our courtship was intense and short-lived; we started planning a wedding four months into our relationship. I once read an article titled: "Planning a Wedding Can Be Hazardous to Your Health." Our experience was quite the opposite. The process was invigorating, challenging in the best sense, and unknowingly, gave us our first clear script for the "We."

On many levels we were a pairing of differences. I was the adopted daughter of Swedish-German Protestant parents raised with many of the privileges afforded an only child. I was serious, independent, somewhat introverted, and bookish. Having been adopted at a time when adoption tended to be stigmatized and surrounded in secrecy, I longed for family, but an overdeveloped sense of gratitude to my birth parents silenced my questions. Roger was the easy-going, funny, adaptable oldest of six in an Irish Catholic family. I was drawn to the whole lot of them like a bee to honey. Dinners at my house consisted of roughly 10–15 minutes of focused silent dining—Roger loved it! Dinner with his family was a raucous affair with constant action, comedy, and antics tied to vying for the last piece of food—I was in heaven!

It was clear to me from early on that we each married the family we imagined we wanted. I got instant siblings and he got to be the only son. I got companionship and excitement and he got attention and peace. In the blush of courtship the differences were attractive and enticing. We thought we could find the right formula to work with those differences and, of course, were clueless as to what that really meant.

Because it was the early 1970s with many lingering remnants of the turbulent 1960s, we felt surrounded by many contradictions. Chicago is a town with solid blue-collar roots and a respect for tradition and, as an only and an oldest, we were raised to honor those influences. Yet, we also strongly identified with our independent beliefs, so figuring out exactly how much difference we could get away with was no easy task. I typified some of the growing pains of the times. For example, while trying to plan a traditional church wedding, I secretly nurtured fantasies of marrying on a grassy hill in Vermont, carrying a bouquet of wildflowers. Roger (he already had the Afro hairdo and Fu Manchu mustache) and I would recite vows that went something like: "I take you for now, as long as we're both cool with it"—you get the idea. Big stretch from my *uber* responsible, conscientious moniker.

Once it became clear to our families that we were serious, the unspoken question that hung over us was "What about religion?" and close on its heels "What about the children?" We certainly could never have said to them we weren't even sure we wanted children. Having been raised in atmospheres where a nod to tolerance cloaked abundant anti-Catholic, anti-Protestant stereotypes, I felt strongly that I did not want to sign the requisite paperwork to raise our future children Catholic. Roger was solidly behind me.

After months of conversation and plotting out various scenarios, we decided we wanted to honor both of the traditions that were important to us and crafted a plan to marry in my childhood church in a service that included a Catholic priest and a Protestant minister. We loved the idea, and in our naïveté, had no sense about what it would mean to make this compromise a reality. We soon learned the rule of the day dictated that we had to petition to Rome for Papal permission to allow Roger to marry in my church. Although this clawed at every one of our liberal sensibilities, we filed the petition and set off to find a Catholic priest sympathetic to our wishes. I well recall our mutual frustration and anger at a set of rules that seemed so antithetical to tolerance, inclusivity, and compassion. Hours of heated debate helped us to create (unwittingly) our first vision of a force and purpose larger than us, a vision that could hold and reflect the essence of our differences while at the same time embracing a third entity—the "We." We scripted every aspect of our ceremony, wrote the vows and the liturgy, and crafted an experience we felt symbolized who and what "We" stood for.

We were married on a muggy early evening in July in a beautiful ceremony officiated by my minister of childhood, our newfound liberal priest, another priest friend of ours, and Roger's uncle, the Monsignor, who showed up at the last minute, vestments in hand. We had no idea what to do with him so we put him on the altar. The Catholics and Protestants, who began the wedding on opposite sides of the aisle (literally), ended the evening laughing, dancing, and having a grand time together. We felt deeply united, gratified by a process that crystallized that unity for us and eager to begin our future together.

As the years raced forward, we applied that process to finding a neighborhood, then a home in which to raise our family, as well as in making most other major decisions. We didn't have the language and often not the skill sets, but in the big-ticket arenas, we somehow managed to keep the "What Is Best for Us" in the foreground.

As time went on and life became exceedingly more complex with two graduate educations, high-pressure jobs, the birth of a son and then a daughter, we gradually became unconscious taskmasters. That vision of "We" got lost in the demands of the day and our couple relationship was no longer our priority. Having gotten off to such a good start in our ability to connect across our differences, we neglected the ongoing, more challenging work of respecting those differences through regularly voicing them in the relationship. Differences at this point went underground, and we regularly took the imagined easy way out of dialogues that might have reignited the spark.

We went through the motions like this until somewhere around the 33-year mark, when we encountered a series of unanticipated, chronic stressors that brought us to our knees. Again, we initially responded with our characteristic teamwork, getting the essentials done, but by now the tank was on empty. We had even lost the will to apply the many relationship skills we had learned through earlier couple therapy. We were two trains operating on completely separate tracks. Having been a "wife" since losing my mother suddenly several months after my 12th birthday, I finally had to admit that I couldn't "fix" things the way I was going and that I was seriously overdue for some self-care. I felt devastated that, as a therapist who specialized in couple treatment, my own relationship was in such dire straits. After years in crisis mode and being together in only the most superficial ways, we silently questioned whether we would continue the marriage. Just at that time, the universe intervened with a creative solution I am forever grateful for heeding. I was offered a visiting professorship at a university on the West Coast and, after considerable soul searching, made the risky decision to take it. It was terrifying—to me, to Roger, and to our adult children who watched their mother pack up at just the point they were cementing serious relationships themselves.

That move turned out to be both the way out and the way home. We were able to use that distance not only to refill individual tanks, but to very slowly and tentatively update one another on who it was each of us was becoming. In tiny baby steps we were able to reach back to that original script and rewrite it to incorporate the voices of two stronger individuals. The self-exploration, which we apparently needed the miles to facilitate, led to individual growth, and that renewal fueled our marriage. Despite the many episodes of distance and disconnection in our marriage, we thankfully never lost total sight of that first vision.

Coincidentally, during that same time, we made the tough decision to sell our family home. For over 36 years, it was the center of our lives—a cherished place of countless celebrations, holiday dinners, neighborhood parties, quiet nights around the fire—the place both of us had lived in longer than anywhere in our lives and our shelter in every sense. It was a big, rambling 125-year-old antique that was filled with charm, but always needed work and attention. Over the many discussions we had on the minutia involved with downsizing and selling, it occurred to me that our house was a metaphor for the "We." Solid in structure, it was also filled with many quirks and flaws that, if unrecognized or cared for, could easily develop into major issues—some that might become irreparable. It dawned on us that we had done a better job of tending to those flaws in the house in recent years than we had to sharing our vulnerabilities with one another in our relationship. Just as we had gotten tired of putting all the time, money, and energy into keeping up our big home, this stressful time pointed out that we had abandoned the upkeep on our marriage. Yet the marriage, just like our beloved home, was always there ready and waiting for our care and attention and promised so much safety and nourishing comfort in return.

While I'm not advocating separation as an automatic fix for relationship stalls, I did learn invaluable lessons about the value of novelty, creativity, and persistence in sustaining long-term, vital marriages. I also learned the degree to which the "We" is a dynamic force. It constantly responds to shifts in each individual partner and to the events that impact them. At some points in a relationship, one person will be better able to hold on to that vision than the other, which is why regular updates on the "state of the relationship" are so crucial. Still a work in progress, our marriage has left behind one solid and reliable structure that no longer worked for us, and we have slowly been evolving a new "marital house" that fits our current life circumstances and needs. This new variation on our We-ness is designed to enable each of us to grow into our best selves, while recommitting to putting the couple first. Remembering the brutal isolation of having given up on one another, we are filled with gratitude and the sense of the mystery and miracle that is marital resilience. Wherever we live, from here forward, "We" are home to each other.

We hope that our personal We-Stories convey our conviction about the importance of helping couples uncover a positive sense of We-ness. This positivity infuses our work with a spirit of joy, and we are dedicated to sharing those blessings with the couples with whom we work. We hope too that this volume encourages other therapists and the couples with whom they work to share similar We-Stories that reflect the power of mutuality. We are living proof that stronger and more resilient relationships can emerge from the recognition and cultivation of the "We."

References

Acitelli, L. K. (1988). When spouses talk to each other about their relationship. *Journal of Social and Personal Relationships, 5*(2), 185–199.

Acitelli, L. K. (1993). You, me, and us: Perspectives on relationship awareness. In S. W. Duck (Ed.), *Individuals in relationships (Understanding relationship processes)* (pp. 144–174). Newbury Park, CA: Sage Publications.

Agnew, C. R., Van Lange, P. A.M., Rusbult, C. E., & Langston, C. A. (1998). Cognitive interdependence: Commitment and the mental representation of close relationships. *Journal of Personality and Social Psychology, 74*(4), 939–954.

Alea, N., & Vick, S. C. (2010). The first sight of love: Relationship-defining memories and marital satisfaction across adulthood. *Memory, 18*(7), 730–742.

Bodenmann, G., Plancherel, B., Beach, S.R.H., Widmer, K., Gabriel, B., Meuwly, N., & Schramm, E. (2008). Effects of coping-oriented couples therapy on depression: A randomized clinical trial. *Journal of Consulting and Clinical Psychology, 76*(6), 944–954.

Gottman, J.M. (2011). *The science of trust: Emotional attunement for couples.* New York, NY: W.W. Norton & Co.

Harvey, J.H., & Omarzu, J. (1997). Minding the close relationship. *Personality and Social Psychology Review, 1*(3), 224–240.

Harvey, J.H., & Omarzu, J. (1999). *Minding the close relationship: A theory of relationship enhancement.* New York, NY: Cambridge University Press.

Jordan, J.V. (1991). The meaning of mutuality. In J.V. Jordan, A.G. Kaplan, J.B. Miller, I.P. Stiver, and J.L. Surrey (Eds.), *Women's growth in connection: Writings from the Stone Center* (pp. 81–96). New York, NY: Guilford Press.

Jordan, J.V., Kaplan, A.G., Miller, J.B., Stiver, I.P., & Surrey, J.L. (1991). *Women's growth in connection: Writings from the Stone Center.* New York, NY: Guilford Press.

Josselson, R. (1992). *The space between us: Exploring the dimensions of human relationships.* San Francisco, CA: Jossey-Bass.

Kayser, K., Watson, L.E., & Andrade, J.T. (2007). Cancer as a "we-disease": Examining the process of coping from a relational perspective. *Families, Systems and Health, 25*(4), 404–418.

McAdams, D.P. (2013). *The redemptive self: Stories Americans live by* (Rev. ed.). New York, NY: Oxford University Press.

Reid, D.W., Dalton, E.J., Laderoute, K., Doell, F.K., & Nguyen, T. (2006). Therapeutically induced changes in couple identity: The role of we-ness and interpersonal processing in relationship satisfaction. *Genetic, Social, and General Psychology Monographs, 132*(3), 241–284.

Rilke, R.M. (1929/1993). *Letters to a young poet.* New York, NY: W.W. Norton & Co.

Rohrbaugh, M.J., Mehl, M.R., Shoham, V., Reilly, E.S., & Ewy, G.A. (2008). Prognostic significance of spouse we talk in couples coping with heart failure. *Journal of Consulting and Clinical Psychology, 76*(5), 781–789.

Rohrbaugh, M.J., Shoham, V., Skoyen, J.A., Jensen, M., & Mehl, M.R. (2012). We-talk, communal coping, and cessation success in a couple-focused intervention for health-compromised smokers. *Family Process, 51*(1), 107–121.

Sarnoff, I., & Sarnoff, S. (1989). *Love-centered marriage in a self-centered world.* New York, NY: Taylor & Francis.

Sharpe, S.A. (2000). *The ways we love: A developmental approach to treating couples.* New York, NY: Guilford Press.

Siegel, D.J. (2012). *The developing mind: How relationships and the brain interact to shape who we are* (2nd ed.). New York, NY: Guilford Press.

Simmons, R.A., Gordon, P.C., & Chambless, D.L. (2005). Pronouns in marital interaction: What do "you" and "I" say about marital health? *Psychological Science, 16*(12), 932–936.

Singer, J.A., Labunko, B., Alea, N., & Baddeley, J.L. (in press). Mutuality and the Marital Engagement—Type of Union Scale [ME (To US)]: Empirical support for a clinical instrument in couples therapy. In K. Skerrett and K. Fergus (Eds.), *Couple resilience across the lifespan: Emerging perspectives.* New York, NY: Springer.

Skerrett, K. (2010). "Good enough stories": Helping couples invest in one another's growth. *Family Process, 49*(4), 503–516.

Skerrett, K. (in press). Relational resilience in couples: A view of the landscape. In K. Skerrett and K. Fergus (Eds.), *Couple resilience across the lifespan: Emerging perspectives.* New York, NY: Springer.

1

WHAT IS THE "WE"?

We begin our investigation into We-Stories by reviewing key features of the most important contemporary approaches to couple therapy. All of these couple therapies share an underlying emphasis on the importance they place on trust and positivity in the couple relationship. We argue that the root of this trust and positivity is consciousness of the "We" in the relationship. But what exactly does it mean to have a We-consciousness? We provide a more formal definition of the seven key elements that constitute the "We," drawing on research and clinical examples. Once we have elaborated our understanding of the "We," we shall be ready to focus on the critical role of stories for couples, and how therapists can help couples leverage these stories to build a more positive and more resilient relationship.

Contemporary Trends in Couple Therapy

The last two decades have been an exciting and in some ways revolutionary period for psychotherapists who work with couples. As Gurman and Fraenkel (2002) detail, couple therapy in the form of "marriage counseling" began in the 20th century as an almost informal practice offered by clergy, physicians, family life experts, and other sundry advice-givers. Equally problematic, a small discipline of "marriage counselors" associated themselves with the tenets of psychoanalysis and dispensed psychoanalytic interpretations of marital problems, often in individual rather than conjoint therapy. Finally, by the early 1960s, with the advent of family therapy and a family systems perspective on marital problems, couple therapy, as we currently understand it, began to take hold. Therapists began to look at the power dynamics, boundary concerns, and communication patterns that define the contours of couple relationships (Bowen, 1961; Haley, 1963; Minuchin, 1974; Satir, 1964). Still, the major theorists of family therapy of the 1960s, 1970s, and 1980s were mostly trained in psychiatry, and their approaches drew less on empirical advances in psychological research and more on their own clinical experiences and personal charisma. Couple therapy borrowed from these theories but did little to carve out a distinct presence in the larger landscape of psychotherapy. The late Neil Jacobson, a psychologist and a pioneer in the scientific study of couple therapy, surveyed the field, including his own efforts at a more rigorously based behavioral couple therapy, and found that only 35% of the couples he was treating were improving and 30–50% were relapsing within one to two years (Jacobson, 1984; Jacobson & Addis, 1993).

Fortunately, since the mid-1990s we have seen successive waves of couple therapy approaches that incorporate advances in scientific findings regarding cognition, behavior, emotion, attachment, and couple interaction (Gurman, 2008). For example, Christensen and Jacobson introduced and provided empirical support for **Integrated Behavioral Couple Therapy (IBCT)**, a cognitive-behavioral approach to couple therapy that features traditional behavioral skills training, but more crucially, an emphasis on mutual acceptance of long-standing emotional concerns or vulnerabilities that each partner brings to the relationship (Christensen et al., 2004; Christensen, Atkins, Yi, Baucom, & George, 2006; Christensen & Jacobson, 1998; Dimidjian, Martell, & Christensen, 2008). In the late 1980s and evolving over the next two decades, Susan Johnson (2004, Greenberg & Johnson, 2010) along with her collaborator, Leslie Greenberg, developed **Emotion-Focused Couple Therapy (EFCT)**, a humanistic-experiential–based therapy that zeroes in on individuals' immediate emotional responses to attachment concerns in their relationship. Similar to IBCT, Johnson's approach addresses the repetitive negative interactions associated with each partner's attachment vulnerabilities and highlights how partners can develop compassion and understanding in the face of these conflicts. Once again paralleling IBCT, EFCT has been tested and found effective in treatment-outcome studies (Denton, Burleson, Clark, Rodriguez, & Hobbs, 2000; Greenberg & Goldman, 2008; Johnson, Hunsley, Greenberg, & Schindler, 1999).

A third groundbreaking force in evidence-based couple therapy can be traced to the well-known studies that emerged from John Gottman's marital laboratory at the University of Washington (what has become commonly known as the "love lab"). Using video coding techniques, questionnaires, and physiological measurement, Gottman had couples spend 24-hour sessions in his laboratory and studied their interactions, emotional responses, and perceptions of their own and their partners' feelings, thoughts, and behaviors. These studies have produced voluminous writings, by Gottman (e.g., Gottman, 1999, 2011; Gottman & DeClaire, 2001; Gottman & Gottman, 2008; Gottman & Silver, 1999) and about Gottman (see Malcolm Gladwell's (2005) account in the best-selling book, *Blink* [2005]), but their take-home message is that conflict in marriage is inevitable; however, it is how we respond to negativity, and even more, our ability to generate positive interactions, that will predict the stability and well-being of long-standing partnerships (Gottman, 1999, 2011).

A fourth critical force in contemporary couple therapy that draws more on philosophical and cultural analysis than psychological science is **Narrative Therapy** (Freedman & Combs, 2008, Madigan, 2011; White & Epston, 1990; Zimmerman & Dickerson, 1996). Narrative Couple Therapy zeroes in on the internalized cultural "stories" that partners in a relationship have learned to adopt as a mutual reality and that often lead to repetitive frustration and disappointment (e.g., "we should have it all"; "we will only be loved if we are beautiful"; "we can find happiness in food and/or alcohol"; "we must outperform our parents"). Its therapeutic focus is to help couples "externalize" these stories and join together in battling their toxic influences. One strategy in this shared effort is to highlight "unique outcomes" or "sparkling events" from past encounters when the couple has effectively united and overcome these negative beliefs and messages. As Freedman and Combs (2008) note, narrative therapy, as a social constructionist and non-positivist perspective, does not tend to engage in quantitative research to support its work; rather it relies on "co-research" and the collaborative testimony and information provided by its participants (clients and practitioners). However, unlike earlier non-empirically based grand theories of family therapy, it is more modest about its claims to a single Truth or theoretical supremacy.

The Common Threads Among Contemporary Approaches

Each of the four major approaches to couple therapy just reviewed defines the emotional process of a relational breakdown slightly differently, but all four emphasize that festering negativity and dilution of positive energy are at the root of marital discord and alienation. And all four see the solution to these problems as based in a greater emotional flexibility and trust during periods of conflict.

More precisely, IBCT sees this relational impasse as a problem with *acceptance*. For example, Christensen and Jacobson (Jacobson, Christensen, Prince, Cordova, & Eldridge, 2000, p. 352) promote "empathic joining, unified detachment, and tolerance building" as methods of *acceptance* in place of efforts to change one's partner. *Empathic joining* means an emotional compassion for the other's concerns; *unified detachment* is an ability to see a relational problem or conflict as a common adversary to be confronted; and *tolerance building* is an increased patience with the other person's behavior that allows for a constructive and modulated response to what is normally a provocative gesture or comment.

EFCT sees moments of severe marital distress as a two-stage reaction to fundamental concerns about safety and security in the relationship. In other words, each partner is experiencing a threat, whether abandonment and/or rejection, to their *attachment bond*. Once an emotional response to this threat is experienced, security strategies (most often some form of pursuit or withdrawal) are initiated. In this way strong negative emotional responses (anger, fear, sadness) are coupled with defensive relational cycles that perpetuate or worsen the rift between the partners rather than draw them closer together. As Johnson (2004) writes,

> A distressed couple is in an absorbing state of compelling, automatic emotional responses and a corresponding set of rigidly organized interactions, both of which narrow and constrict interaction and experience. (p. 41)

EFCT responds to this destructive cycle by a strategy of what Johnson calls "within" and "between." In other words, the therapist seeks to evoke strong emotion *within* each partner during the session and then works on expanding his or her experience of that emotion to support the reframing of the interaction *between* the partners. For example, a wife may bear great anger at her husband for his emotional remoteness and often criticizes him for his "cluelessness." The husband responds to this frequent negativity by even greater efforts to withdraw and avoid close contact. In the session, the emotion-focused couple therapist may help the wife to explore her anger and find the sadness and hurt beneath her frustration. In accessing this hurt, the wife may also speak more vulnerably about her loneliness and of her softer desire for closeness with her husband. In turn, the therapist may ask the husband to register emotionally what it is like to be needed so deeply and then ask him whether he had previously realized how much he is loved. The husband may find new compassion and encouragement from this awareness and resolve to take new steps to change the attack/withdraw pattern that has been dominating the couple interaction. Undergirding what Johnson (2004, p. 315) calls the "softening process" is a willingness to trust—to believe that there will be reciprocity if one member of the couple finally reaches out to the other.

A foundation of trust and a belief in the value and viability of the relationship is also what Gottman (1999, 2011) sees as the key to the sound "marital house." In one of his more remarkable findings, Gottman and colleagues (Gottman, Coan, Carrère, & Swanson, 1998) determined that they could predict whether a newlywed couple would be together and happy, together and miserable, or divorced six years later. The basis of this prediction was a 30-second difference in positive emotion during a 15-minute conflict discussion recorded in the love lab in their first year of marriage. The key aspect of this difference is that stable and happy couples learn to use positive emotion to deescalate their arguments and fights. Through humor, affection, and genuine interest in the concerns of the partner, the couple moves the "negative needle" in a more positive direction, allowing each partner to take a breath and engage in self-soothing. Gottman calls these shifts toward the positive in the midst of a negative interaction *repair efforts* resulting in a *positive sentiment override* that defuses the conflict.

For practitioners of Narrative Therapy, the building up of trust in distressed couples is through their ability to develop an alternative story to their current experience of conflict and unhappiness. The raw material of this more positive story can be found in their past recollection of unique outcomes. For example, Freedman and Combs (2008) described a couple who are both writers and have been undergoing power struggles and competitive conflicts, magnified by their impending move to take joint positions in an English department. By helping the couple to identify recent "sparkling events" where they worked together and appreciated each other outside the realm of their writing careers, the therapists encouraged the "reauthoring" of the couple's story to highlight their complementary differences and strength as a part of the same team. Equally important, the telling of their story promoted a better vision of the couple's future together. This positivity was clearly being overlooked due to the "problem-saturated" narratives that had dominated the couple prior to treatment. Freedman and Combs (2008) wrote,

> We work to help couples notice the influence of restrictive cultural stories in their lives, and to expand and enrich their own life narratives. We strive to find ways to spread the news of triumphs; to circulate stories of accomplishment, fulfillment, and meaningful struggle in order to keep them alive and growing. (p. 232)

Across these four diverse therapeutic perspectives, the critical element of change for the couple is **recourse to positive feelings and a shared faith in each other**. But how does the couple access this positivity so that it can emerge like a life preserver in the nick of time and save them from a sea of hostility and recrimination? Clearly, most distressed couples that come in for treatment do not have the magic "5 to 1" ratio of positive to negative emotion that Gottman uncovered in stable and happy couples. To appropriate a metaphor from Gottman (1999), we are essentially asking, what provides the positive energy to keep the "marital house" warm, inviting, and livable for the couple? If **acceptance**, **attachment security**, **repair efforts**, and **sparkling events** are key resources to overcoming marital distress, from what marital resource do troubled couples derive this fuel?

The "We"

Our answer is that the source of positive energy for couples lies in a **shift in consciousness** that translates into a series of daily practices. Distressed couples will learn to tap the positive elements of their relationship or learn how to generate them by shifting from an individual consciousness of what each partner needs or wants to a **consciousness of the relationship or the "We."** Or as Taibbi (2009, p. 11) succinctly puts it,

$$1 + 1 = 1 + 1 + 1$$

which signifies "two people who are balanced and individually strong but who have created something else—the two has become three, and the third is the relationship between them that they share and nurture."

When we talk about couples working through their patterns of conflict and distress to build this stronger connection, we are really talking about forging resilient relationships. Resiliency is the ability to bounce back after challenges and to learn and grow from adversity. **Relational resilience**, as exemplified in **We-ness**, consists of a capacity for working together, interpersonal sensitivity, and generosity, as well as a willingness to set boundaries and give space with a confidence that both separate and coordinated action will lead to mutual benefit.

The Seven Elements of the "We"

The following characteristics are the key attributes of the "We," and we shall return to them repeatedly throughout this volume:

- Security
- Empathy
- Respect
- Acceptance
- Pleasure
- Humor
- Shared Meaning and Vision

Security

Security entails a willingness on both partners' parts to acknowledge the primacy of their relationship in their lives. There are many ways that we help couples to think about the extraordinary miracle it is to have another person share a life with you—to experience concern for your disappointments; to express joy at your successes; simply to remind you of an appointment; or warm a bed with you on a winter night. We strive to reorient couples back to this basic shared commitment and the most elemental gratitude each partner can have for this bond. We tell them to think of a famous movie star living in a Malibu mansion, recently on the cover of *People* or *Us*, wealthy and glamorous, a supposed object of envy in our culture. And then acknowledge that any one of those stars lying in that Malibu bed alone would trade their celebrity in a heartbeat for the loving relationship that the couple can build together.

True relationship security means prioritizing the relationship as the most important commitment in the couple's life. This seems simple on the couple's wedding day, and then day-to-day life becomes increasingly more complicated. Demands at work, the arrival of children, aging parents, community and religious commitments—it gets easier and more routine to move the relationship lower and lower down the list of "must do's" and "can't do without's."

The essence of our focus on the "We" is to reverse this slide and challenge couples to reprioritize their relationship. Often couples with children will say, "But our children have more pressing needs." Our simple response, and it is not at all glib, is that the greatest gift that you can give to your children is to offer them evidence of a loving and positive partnership. When they experience their parents in a unified and affirming relationship, their lives will inevitably gain in safety, structure, and happiness. For the distressed couples who have spent years constructing what Harville Hendrix (1988) calls "exits" from genuine intimacy, this reprioritizing process is a challenge, but it is essential if they are to achieve the hard work of change. Each partner needs to know that the other one is "all in." We like to tell couples about one husband who worked in construction and taped the following sign to his dashboard, so he would be sure to remember his commitment as he drove to work each morning and drove back home each night:

COUPLE FIRST

Empathy and Respect

One of the greatest virtues of EFCT is its ability to use immediate emotional experiences in the therapy session to engender **empathy** in a partner for the other partner. Seeing pain or hurt behind a partner's anger or withdrawal is a sudden reminder of connection. However, so often in our work when we get to this point, we often find that this awareness is short-lived and the partner retreats back into a familiar feeling of resentment and confusion.

Lasting empathy takes hold when each partner also feels that his or her own feelings are being acknowledged and respected as well. Empathy and concern for the other need to come in the context of self-care and self-respect. Whenever we begin to work with couples to refocus on the "We" and the importance of their relationship, we often encounter a fear that we are asking the two partners to submerge their own identities or give up their autonomy. Traditionally, many women have been forces of nurturance and self-sacrifice in their relationships; the prospect of making the "We" a priority seems either redundant or counterproductive to their hopes for greater autonomy and self-expression in the relationship. In confronting this legitimate concern, we immediately return to Taibbi's formulation of the 1 + 1 + 1. True We-ness means that two "I"s live inside the "We" and that there must be **respect** for each of these separate individuals to grow independently and together.

One of us (JAS) has a distant cousin whom my wife and I would see every few years when we traveled to California. Whenever he would meet us, his wife and he would be wearing identical matching sweatshirts. **This is not what we mean by the "We"!** Creating a true sense of We-ness in a relationship means creating more room for each partner to express and act on their individuality confident in the support and security that their partner provides. In fact, a partner who embraces the "We" strives to help his partner reach her dreams more ardently, precisely because he knows that his partner is wishing and working for the same in his life. This acknowledgment and support of difference in the couple is the deepest form of empathy or what Skerrett (2013) calls "flexibility to see self and other within the We." Compare this with a relationship in which each partner is zealously protective of his or her individual needs and vigilant about how much their partner might interfere with their efforts. In this latter case, each partner sees himself or herself as pursuing their dreams *in spite of* their partner rather than because of them. Feeney (2007) identified the ability to grow within the "We" as a "paradox in close relationships where accepting dependence promotes independence" (p. 268).

In order to accomplish this goal of cultivating individual growth within the larger relationship, partners have to work at cultivating an awareness of their own needs, as well as an awareness of the needs of their partner. Even more, both partners must learn to articulate and express their needs respectfully. For example, Kristen and Rich were extremely different in their need for communication during the course of the week. Kristen liked to touch base during the course of the day and Rich could go the whole day without a text or phone call. Kristen felt that Rich's lack of contact was a sign that he did not care; Rich felt that it was just an indication of how busy he could get at work and that his silence said nothing about his feelings. We asked Kristen how she handled this difference, and she replied,

I realized that he felt that I was nagging him or needy, so I
decided to just shut up about it. I have tried to put my focus on
my own job and not worry about it, but it continues to bug me.

In working on developing a We-consciousness with Kristen and Rich,
we explained that suppressing a legitimate need supposedly to help the
relationship is like putting a **pebble in your pocket** and over time that
pebble is followed by similar pebbles until you are pulled down by a huge
weight of resentment. Awareness of your own need and respect for that
need requires a respectful but continued expression. To build a true
"We," Kristen was able to say to Rich, "I do want some contact, even if
it is not as much as I would ideally like." In response, Rich modified his
approach by sending a text or making a brief call; he felt that he could
do this without compromising his own integrity. These shifts in behaviors that acknowledge the other partner's needs, while still honoring
one's own, are what Hendrix (1988) calls "stretching" on each partner's
part. They also reflect what developmental psychologists call a "theory of
mind"—the capacity to step out of one's own thought process and grasp
(and ultimately feel) what is going on in the other partner's head. True
empathy and true respect!

A critical factor in taking these steps is the awareness of the relationship itself. In confronting this dispute, we coached the couple to ask the
fundamental question, **What is Best for Us?** It might be good for Rich
to go through his busy day without distractions, but is it good for his
relationship if Kristen's resentment is slowly building? Similarly, he could
call and text multiple times in the course of the day, but if each contact
builds his annoyance, they have moved no closer to a healthier "We."
When the health of the relationship is set as the ultimate objective, then
the reduction of resentment and the respect for each individual within
the "We" remain paramount.

Acceptance

Returning to the IBCT perspective, We-ness ultimately means an **acceptance** of the imperfections and vulnerabilities that each partner brings
to the relationship. A theater professor with whom one of us co-taught a
course used to employ the following exercise to help actors get in touch
with the vulnerability of their characters. The two actors would sit very
close, face-to-face. One would begin the exercise by saying, "I could be
hurt by you." The other responded in kind, "I could be hurt by you"
and the remainder of the exercise was to alternate repeating the phrase
while looking in each other's eyes. Needless to say, it could often bring
one or both of the participants to tears.

Living inside a true "We" is living with this reciprocal awareness of the fragility of each partner and the recognition of how much care such awareness requires. Jordan (2010) and Skerrett (2013) describe this as "mutual engagement in supported vulnerability." It is a willingness to stand naked in front of the other person and say, "Here I am, flaws and all" and know that your partner is willing to do the same, and that it is good enough for both of you. Interestingly, we have found in our work with couples that the most challenging part of helping partners achieve this joint vulnerability is not a partner's willingness to accept the other partner's imperfections, but rather the partner's own unwillingness to accept his or her self-perceived flaws, compounded by a skepticism that the other partner truly would accept them as well.

Garrett and Duane were a couple that exemplified this difficulty. Garrett had grown up in a high-powered, extremely successful family of physicians (both parents and his two older brothers were all MDs), but he was the one child who had not become a doctor. Not inclined toward science, he had worked with at-risk youth and become a beloved social worker at a large community mental health center. Despite his fine work and the high praise he received from his coworkers and clients, Garrett always measured himself against the yardstick of his parents and older brothers. Unfortunately, these feelings of self-doubt had built up a strong defense against the belief that anyone might find him worthwhile, and even more, worthy of love. Nothing confounded his partner, Duane, more than Garrett's unwillingness to accept his own goodness and inherent value. Duane would endlessly tell Garrett that he loved him, but Garrett could not seem to trust fully in these declarations. Duane felt pushed away and frustrated. In response, we worked closely with them on building a stronger and safer "We" that would give them more room to allow these vulnerabilities to be supported and accepted.

Finally, they came into therapy and recounted a pivotal night in bed together. Duane had just made an affectionate statement to Garrett, but Garrett had been down all day, blaming himself for a negative interaction at work. Duane told Garrett again that he loved him, but Garrett said that it was hard for him to believe that anyone could love such a "fuck-up." Duane had finally had enough. He spoke clearly to Garrett and told him that he did love him, but that he wasn't sure how much longer he could put up with this. He felt pushed away and that his love was being devalued and treated as superficial or phony. He said that if Garrett could not love himself, then maybe this was sending a message that the love he was offering was a mistake.

Now faced with the real prospect of losing Duane, at last it clicked for Garrett—that Duane truly did love him and that the only real impediment to their relationship was his unwillingness to give himself over to this idea. He was using his self-doubt to protect himself from true vulnerability and acceptance of Duane's love. He told us that he still had a lot of work to do on having more self-confidence, but he was no longer willing to doubt that he was worthy of the gift that Duane was offering. Duane felt an extreme sense of validation from this leap of faith, and that his own vulnerability had finally been rewarded.

Acceptance of self and acceptance of the other, patience with the shortcomings that are inherent to being human—this attitude engenders a wisdom that grows stronger over the course of a long-term relationship and leads to the deepest resilience in times of stress and challenge.

Pleasure and Humor

Thus far, we have made the "We" sound rather heavy and somber, but the essence of the relationship should also include pleasure, humor, and passion. No partner in a couple ever went to the altar saying, "I know that I want to build my 401k with you and make sure that there is an equitable distribution of domestic chores." Couples marry with visions of romantic vacations, ardent lovemaking, dinners with good friends, and casual Sundays eating a late breakfast and reading the newspaper together. Through it all, they imagine forging an ever-deepening friendship with each other.

Obviously, the couples we tend to see in therapy have strayed far from this vision. Our job is often to bring them back to this aspiration—to help them find the humor and fun that were central parts of why they got together in the first place. We seize any moment of shared humor that we observe between them. We highlight the good acts that they do for each other and encourage them to continue and slowly build on them. We initially prohibit grandstanding acts of buying flowers, surprise gifts, big nights out. Instead, we talk about simple acts of kindness—handing the towel to your partner when she steps out of the shower, making his coffee before he gets up, agreeing to watch a favorite TV show rather than going to your office to surf the Internet, volunteering to do the bedtime rituals for the kids on a day that's not your usual routine. And in all cases, such acts must be followed by explicit acknowledgment—in other words—a "thank you." We call any act of kindness "**gift-giving**," and we have been stunned to see how many of these micro-moments can pass in a session without the partner noticing them and registering gratitude. Robinson and Price (1980, cited in Gottman, 2008) found that happily married partners were aware of almost all of the kind gestures of their spouses, while distressed partners registered only half of these behaviors. With many distressed couples, no slight, however trivial, will be overlooked, and yet numerous subtle loving acts will land and vanish, like a spare snowflake on an asphalt drive. We purposely disrupt this pattern by asking partners to say their explicit thank you's to each other while making eye contact. They often describe that they feel self-conscious doing this and repeating it at home, but then they soon notice that it starts to make a difference in how they treat each other.

Once couples start to shift their mindset back to seeing the "We" as a source of pleasure rather than repetitive frustration, they are more ready to engage in the exercises endorsed by Gottman (2008, pp. 153–154) that promote "love maps," building a "culture of appreciation and respect," "increasing and savoring positive affect," and "building affection, good sex, romance and passion." Once they can see the positive potential of the "We," they are ready to take up Gottman's "Love Map Card Deck" or his "Salsa Deck" as a means to greater pleasure in their lives together.

Silvio and Amelia were a couple that had built up a powerful wall around sexual intimacy. Silvio had a chronic back injury and worried about his sexual performance, not to mention his fear of reinjuring his back while making love. Despite his reticence, Amelia was desperate to reconnect with him physically, and this tension between them created ongoing conflicts and alienation.

At the same time they continued to work together every day in raising their three children, negotiating their finances, managing their extended families. When not focusing on their sexual problems, they were considerate, loving, and engaged with each other. Still, Amelia could not accept the possibility that they would live without sexual contact, and Silvio felt deeply threatened and defensive in response to her frustration.

As I (JAS) embarked on direct efforts through the technique of sensate focusing to reduce their anxiety and build up their positive physical connection in small steps, they both emphasized their shared story of disconnection from each other. Silvio said to me, "What's the point of this exercise that you want us to do—the best predictor of future behavior is past behavior." Amelia agreed with a downcast look, "We've tried so many times before, but nothing changes." I pointed out that if past behavior predicted future behavior, they had plenty of reason for hope. I asked them to consider a number of shared moments that I had just witnessed in the current session. Silvio had stopped on the way to therapy to buy coffee for Amelia. Amelia mentioned that she had been dying to tell Silvio about something that happened at her work. They shared a laugh about their youngest son's disaster of a bedroom. I asked them, "Aren't these examples of 'past behaviors,' along with the hundred other ways that you daily think of and attend to each other's needs? Isn't your relationship a record of support and affection as much as it is one of alienation? Wouldn't it be more effective to concentrate on the gratitude you feel for each other's acts of good will rather than on your setbacks as you take these steps toward regaining intimacy? You have a story of kindness that exists just as powerfully as your current story of discord."

In the chapters ahead, we shall address exactly how couples can learn to leverage the positive stories of We-ness in their relationship and how to find more uplifting meaning in the stories of struggle. As EFCT emphasizes, positivity grows out of immediate emotional experience in the present moment, but the capacity to notice that brief quasar of kindness is born from knowledge of past benevolences. We must use our storehouse of positive memories shared with our partners to heighten the value of the current positive interaction or as Gottman (2008) writes,

> It is like periodically lifting out of one's memory a many-faceted jewel, each face of which contains a lovely and loving memory of how the partner or the relationship has enriched one's life. (p. 154)

Shared Meaning

In studies of both individuals and couples, the capacity to draw meaning from life experiences and to see a larger purpose to one's existence has been associated with higher levels of adjustment and greater subjective and psychological well-being (Bauer, McAdams, & Pals, 2008; Blagov & Singer, 2004; King, Hicks, Krull, & Del Gaiso, 2006; Lyubomirsky, 2007). In particular, individuals who are able to grow from adversity and finding meaning in traumatic events often show better long-term outcomes than individuals who are unable to build a meaningful context from these events (Joseph & Linley, 2006).

Ultimately, the "We" is a statement of meaning about the relationship and about each partner's life trajectory. Individuals who have grasped the "We" see themselves as engaged in a lifelong project—the building and sustaining of a structure that they have created and that is unique in the world. We encourage them to see their relationship as belonging to them; they build its private language, rules, symbols, rituals, and meaning systems. We like to tell them that their being together in the way they want to be is "off the grid"; they can bring their own style, ingenuity, and spontaneity to the relationship and need not involve any material purchase or consumer activity. In other words, their relationship, treasured and savored, in their home, and behind their bedroom door, is an act of radical freedom that they can share together. We will never forget the pleasure we saw in the face of an executive husband in our practice as he confessed how much fun he was having in his marriage once he embraced the "We." It was the first time he had bucked the corporate system in his life. "I kind of like being a rebel," he told us.

We once worked with a couple that had the last names of Zimmerman and Rosenstein. Each partner came from very close families, and their respective parents continued to play strong and, at times, intrusive, roles in their married life. Once we began to discuss the "We" with them, we examined how important it was for them to establish their own married identity, separate from their families of origin. Too often, they used the value systems of their parents (not infrequently supported by comments from their parents) to judge their partner as falling short or not doing things right. Zimmermans always went to Sabbath services on Saturday mornings and Rosensteins on Fridays. Zimmermans believed that young children should be free to play and not tracked into achievements. Rosensteins felt that children should be exposed to an instrument or sport as early as possible to give them a head start in life. Our sessions devolved into Talmudic debates with each partner quoting the "scripture" according to Zimmerman or Rosenstein.

In the spirit of the "We," our intervention was simple—we asked them what the **Zimmersteins** thought was the right thing to do. They were their own couple—a unique combination that they had created that belonged to neither the Zimmermans nor the Rosensteins. It was time for the Zimmersteins to carve out their own turf and personal vision in the world. This, of course, meant creating some necessary boundaries that pushed back the all too well-meaning relatives and allowed the Zimmersteins to begin to flourish on their own. "What do the Zimmersteins want and what have they decided to do?" became a powerful catchphrase and touchstone as this couple pursued a meaning and purpose in their relationship distinct from their families of origin.

As we explore other couples' stories in greater depth in the chapters ahead, we shall see how their ability to define a sense of shared purpose and to use stories to highlight these meanings is critical to the positive energy that thriving couples possess.

To summarize the seven basic elements of the "We" that serve as the foundation for our therapeutic work with couples, we developed the following acronym:

Security

Empathy

Respect

Acceptance

Pleasure

Humor

Shared Meaning and Vision

This spells out SERAPHS, which as defined by the dictionary, are "angels of the highest order." We can think of no better way to characterize the spirit of the "We"—that it can bring out the "better angels of our nature," as our noble President Lincoln once said about the threats to a different kind of union!

Finding the "We" in Stories

As we move to the next chapter, we address the following question: If a shift in consciousness from the "I" to the "We" is the critical factor in building trust and positivity, how can we, as therapists, accelerate this process and put it to work for our clients? Besides explaining the elements of the "We" and exhorting them to believe more deeply in this possibility, how do we help them achieve this shift in thinking, feel it in their relationship, and then take action in their life together? Couple exercises can help, and we have included two in this chapter (see "Resilience Boosters for Couples" and "Boosting Your Relational Positivity Ratio"), but we believe something more fundamental can help as well.

We have found stories to be a powerful intervention to achieve the goal of building We-ness. When couples look at how they narrate their separate and shared lives, and how they use stories as forceful communications to each other, they begin to see the hold that stories have over their emotions and feelings of trust.

In the next chapter, we go deeply into the question of what stories mean for couples—how they organize past, present, and potential future experiences of the relationship. Having fully grasped the power of stories in couples' lives, we will be ready to show how they can be a force for success in building a lasting "We."

References

Bauer, J., McAdams, D. P., & Pals, J. L. (2008). Narrative identity and eudaimonic well-being. *Journal of Happiness Studies, 9*(1), 81–104.

Blagov, P. S., & Singer, J. A. (2004). Four dimensions of self-defining memories (specificity, meaning, content, and affect) and their relationships to self-restraint, distress, and repressive defensiveness. *Journal of Personality, 72*(3), 481–511.

Bowen, M. (1961). Family psychotherapy. *American Journal of Orthopsychiatry, 31*, 40–60.

Christensen, A., Atkins, D. C., Berns, S., Wheeler, J., Baucom, D. H., & Simpson, L. E. (2004). Traditional versus integrative behavioral couple therapy for significantly and chronically distressed married couples. *Journal of Consulting and Clinical Psychology, 72*(2), 176–191.

Christensen, A., Atkins, D. C., Yi, J., Baucom, D. H., & George, W. H. (2006). Couple and individual adjustment for 2 years following a randomized clinical trial comparing traditional versus integrative behavioral couple therapy. *Journal of Consulting and Clinical Psychology, 74*(6), 1180–1191.

Christensen, A., & Jacobson, N. S. (1998). *Acceptance and change in couple therapy: A therapist's guide to transforming relationships.* New York, NY: W. W. Norton & Co.

Denton, W. H., Burleson, B. R., Clark, T. E., Rodriguez, C. P., & Hobbs, B. V. (2000). A randomized trial of emotion-focused therapy for couples in a training clinic. *Journal of Marital and Family Therapy, 26*(1), 65–78.

Dimidjian, S., Martell, C. R., & Christensen, A. (2008). *Integrative behavioral couple therapy.* New York, NY: Guilford Press.

Feeney, B. C. (2007). The dependency paradox in close relationships: Accepting dependence promotes independence. *Journal of Personality and Social Psychology, 92*(2), 268–285.

Freedman, J., & Combs, G. (2008). Narrative couple therapy. In A. S. Gurman (Ed.), *Clinical handbook of couple therapy* (4th ed., pp. 229–258). New York, NY: Guilford Press.

Gladwell, M. (2005). *Blink.* New York, NY: Little, Brown.

Gottman, J. M. (1999). *The marriage clinic: A scientifically based marital therapy.* New York, NY: W. W. Norton & Co.

Gottman, J. M. (2008). Gottman method couple therapy. In A. S. Gurman (Ed.), *Clinical handbook of couple therapy* (4th ed., pp.138–164). New York, NY: Guilford Press.

Gottman, J. M. (2011). *The science of trust: Emotional attunement for couples.* New York, NY: W. W. Norton & Co.

Gottman, J. M., Coan, J., Carrère, S., & Swanson, C. (1998). Predicting marital happiness and stability from newlywed interactions. *Journal of Marriage and the Family, 60*(1), 5–22.

Gottman, J. M., & DeClaire, J. (2001). *The relationship cure.* New York, NY: Crown.

Gottman, J. M., & Gottman, J. S. (2008). *Gottman method couple therapy.* New York, NY: Guilford Press.

Gottman, J. M., & Silver, N. (1999). *The seven principles for making marriage work: A practical guide from the country's foremost relationship expert.* New York, NY: Three Rivers Press.

Greenberg, L. S., & Goldman, R. N. (2008). *Emotion-focused couples therapy: The dynamics of emotion, love, and power.* Washington, DC: American Psychological Association.

Greenberg, L. S., & Johnson, S. (2010). *Emotionally focused therapy for couples.* New York, NY: Guilford.

Gurman, A. S. (2008). The comparative study of couple therapy. In A. S. Gurman (Ed.), *Clinical handbook of couple therapy* (4th ed., pp. 1–26). New York, NY: Guilford Press.

Gurman, A. S., & Fraenkel, P. (2002). The history of couple therapy: A millennial review. *Family Process, 41*(2), 199–260.

Haley, J. (1963). *Strategies of psychotherapy.* New York, NY: Grune & Stratton.

Hendrix, H. (1988). *Getting the love you want: A guide for couples.* New York, NY: Henry Holt & Co.

Jacobson, N. S. (1984). A component analysis of behavioral marital therapy: The relative effectiveness of behavior exchange and communication/problem-solving training. *Journal of Consulting and Clinical Psychology, 52*(2), 295–305.

Jacobson, N. S., & Addis, M. E. (1993). Research on couples and couple therapy: What do we know? Where are we going? *Journal of Consulting and Clinical Psychology, 61*(1), 85–93.

Jacobson, N. S., Christensen, A., Prince, S. E., Cordova, J., & Eldridge, K. (2000). Integrative behavioral couple therapy: An acceptance-based, promising new treatment for couple discord. *Journal of Consulting and Clinical Psychology, 68*(2), 351–355.

Johnson, S. M. (2004). *The practice of emotionally focused couple therapy* (2nd ed.). New York, NY: Routledge.

Johnson, S. M., Hunsley, J., Greenberg, L., & Schindler, D. (1999). Emotionally focused couples therapy: Status and challenges. *Clinical Psychology: Science and Practice, 6*(1), 67–79.

Jordan, J. (2010). *Relational-cultural therapy*. Washington, DC: American Psychological Association.

Joseph, S., & Linley, P. A. (2006). Growth following adversity: Theoretical perspectives and implications for clinical practice. *Clinical Psychology Review, 26*(8), 1041–1053.

King, L. A., Hicks, J. A., Krull, J. L., & Del Gaiso, A. K. (2006). Positive affect and the experience of meaning in life. *Journal of Personality and Social Psychology, 90*(1), 179–196.

Lyubomirsky, S. (2007). *The how of happiness: A scientific approach to getting the life you want*. New York, NY: Penguin Press.

Madigan, S. (2011). *Narrative therapy*. Washington, DC: American Psychological Association.

Minuchin, S. (1974). *Families and family therapy*. Cambridge, MA: Harvard University Press.

Robinson, E. A., & Price, M. G. (1980). Pleasurable behavior in marital interaction: An observational study. *Journal of Consulting and Clinical Psychology, 48*(1), 117–118.

Satir, V. (1964). *Conjoint family therapy*. Palo Alto, CA: Science and Behavior Books.

Skerrett, K. (2013). Resilient relationships: Cultivating the healing potential of couple stories. In J. Jordan and J. Carlson (Eds.), *Creating connection: A relational-cultural approach with couples* (pp. 45–60). New York, NY: Routledge.

Taibbi, R. (2009). *Doing couple therapy: Craft and creativity in work with intimate partners*. New York, NY: Guilford Press.

White, M., & Epston, D. (1990). *Narrative means to therapeutic ends*. New York, NY: W. W. Norton & Co.

Zimmerman, J. L., & Dickerson, V. C. (1996). *If problems talked: Narrative therapy in action*. New York, NY: Guilford Press.

BOOSTING YOUR RELATIONAL POSITIVITY RATIO

Count the blessings in your relationship.

Try for 3 times each week.
Transform ordinary events into blessings.

Count the kindnesses you extend toward your partner. Notice his or her reactions.

In addition, select a Kindness Day each week in which you step up your kindness to a new or higher level. For example, weed your neighbor's garden, volunteer at a soup kitchen, participate in a local sing-a-long in an extended care facility.

Visualize your future successes as a couple.

As you imagine, linger over every detail.
Share the visualization experience with your partner.

Cultivate healthy distractions.

Keep a list of the things each of you do individually to get your mind off your troubles.
Which of those can you do together?

Establish gratitude rituals for your relationship.

For example, share the things for which you're grateful each night before bed, give thanks together before a meal, throw a small celebration to honor one another's successes and accomplishments.

Devise ways to increase your experiences of inspiration, wonder, humor, awe, and hope in your partnership.

RESILIENCE BOOSTERS FOR COUPLES

Gratitude Lists

Make a list of all the things you are grateful for and add to it weekly.

Exchange lists with your spouse and talk about it on a regular basis.

Pleasure Breaks

Find one thing that brings you pleasure and do it daily.

Identify a pleasure you and your spouse share; plan a way to do it weekly.

Signature Strengths

Visit the website: www.authentichappiness.org.

Identity your signature strength and have your spouse do the same.

Plan a night together in which each of you use your highest strengths.

Increase Optimism and Hope

Practice finding the universal causes of good events as well as the temporary and specific causes for misfortune.

Practice disputing your pessimistic thoughts:

Recognize them.

Treat them as if they were uttered by an external person (a rival whose mission in life was to make you miserable).

Stand back and check the evidence for your pessimistic belief.

Examine the alternatives.

Ask how useful it is to hold onto the pessimistic belief.

Thankfulness

Thank one person a week for something that person said or did that added to the quality of your life.

2

THE POWER OF STORIES
IN OUR LIVES

Most of us love a good story. In fact, pay attention to how you feel as you read the words, "Once upon a time." We can almost feel our bodies ready and primed for a well-told tale that we can lose ourselves in. We all have stories to tell and are just dying for people to listen.

Many academic disciplines have embraced the study of stories—from cultural anthropology to social and developmental psychology to cognitive neuroscience. These various approaches concur on a number of points. First, stories are universal as they can be found in every human culture on the planet. They are found across the life span, from the youngest child to our oldest elders—stories give shape to human interactions. They are also a wonderful example of the ways in which emotion and analytic thinking are intertwined; the logical left hemisphere needs the emotional context and autobiographical data of the right hemisphere to have a personal story make sense (Siegel & Hartzell, 2003).

Therapists are in the story business. We listen, struggle to understand, and then work to help clients shape their narratives in ways that support change. We are regularly fascinated by the infinite ways that clients craft stories to make sense of their world, and we are particularly fascinated by the unpredictable, unconventional, even surprising stories we hear daily. We respond to the magnetic pull of stories of pathos, destruction, heroism, and quiet courage and routinely ask questions like: What made this story turn out this way rather than that?

For example, one evening I (KS) saw Mark and Lee and later Emma and John. Mark and Lee had been married for 12 years and had sought therapy to interrupt the escalating screaming matches in which they regularly engaged. We had had only three sessions, and while they had taken a few steps to contain their volatility and substitute more constructive dialogue, they seemed far from stable. Their communication was still peppered with foul language, eye rolls, and other gestures of disgust. Emma and John, on the other hand, were the epitome of politeness and calm. Sessions with them were marked by careful turn-taking; considered, well-crafted opinion-giving; and patient listening. We had met five times previously with the goal of helping them examine their impasse around whether or not to have a third child.

Mark and Lee came to our session that night professing gratitude and claiming that their work was done and they could stop. Later, Emma and John arrived for their hour, both looking depressed and uncharacteristically tearful. Emma announced that they wouldn't be back because John had revealed his six-month attraction to a coworker. He was seeking a separation from Emma to explore the other relationship "with a clear conscience."

Conventional wisdom might have predicted Mark and Lee to be the couple headed for separation and/or divorce, and John and Emma, the ones to negotiate a mutually agreeable action plan. These are the kinds of experiences that keep our therapeutic lives interesting (as well as a little frustrating). So how can we understand these couples?

One way of understanding the behavior of Mark and Lee and John and Emma is to examine the stories each had about the kind of relationship they were in and about the kind of relationship they believed they wanted. In looking closely at their stories, we might consider the degree of We-ness that their different narratives invoked. Additionally, we might evaluate the match between the stories that they told and the nature of the relationships that they actually presented in session.

Mark and Lee both grew up in warring households and, for better or worse, this was the template by which they graded normalcy. In each partner's individual stories, as well as in their shared stories of their relationship (what we might define as their **Couple Story**), both viewed fighting as caring and passionate connection. Neither wanted to change the basic story template; they just wanted help in learning how to turn down the volume. They also both valued loyalty and believed it was essential to go the distance once committed. Gottman and Gottman (2008) have detailed extensive research to show that volatile couples who know how to make up and who experience an underlying love are likely to remain together and maintain a stable bond. Mark and Lee felt a shared bond in their intense emotionality; one might say that their story reflected the following message: "We may seem loud and angry at times, but this is the language that we speak and its volume is grounded in passionate caring, not discord." It is this narrative movement from emotional conflict to an endpoint of caring that then elevates their story from simply a Couple Story to a **We-Story**.

John and Emma, on the other hand, presented a surface relationship that may have looked and sounded functional to outsiders, but it didn't meet each partner's individual needs and certainly was not connected to a shared We-Story. John's background led him to desire more companionship and intimacy than the current relationship provided. Emma's individual story template placed family obligations, including extended family, as more important than her marital priorities. She tended to devalue John's requests to be a bigger priority in her life. John's parents had modeled a highly committed partnership and he could not make sense of how Emma did not put their relationship first. These two partners had very different visions of what a happy, fulfilling relationship should look like, and this disconnect grew more critical as time went on. In terms of our **SERAPHS** perspective on We-ness, they had not arrived at a **Shared Meaning and Vision** for their relationship. As therapists, we often see couples that end up tolerating a relationship that is a misfit for each individual's personal story. One critical intervention that we can offer is to help couples mesh their individual stories into a more constructive shared We-Story. To do so, each partner must learn to modify familiar expectations and move a bit more in the direction of their partner. Out of this mutual accommodation a new more mutual story can emerge.

In this chapter, we take a look at the broad role of stories in our lives, first from an individual perspective and then from a couple perspective. We then define more fully our concept of the We-Story and provide some examples of the different types of We-Stories that couples may generate. With our definitions of We-ness and We-Stories in place, we will be ready to move forward to applications of these concepts in couple therapy— first with how we assess couples' initial levels of We-ness and then how we help them to craft We-Stories that are "good enough" to encourage greater mutuality.

The Role of Stories for Individuals

At the heart of this book is the conviction that human beings are first and foremost meaning-making beings, and that our essential way of making meaning is through narrative. It is no news that 21st-century life is very complex. Stories allow us to make sense out of otherwise confusing or random events. They help us understand some of the decisions we have made and create something sensible out of the daily chaos of our lives. They can also shape our futures by offering a template for our goals and desires. In particular, telling stories of struggle that turn out well may give people the hope they need to take initiative and fashion productive lives (McAdams, 2013).

Interest in the storied self coalesced in the therapeutic community in the 1990s with the postmodern and social constructivist approaches offered by Gergen (1991) and others (Shotter & Gergen, 1989), as well as the contributions of Narrative Therapy (Freedman & Combs, 1996; Madsen, 2009; White & Epston, 1990; Zimmerman & Dickerson, 1993). At the same time, an emerging movement in personality psychology also focused on "narrative identity" and how individuals use life stories to create a sense of unity across past, present, and future selves (Lieblich, McAdams, & Josselson, 2004; McAdams, 2001, 2013; McLean, 2008; Singer, 2004; Singer, Blagov, Berry, & Oost, 2013). These authors maintained that the meaning of life events come from the stories people tell themselves and each other, and as such, constitute the shape of their lives and relationships. From their perspective, therapy is fundamentally a process of story reformulation and repair.

More recently, Gottschall (2012), in *The Storytelling Animal* chronicled how narrative is stitched intrinsically into the fabric of human psychology. Etymologically, narrative is rooted in the Sanskrit word *gna,* which connects to Latin words for both "knowing" (*gnarus*) and "telling" (narrative), which reminds us that the story is a universal tool for absorbing knowledge and expressing it (Abbott, 2008). This also underscores the necessity both to know our own stories, as well as to tell them.

Although the quest to understand the nature of consciousness is ancient, emerging interdisciplinary work in cognitive neuroscience and epigenetics indicate that consciousness itself is a narrative process. Storying is a primary activity that actually precedes language (Randall & McKim, 2008). Another way to put this is that we are born with the neurological equipment necessary to conceive of ourselves as distinctive human selves participating in events over time. We now know that this conception takes a narrative form. A key researcher in the neuroscience field, Antonio Damasio, states: "Self is the feeling of what happens when your being is modified by the act of apprehending something" (1999, p. 10). Developmentally, then, selfhood is a continuum that extends from an unconscious state to a fully evolved self-consciousness. The self becomes conscious of itself only through the process of perception and representation of either an external object or an internal memory. This representational process is fundamentally narrative when it applies temporal parameters, and as such, displays qualities such as event sequences, plot, and causal outcomes. Such a highly developed, complex level of awareness ultimately allows us to have a life story, and it is through this expansive consciousness that we craft a coherent self across time. A coherent self can also be thought of as a coherent story (Bruner, 1990; McAdams, 2013; Sarbin, 1986). Research suggests that life stories begin to be actively constructed in late adolescence/early adulthood (Csikszentmihalyi, 1990; Habermas & Bluck, 2000), and once begun, are works in progress that continue across the adult life course.

A life story can also be thought of as akin to a "personal myth" about who we are deep down, how we got this way, and what our life experience all means (Gottschall, 2012). Our life stories are who we are, but, of course, do not represent an objective account (Spence, 1982). Rather, our life story is a carefully shaped narrative that is rampant with selective forgetting and skillfully spun meanings. When my (KS) children were teenagers, they used to call this "selective memory." I, of course, seemed to be the only one in the family who suffered from this condition, as I was reminded regularly with statements like, "I never said that" or "Don't you remember I told you I was going to Dave's house, not Matt's?" They were always convinced my memory was driven by forces designed to ruin their good times, and I was convinced their memories were driven by secret pacts concocted to see who could make me crazy first. It took me many years to appreciate that memory isn't an outright fiction, but more like a fictionalization, or least a reconstruction of episodic memories interacting with our desires, long-term goals, and self-schemas (Conway & Pleydell-Pearce, 2000; Conway, Singer, & Tagini, 2004; Singer et al., 2013).

As therapists, we've been trained to help couples distinguish fact from fiction—to separate the stories they tell themselves from what actually goes on in relational interactions. But contemporary neuroscience tells us that such a clear separation simply isn't the way we're wired. Rather, we shape the facts of a relationship to conform to our personal fictions. As Schacter and Addis (2007) have demonstrated, there is considerable overlap in a neural circuit called the "default network," which is responsible for both remembering and imagining. Oliver Sacks, in a recent essay in the *New York Review of Books* (February 21, 2013), claimed that there is no mechanism in the mind or brain for ensuring the truth of our recollections, and that all events are experienced in a highly subjective way. Thus, there is no easy way to distinguish a genuine memory or inspiration from those that have been borrowed or suggested; memory is dialogic—arising from interconnections and conversations among many minds. Research with couples suggests that stories are a very powerful source of self-persuasion, and highly internally consistent, so that evidence that doesn't fit the story gets left behind (Holmes, 2012).

Neuroscience is also helping us to understand that one of the chief functions of our brain is to simulate potential challenges—to play out scenarios without the risk of attempting them *in vivo*. Parents will recognize that play serves a similar purpose in the lives of developing children. Playing out the "what ifs" in our mind is the optimal way to test and refine our decision-making and change our behavior. Crafting stories allows us to do just that. Constructive changes in the patterns of neurotransmission are most likely to happen when we are curious and emotionally engaged. Therapists seek out and emphasize stories because we appreciate their mesmerizing quality, their "stick-ability."

An equally important contribution from narrative psychology is its emphasis on the role of stories as moral-driven and meaning-making. This aspect has great significance for couple relationships. Not all stories are created equal and for a particular story to really work, it has to have a particular moral quality. Think of how much more we're drawn to the story of the good guy who profits and becomes successful than we are to the story of the good guy who becomes paralyzed in a hit-and-run accident. The stories of Lee and Mark demonstrate several moral themes with a redemptive twist; arguing is acceptable because it represents passionate caring and true engagement; for these two, loyalty to one another trumps all other virtues and vices and is the ultimate yard-stick. In our own research (Baddeley & Singer, 2008), we have found that individuals who have lost a loved one are much more likely to find a sympathetic audience and seem more desirable as friends and intimates if they tell their stories of bereavement with a more redemptive ending than if they let their stories remain weighted down with grief and futil-ity. As McAdams (2013) has repeatedly demonstrated, individuals and couples in our society function more effectively and have better physical health when they can link their personal stories to endings that convey growth, uplift, and renewed possibility.

We all try to get one another's attention and influence each other through the stories we tell. Stories that reflect particular virtues are more likely to engage a listener and sustain influence. Aesop knew this with his fables, but it turns out that recent neuroscientific findings are ver-ifying this fact—our brains are less likely to absorb stories that lack a moral or meaning-making component (Gottschall, 2012). It seems that stories serve the biological function of encouraging prosocial behavior—of teaching us how to get along, the rules to play by, and the rewards we will reap when we do. Simply put, we are hard-wired to both create and tell moralistic stories in order to bind us together as a species. As a group-level adaptation, stories are an important protective mechanism for our gene pool, as they promote cooperation and suppress selfish-ness. Of course, the kinds of stories that can be told and the particular virtues extolled are socially constructed and culturally specific. Within and between different societies, different narrative traditions shape their own standard of story content and moral message.

An expanding amount of research suggests that the stories in which narrators draw lessons about the self, important relationships, or life in general ("life lessons") are especially associated with better adjustment and greater emotional maturity (Blagov and Singer, 2004). It seems we are drawn to those narratives in which we can learn how a protagonist gains insight, wisdom, or self understanding from a series of recon-structed life scenes (Thorne, McLean, & Lawrence, 2004). McAdams (2013) identified the "redemptive life narrative" as one told by highly generative midlife Americans in which an innocent but highly principled protagonist transforms chaos into order, turns suffering to advantage, or overcomes many contrasting desires and ultimately gives back to oth-ers the advantages he has gotten along his journey. Having a redemptive story behind you provides the hope—even confidence—that your efforts will bear fruit in the long run. Such rags to riches, self-help, conversion tales run through American cultural history and are recognized in Amer-ican society as accounts of the "good life."

Individual stories also powerfully structure lessons about gender, race/ethnicity, power, time, and development. They answer questions like: How does a Latino middle-aged man working in Southern California react to his male partner's extramarital affair? Or how does an 82-year-old Asian American woman respond to the request of her daughter to take in the daughter's drug-addicted homeless boyfriend? How does an African American couple address the retirement of the husband after a productive 30-year career in sales, especially when the wife continues to work? Contextual issues are deeply embedded in the stories we tell ourselves as well as those we tell others and shape both meaning-making and interactions between partners.

Couple Stories and We-Stories

Just as individuals have stories, each individual in a committed relationship holds a conception of a joint or couple story he or she believes is shared. We define a **Couple Story** as a story that the two members of the couple jointly tell about their experiences in their relationship. It may describe their meeting, courtship, early years of their partnership or marriage, their ongoing experiences up to the present moment, or even convey their expectations about the future of their time together. This Couple Story reflects the joint narrative of the couple's connection or lack of connection to each other. This narrative may be agreed upon or disputed by each member, but it is the record of what they each present about their shared lives together rather than stories of their individual experiences prior to the relationship (see Figure 2.1).

In defining the Couple Story, it is critical to emphasize: **Not all Couple Stories are We-Stories.** Indeed, many couples in therapy may narrate a story of their relationship that highlights their tension, disconnection, or outright hostility toward each other. However, for couples that have explicitly requested that we work with them to sustain and improve their relationship, our job is to find ways to uncover and cultivate We-Stories

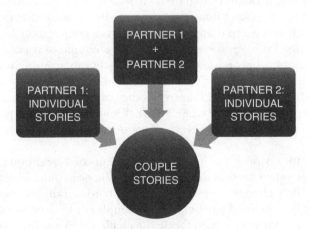

Figure 2.1. Individual and Couple Stories

that are positive antidotes to stories of rancor and frustration. We-Stories express one or more SERAPHS elements and affirm the commitment and mutual caring that are the bedrock of a strong relationship. We-Stories provide the couple a sense of meaningful coherence and guidance for engagement. For example, when asked for their We-Story, Mary offered this tale of her 58-year marriage:

> We got married at a time when that was what people did. I wouldn't say we knew each other very well, but there was a spark and I wanted a family. Ed was hard-working and honest and seemed to care about me, so we decided to marry. We really had no idea what was ahead. We had four children close together and when our fifth was born with cerebral palsy, we said "No more." Ed worked a lot of jobs and was always gone, so I had the work of the kids pretty much alone and our last child was a real problem. I just kept my nose to the grindstone, but we slowly became like two workhorses—plodding along next to each other with no connection. At the time I wouldn't have called myself depressed but when I look back at it, that's what I was. I did what was necessary and was good with the kids but that was it. Things got to a turning point when the older four were grown and out of the house, and we were starting to slow down and realized we couldn't manage Kevin (5th child) alone anymore. Ed had a few health scares and that was like a wake-up call for us. Somehow we managed to slowly get out of our rut and start talking like we never had—about what options we had and about how we felt about Kevin and his needs. None of our other kids were in a position to help us so we made the hard decision to put Kevin in a home for the disabled close to where we live. It killed us, but in a funny way, brought us together—maybe because we started talking again. It's easier now to talk to each other about what we like or want, and we're doing more of that as a couple than we ever did. Now I'd have to say that we're like a couple of rocks someone kept in their pocket too long. They bump around and rub together and wear off the sharp edges so that they're smoother. The sharp edges are still there, but they can toss around together or lie side by side, and when you stick your hand in your pocket and remember they're there, it's comforting.

Mary's story typifies the narrative ingredients of a beginning, middle, and end as well as tension and a problem to be overcome. We can follow Mary and Ed's changes over time from the hard-working, somewhat distant though committed partnership to a couple confronted by a challenging dilemma. Their choice to tackle the challenge as a team appeared to reengage them as a couple and set them on a more interactive path going forward. In their We-Story, we hear the shift from an earlier independent, individualistic relationship to one of greater partnership and connection.

A We-Story may flow seamlessly out of one or both partners' individual story (or not), and each partner may tell the same We-Story (or not). And as individuals have many stories to tell, so, too, do couples have multiple stories. There is the story of how we met, the childbirth story, the story of buying our first home, the story of a job layoff or a partner's illness, and on and on. The couple prioritizes certain We-Stories, elevating them to favored status. Listeners, whether it be a child, friend, or therapist, can often become co-contributors to story creation, as they react differentially to each aspect of a story.

These favored stories may include what Alea and Vick (2010) have called "**relationship-defining memories**," which are accounts of how couples first met or first recognized the potential for a lasting love relationship. More vivid, positive, and well-rehearsed relationship-defining memories have been linked to higher levels of marital satisfaction (Alea & Vick, 2010; Alea, Singer, & Labunko, in press). Alea et al. (in press) also found that couples' memories of strongly positive and strongly negative events from their relationship differ in the use of the pronoun, "We." This study demonstrated that, regardless of the emotional valence of the couples' memories, memories with more "We" statements were linked to greater marital satisfaction. This effect was strongest for women, a finding that parallels the results of Singer, Labunko, Alea, and Baddeley (in press) who found that women showed greater sensitivity to ratings of mutuality in their relationship than their husbands (see Chapter 3, this volume for detailed discussion of these findings). Alea and Bluck (2007) additionally demonstrated that the sharing of more personally significant relationship memories produced greater intimacy among couples, and this effect was particularly true for women. All of these findings, as a whole, point to the particular potency of We-Stories, and especially those that highlight a We-consciousness, whether these memories are of initial encounters or subsequent shared experiences.

Let's take a look at an example of a relationship-defining memory (or We-Story) told by another long-married pair. It was obvious that the story was an oft-told tale, craftily shared, perfectly timed, peppered with head nods, anticipatory smiles, and looks exchanged that said, "Wait till you hear what comes next."

> So my girlfriend set us up, I was almost out of high school, not sure of my next step and I liked the idea of going out on a date with an older man. (I was 27.) We double-dated with my girlfriend and her boyfriend and had an okay time, but I can tell you it wasn't love at first sight for me. (It sure was for me—I

thought she was the most beautiful girl I had ever seen.) So he called after that and I figured I'd give him another chance, but then it took awhile for us to agree on a time and the next thing I hear, he tells me he has to go back home to Kansas City because his Dad is really sick and they needed him on the farm. So then, I never heard anything for like 5 years and I got married and forgot about him. (I never forgot about her—I thought about her every day and plotted how and when I could get back to Chicago.) So my marriage didn't really work out. Thankfully, we never had any kids, but I felt bad about myself and about what happened for a long time. One day, that same girlfriend says to me, "Hey, Jack is back in town and has been asking after you. Can I give him your number?" I told her why not and we went out for drinks and that was that. **That** was love at second sight we like to say! (It was always first for me 'cause I never stopped believing you were the one—I just had to convince you!)

We-Stories can be told in response to a direct question like those above; told in bits and pieces by alternating narrators over time; or inferred, interpreted, and understood from the deep listening that typically occurs in the therapy room. What this particular story contains are seeds for many successful We-Stories—a redemptive ending; a mythology of true love (as expressed here by the husband first); a dynamic of loyalty and patience, in this case also embodied by the husband's role in the relationship. All of these story elements are templates for how this couple understands their sense of We-ness and how it constructs a shared vision of the relationship. In this story, we see key elements of SERAPHS that constitute the essence of We-ness. There are **A**cceptance, **P**leasure, and **H**umor—as depicted in the wife's willingness to give Jack a second try; Jack's willingness to look beyond his wife's first marriage; and the clear affection and humor with which each partner contributes to the shared tale.

The contrasting individual stories of Jesse and Sandra, as well as their Couple Story, typify those we more commonly hear in our consulting practices during our initial sessions with a couple in distress. Jesse and Sandra were successful attorneys in their late 50s, married for 24 years who were seeking counseling to "make a decision about the future of their marriage." They had two young adult daughters together and shared life with Jesse's three adult sons from a previous marriage. Both described their marriage as "working reasonably well—we are compatible workaholics who are devoted to our family." They had managed to merge their busy lives and felt that they had achieved a shared routine gracefully. In this sense their Couple Story seemed superficially happy. However, their individual stories were quite different from the Couple Story. Jesse viewed Sandra as emotionally distant, a "cold fish" who was always more interested in work than him. He knew that this, in part, rationalized the five-year love affair he was conducting with an unmarried colleague and helped assuage his periodic feelings of guilt. He was convinced that if he told Sandra of his dissatisfaction, she would be "unbearably hurt" and he took great pains to keep this affair secret. Sandra's private individual story described Jesse as "a terribly needy man" who she figured had had multiple affairs throughout the course of their marriage. She found their different emotional styles to be irreconcilable and her "don't ask don't tell" policy an effective solution.

What happened for Jesse and Sandra is common in many long-term relationships. As partners begin to get to know one another in the early days of their relationship, they begin to project their own thoughts and feelings onto the other and create a Couple Story that has less and less to do with what the other is really like and more to do with what each imagines the other to be like. Then the partner's behaviors come to be perceived through the lens of these characterizations and each acts in ways that shape the behavior of the other in order to make the portrait a better match. So despite the fact that Jesse and Sandra shared the initial story of a "happy union," both individuals found themselves playing a role that they never imagined when they first married. Their Couple Story portrayed mutual efficiency on the surface but papered over deep divides below their "transactional" partnership. Eventually, their Couple Story and the related ways it shaped behavior became constraining and incompatible to their preferred view of their better selves. The marriage ultimately collapsed under the strain.

Why would couples like Jesse and Sandra maintain a Couple Story so discontinuous from their individual ones? Here again, we see the essential function of story making—to help us make sense of life and then follow that outline in a consistent way. None of us would want to stay in a relationship that didn't make sense in the context of what went on before, thus we perceive new events in terms of old stories. The "We are happy, compatible workaholics" story enabled Jesse and Sandra to stay together and maintain their priorities—success in the workplace and devotion to family unity. However, it had few genuine elements of We-consciousness holding it together. Despite the painful subplots of their individual stories, and the lack of any underlying connection, they embraced the couple fiction to keep their agreed-upon priorities afloat. This was a temporary and ultimately costly bargain.

Often such disconnects between individual and couple stories reflect a sense of threat felt by one or both partners. The individual stories of both Jesse and Sandra registered as a "threat," both to self and other and whether or not the threat registered consciously, they devised a compensatory Couple Story that would, in effect, hold the tension created by the individual stories. These survival skills are often at odds with openness, receptivity, and higher thought—the skills we call relational thinking.

Usually, partners resort to a "cover story" because they lack the relational skills necessary to shift the interaction into a more open and challenging discussion that would ultimately allow genuine We-ness to build. Simply put, a rigid reactivity is our fight-flight-freeze survival reflex; receptivity is our experience of being safe and seen.

Defining the Functions and Features of We-Stories

Dan Siegel's (2012) work has particular relevance for us in his writings about interpersonal neurobiology and neuroplasticity and his description of the neurobiology of the "We." He was one of the first to connect the idea of a coherent story to a coherent mind and identify the importance of integrative communication—when individuals are honored for their differences and become linked through respectful and compassionate communication. What makes a coherent narrative is the flexible blending of the left and right modes of processing. When the left-mode drive to explain and the right-mode nonverbal and autobiographical processing are freely integrated, a coherent narrative emerges.

Gottman and Silver (2012) wrote that a critical component to couple functioning is the capacity to share their stories, find meaning, and dream out their lives together—this is how trust is developed, cultivated, and sustained over time. Leslie Greenberg (2010) has discussed the concept of an "emotional handle"—a metaphor, story, or phrase that serves as a shorthand placeholder for a more elaborate psychological and/or relational concern. Couples' stories function as the emotional handles that couples grab on to in order to express to each other and to others outside their relationship fundamental themes and defining elements of who they are together. When couples can find the We-Stories among their repertoire of Couple Stories, they are able to leverage their imagery, metaphors, and shared visions toward hopeful and affirming ends.

In general, Bluck (2003) has argued that autobiographical memory-telling serves three primary functions: (1) self-understanding; (2) a directive function (aiding in goal definition and guidance); and (3) a social function (intimacy building and communication). We see We-Stories as having four similar roles that all serve to cultivate We-ness.

Putting all that we have said previously about the nature of stories and We-ness together, we might define We-Stories more formally as carrying out the following four functions: they

1. shape the couple's mutual identity;
2. provide meaning and purpose in the couple's life;
3. serve as guides for interaction in the moment and templates for future growth;
4. serve as a repository of the couple's wisdom and a vehicle for transmission of the couple's legacy.

These four functions are usually merged in a **vivid image or metaphor that serves as symbol or touchstone for the relationship.** We will explore how each of these dimensions can be identified and worked with in couple therapy in future chapters, but we will briefly outline each dimension in the following discussion. In addition, we also define what we see as the essential structural features of We-Story narratives. In order to be an effective or **Good Enough** We-Story, these structural features should be in place as the couple tells their story. Just as important, we also acknowledge the power of "stuck" Couple Stories that serve a destructive and defining role in couples' lives. Chapter 5 addresses these negative Couple Stories and how to break through the impasses they create.

1. Couple Identity Shapers

The moment a couple walks in the door and extend their hands in greeting, the therapist has her or his first encounter with the notion of identity. Whether it is: "Hi, we're the Joneses" or "Hello, I'm Bob, he's Bill," or "Hi, I'm Jessica Williams"—"I'm Sam Kennedy," we are given important information about the way this particular couple has chosen to present themselves to the world at large.

Once we ask the couple to tell us a brief history of their relationship, we are further launched into multiple dimensions of couple identity shaping. It might be helpful to think about the Couple Stories that emerge from their history as coming in two forms—a micro- and macro-format (Angus & Greenberg, 2011, p. 5, refer to these in their narrative-informed EFT as "micro-narratives" and "macro-narratives"). Think of the *micro-stories* as the specific narrative episodes the couple chooses to share—their first encounter (or "relationship-defining memory"), their wedding day, birth of a child, a discovery of an infidelity, a response to a parent's death. These more defined narrative episodes are all rich stories that have the potential for the defining characteristics, repetitive themes, and metaphors that we highlighted previously. In Chapter 5, we discuss how to collect, link, and analyze these Couple Stories to extract what narrative psychologists call "scripts" (Siegel & Demorest, 2010; Tomkins, 1979, 1987) that reflect key emotional patterns and relational themes that are crucial to the couple.

The **macro-story** is the big picture that the couple paints of their overall story. Here, the lens is pulled back from individual episodes to take in a sweeping portrayal of the couple. For example, Peggy and Wilson described their relationship history in the following way:

> We met during a meditation retreat at a Buddhist Center in
> Western Mass. and our commitment to meditation has been a
> guiding light in our relationship. Whenever things go awry, we
> know it is time to get back to our basics—whether it means going
> to a retreat or simply building in more time for meditation into

our weekly routines. People always say how children screw your balance up, but we just threw them in carriers and pressed them to our chests during our reflection times. Now with kids at that middle school age, our friends ask us why they seem so quiet and stable. We tell them that they started meditating before they could speak.

No single incident receives any in-depth focus in this macro-story, but as a whole, it richly conveys the positive identity and defining features of this couple, making it a good candidate for a We-Story. Indeed macro-stories are likely to express many of the couple's conventions, rituals, and customs. However, they may also reveal the familiar areas of division or difference to which the couple repetitively returns. Implicitly, macro-stories convey the shared and/or conflicting values of the couple: "Are we city people or suburban people?" "Do we believe in public education or private?" "Are we spiritual or religious?" "Do we merge our money or keep it separate?" "Are we a deeply trusting or deeply doubting couple?" As we pointed out earlier, once a narrative is set in place, it can solidify and become a poor reflection of a couple's life 2, 15, or 30 years into the relationship. One of the key jobs of the couple therapist is to help keep these stories dynamic, fluid, and representative of the current life of the couple. In this way, they have a greater chance of representing the couple's current sense of themselves more accurately.

2. Making Meaning and Purpose

Stories help couples make sense of the complexities of their experiences— from the philosophical to the mundane. They provide everything from a rationale for the marriage itself: "We got sick of keeping two apartments and always moving back and forth" to explaining a period of bad luck: "We really got distracted and let our finances get out of hand" to addressing the illness of a child: "We were preoccupied with ourselves; we never gave her enough attention until it was too late and she was really sick." The scientific study of meaning has repeatedly demonstrated that people who believe their lives have meaning or purpose appear better off on a variety of measures (King, Hicks, Krull, & Del Gaiso, 2006; Lyubomirsky, 2007). The creation of meaning—understanding where we've been, where we are, and where we're going—is one of the most human and critical tasks we face. It is also a vital part of couple resilience (Walsh, 2006), and those who find meaning following adversity or traumatic life events report better outcomes than those who do not (Janoff-Bulman & Yopyk, 2004). Ongoing research suggests that once couples develop a common understanding and a sense of shared purpose, they can begin to take more effective action on their own or the other's behalf (Skerrett, 2013). Couples who constructed a unified meaning for a cancer diagnosis (specifically defining it as "our problem") found that it lent coherence, provided direction, and helped them manage the accumulation of stressors and illness demands (Skerrett, 1998).

Ellen, a successful biologist, had been diagnosed with breast cancer. Bob, her husband of 31 years, was both distraught and confused at her unwillingness to follow the recommendations of her oncologist. He tried supporting, cajoling, sympathizing, fighting—all to no avail. She was resolute in her denial and refusal to initiate treatment. After several weeks of therapy in which she struggled to make sense of her diagnosis by applying her logical, scientist mind, she came to believe that her diagnosis was a "retribution" for earlier sins and decided to initiate treatment. Although this "insight" struck both the therapist and her husband as judgmental, what was critical was the fact that it made enough sense to Ellen to mobilize her, and, of course, the outcome was a profound relief to Bob. Bob was willing to buy into this story for Ellen's sake, and they were able to allow it to guide them to the treatment she required.

This example worked out well, but it also illustrates why narrative psychologists have recently been more cautious about the value of meaning-making in stories. In general, early research (Bauer, McAdams, & Pals, 2008; Blagov & Singer, 2004) pointed to the connection between meaning-making and better adjustment as well as higher levels of subjective well-being. However, recent research has emphasized that this meaning-making must be coherent, flexible, and accurate (Singer et al., 2013), while McLean and Mansfield (2010) have identified certain circumstances in which meaning-making may overcomplicate positive experiences or interfere with more adaptive repressive coping (Bonanno, 2005). In Chapter 5 of this volume, we highlight how partners can assign rigid interpretations or undermining meanings to Couple Stories that then perpetuate distance and distress within the relationship. Stories direct us toward meaning, but for couples clearly some meanings are likely to be healthier and more growthful than others. We-Stories assign positive meaning or a shared optimistic vision to a couple's life experiences, which in general is a healthy and adaptive process. However, pasting positive meanings on experiences when they are not justified or when this creates an incoherent or hypocritical narrative is a danger to which both the couple and the therapist should be alert and watchful. Redemptive endings of Couple Stories need to be earned; they cannot simply be wished for and imagined in the face of a contradictory reality.

3. Guides for Engagement; Vehicles for Change and Growth

Stories are a rulebook of sorts, establishing what will work, what won't, what the parameters are for connection and disconnection—the how-tos for the human condition and its triumphs and disappointments.

We know that the emotions evoked in stories play a central role in the couple's ability to galvanize change and guide healing (Fosha, Siegel, & Solomon, 2009). The intimacy of a committed relationship enables emotions to enrich, rather than enslave, our lives. The influential "broaden and build" theory of Fredrickson and her colleagues (2002, 2005) suggests that positive emotions (1) broaden attention and thinking; (2) undo lingering negative emotional arousal; (3) fuel psychological resilience; (4) build consequential personal resources; and (5) trigger upward spirals toward greater well-being in the future. Since these effects of positive emotion accumulate and compound over time, they carry the capacity to transform individuals (and by extension, couples) for the better, making them healthier and more socially integrated, knowledgeable, and effective (Fredrickson, 2006). In her latest book, *Love 2.0*, Fredrickson (2013) defines love on a bodily level as micro-moments of connection between people. When the brain registers love, it triggers the release of the hormone oxytocin, as long as that feeling is shared, matches up with the brain activity of the other, and comes with a mutual motivation to invest in each other's well-being. She claims that this positivity process ultimately alters our cellular architecture and sets us up for healthier lives. Because these micro-moments are always renewable, love—more than other positive emotion—holds the key to improving our mental and physical health and lengthening our lives.

This makes a very strong case for assisting couples to create a culture of positivity. If the relationship itself and the ways in which it is storied can be viewed as a source of positive emotion, couples are much more likely to view the relationship as an entity that nourishes, sustains, and is worthy of time and attention. This last point cannot be overstated—too often long-married couples take their relationships for granted; they are grateful for the security they provide, but they do not look to the relationship as a primary source of positive emotion and pleasure. It is treated as the safe backdrop that allows them to find enjoyment in their children, their work, their hobbies, and their friendships. Our "We" orientation and our interest in cultivating We-Stories redirects couples back toward their relationship as a fundamental, if not the primary, source of positive emotion and pleasure in their lives. Our "couple first" orientation is not simply for the sake of a stronger marital bond, but rather we believe this approach is the best way to regenerate strong positive emotion and joy shared between the members of the couple.

Couples that can draw on a powerfully positive We-Story have a great resource to enlist whenever they need validation to work through conflict and find the positive focus in the relationship. Here is an example of how Ted and Sylvia found a story that serves as their "go to" We-Story (Singer, 2005) to draw on whenever they were in need of reassurance regarding their love:

For so long, I had been doubting that Ted still loved me. We had both retired and I thought that meant we would spend more time than ever with each other. Instead, he was out several nights a week at political meetings and events. I begged him to ease up on his schedule, but he told me that I was nagging him, and it wasn't as bad as I made it out to be. He kept saying, "It's no big deal." But it was a big deal to me and nothing I could do seemed to change his mind. I really started to withdraw after a while, and we did less and less together. Then one night, he woke me up, and he was crying. I had barely ever seen him cry and I asked him, "What's wrong?" He told me that he was frightened that I didn't love him any more—that he would lose me. Well, I started to cry too and my heart just melted. We talked for a long time, and he said that he saw where he was wrong and would cut back to have more time with me. That was a year ago and we have been so much happier since then. He still goes to meetings, and I am happy that he does, but he definitely has made our time together a priority.

Ted and Sylvia's story of their "Middle of the Night Confession" is a signpost that guides them—it is their version of the Hibiscus story that tells them what the "True North" of their relationship is and what principle they must always follow—**Put the Couple First**.

4. Repository of Couple Wisdom

Wisdom has played a key role in the attempt to understand the positive nature of human behavior since the time of Aristotle (see the more recent review of empirical research on wisdom by Staudinger & Glueck, 2011). However, despite the burgeoning evidence of the mental and physical health benefits associated with positive relationship functioning, the relational dimension of wisdom has received less attention.

We propose that the development and cultivation of a "We" perspective can be thought of as the epitome of relational wisdom. Defined as the capacity to develop and maintain a collective mindset of mutuality, or We-consciousness, it involves capacities for self-reflection, attunement to self and other, the interpretations of rules and principles in light of the uniqueness of each situation, and the ability to balance conflicting aims. We see it as the master virtue of relationship development, related to virtues of knowledge, curiosity, generosity, gratitude, and compassion. It is built through mastering challenges, and cultivated across the life span of the partnership.

These qualities of relational wisdom emerge through dialogue and shared memory—the vehicle of storytelling. The resulting We-Stories become the touchstones to what is most precious and vital in the relationship and can be passed forward to the generations that follow. If this is true, how can we as therapists foster such life-affirming, positive stories? What even goes into the making of such stories? Is there such a thing as a "good story" or perhaps a "good enough story"? We will turn to a brief exploration of these questions now.

The Structural Features of the Good Enough We-Story

Fortunately, there has been considerable interest in the empirical study of stories—their composition, construction, plot, outcomes, and their relationships to various states of well-being (e.g., McAdams, 2001; McLean, Pasupathi, & Pals, 2007). Researchers (Siegel & Demorest, 2010; Singer & Bonalume, 2010) have also begun to identify how key factors in healthy narrative identities translate into useful information for client assessment and treatment. Of the various building blocks identified as aspects of narrative identity, the life story is the largest (Singer et al., 2013).

The couple's We-Story in its macro-narrative form is at a similar level of conceptual and empirical complexity. As we have defined it, the couple's macro We-Story reflects a mutual identity that couples describe as experiences of We-ness, the overall lived experience of their relationship accumulated over many years of events and episodes. It is evidenced by a kind of thinking that reflects reciprocity and integration of the other's perspective in one's own. Therapists recognize that couples frequently and spontaneously use the words "we" and "us" in talking about this quality (Skerrett, 2010). The property is not only challenging to grasp conceptually, but daunting to define empirically. Fortunately, this "We" property in storytelling is also getting increasing attention from a variety of perspectives.

We-ness has been assessed in pictorial diagrams (e.g., Inclusion of Other in the Self scale; Aron, Aron, & Smollan, 1992), scalar-type questionnaires (e.g., Marital Engagement–Type of Union Scale; Singer et al., in press), the use of pronouns in conversations, memories, and descriptions of relationships (Agnew, Van Lange, Rusbult, & Langston, 1998; Buehlman, Gottman, & Katz, 1992; Honeycutt, 1999; Seider, Hirschberger, Nelson, & Levenson, 2009; Simmons, Gordon, & Chambless, 2005), and the extent to which couples, when engaged in conversation, have linguistic matching (Ireland & Pennebaker, 2010). There is considerable work being done around the relationship of "We-talk" to broad areas of communal coping and couple adjustment to illness and disability (Connor, Robinson, & Wieling, 2008; Skerrett & Fergus, in press), as well as associations to relationship satisfaction in distressed couples (Williams-Baucom, Atkins, Sevier, Eldridge, & Christensen, 2010) and in young, dating couples (Slatcher, Vazire, & Pennebaker, 2008). Measures of We-ness are proving to be fertile ground for understanding the couple experience.

Our own notions of what makes for a **Good Enough We-Story** evolved from work with self-defining memories (Blagov & Singer, 2004), relationship-defining memories (Alea & Vick, 2010), and Couple Story projects (Skerrett, 2010, 2013). There is overlap between the notions of "self-defining and relationship-defining memories"—snapshots of significant images seen as characteristic of the self or relationship— and "themes" or "scripts"—patterned, recurring issues that give shape and continuity to stories and serve as guides to decision making. What these "We-oriented" memories and themes have in common are certain essential features that make them "good enough" to highlight a sense of connection in the couple. We borrow the phrase "good enough" from Winnicott's (1957) concept of the "good enough mother" who conveys a fundamental love and acceptance that fosters positive growth in the developing child. The Good Enough We-Story consists of the following four structural features:

1. An active, conscious interpretation of life experiences that clarifies how one got from point A to point B
2. An internal consistency or overall coherence
3. An overall theme of resilience and/or a redemptive recasting of negative events into positive meaning
4. A lesson or understanding about the value of the couple's relationship, and perhaps, relationships in general.

Effective We-Stories combine these features into compelling and persuasive narratives that are memorable, maintain a story-telling vitality, and offer a clear lesson about the value of mutuality. In Chapter 4, we explain how to work with couples to build Good Enough We-Stories, but here are some edited examples—first from two couples who are part of an ongoing project on Couple Stories and then from two couples in ongoing couple treatment. The first two stories are macro-stories. Observe how they take the listener on a more temporally extended journey toward a resilient result. They employ a metaphor (the balloon for Amy and Bob, the jewel for Mark and Max), and they are expressed in a "We"-rich language that references security, empathy, respect, acceptance, pleasure, humor, and shared meaning and vision (SERAPHS). In acknowledging this shared meaning, the couple conveys the idea that both partners are in this together and building toward something larger than themselves. Each of the narratives is "good enough" in the sense that it has an identifiable narrative sequence, an overall coherence, redemptive ending, and ultimately conveys a shared relational vision (see Figure 2.2).

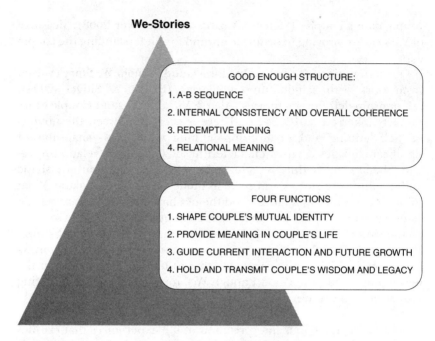

We-Stories

GOOD ENOUGH STRUCTURE:

1. A-B SEQUENCE

2. INTERNAL CONSISTENCY AND OVERALL COHERENCE

3. REDEMPTIVE ENDING

4. RELATIONAL MEANING

FOUR FUNCTIONS

1. SHAPE COUPLE'S MUTUAL IDENTITY

2. PROVIDE MEANING IN COUPLE'S LIFE

3. GUIDE CURRENT INTERACTION AND FUTURE GROWTH

4. HOLD AND TRANSMIT COUPLE'S WISDOM AND LEGACY

Figure 2.2. The Structure and Functions of We-Stories

Amy and Bob

One of the main reasons we got married was to have kids—
we're both crazy about kids. We never ever imagined it wouldn't
happen. We tried for years and I think my denial (wife) made
it worse—I just couldn't get it in my head that we might not be
able to have kids. When we finally went to a fertility person and
got the dreaded diagnosis, we went into some kind of collective
shock. We got depressed and stayed that way for a couple years.
Now we know we were probably mad and taking it out on each
other. We were like a bright balloon that someone took the air
out of. One day my sister in law, who we're very close to, brought
over a stray dog her kids wanted them to keep, but they didn't
have the room. She pushed us to take it and something kind
of clicked. It was a really good dog, but beyond that, I think
we were ready to snap out of our pit. We started to talk about
the possibility of fostering dogs—we had the space, certainly
the love and the need was there. So in a way, we re-inflated our
own balloon and started taking in dogs. It has really brought
our relationship back to life, and we feel like we have a purpose
again. It has brought us even closer and way happier.

Mark and Max

We probably had to work harder than a regular couple to feel like a couple. I'm sure part of it's being gay . . . we didn't even come out until we were in our late thirties, and his family really only started to accept our relationship last year. We had both had a lot of very bad relationships before we got together—some really abusive. When we hooked up, we both felt like we had found a jewel (right—in the rough!), and we wanted to do everything we could to treat each other right so as not to lose each other. We've gone through some very rough patches—mostly related to our family's opposition to our desire to marry, but it has only made us stronger and more determined. We think of the jewel and are even working on a way to put that image into our marriage ceremony somehow.

These next two more micro We-Stories focus in on a specific moment—taking the mother-in-law to lunch and the wife's wearing of her husband's dogtags. These specific events reference examples of healing gestures made on behalf of the other that express mutuality and overall appreciation. These stories serve as points of leverage to move distressed couples toward a positive trajectory and momentum—from negativity and isolation back on the path toward the "We."

Beth and Jamie

We've been touch and go for so long now . . . so much distance and so little ability to hear and see each other realistically. The fighting only dug us in deeper ruts. We really turned a corner when you reached out to my mother and offered to take her to lunch; our relationship with my family has been so bad and it so tore me up. That gesture totally touched my heart; you knew how much that might mean to me and you didn't even ask, you just did it. Since then, we've been talking more about those sensitive parts of each other—what we most love about each other, what we've been burying. We both had the sense that we could remember and feel what we felt for each other and how much we still do care.

Kim and Allen

My re-enlistments have been a big thing between us; I never felt like she got why I did it or how much I was trying to keep our family afloat. It got to where we couldn't even talk about the Army or any of what happened to me over there—she just had such an attitude. Then one day she came out wearing my dog-tags that I'd given her when we first started going out—it was the first thing I gave her that showed I was getting serious about her. The fact that she took that out and wore them made me feel like she still cared and like she did know me after all and would understand what that meant to me. Now it's like a symbol between us—she's gone back to wearing them a lot and we both just smile because we remember what it means.

This chapter began by reviewing the central importance of storytelling in human understanding and interaction. We examined some of the key features of stories that individuals tell about their own lives and then moved on to the concept of the Couple Story—or the stories that the two members of a couple tell about their shared experiences as a couple. We then introduced one particular form of Couple Story—the "We-Story," which is a couple narrative that conveys relational connection by emphasizing one or more of the seven SERAPHS that define We-ness. We-Stories serve four vital functions of providing identity, insight, guidance, and wisdom that the two partners experience as the mutual rewards of their relationship. Additionally, they are characterized by a vivid image, metaphor, or catchphrase that expresses succinctly some essential positive theme that the couple embraces. One subtype of the We-Story is a relationship-defining memory that is an "origin" story of how the couple came together. In considering how couples might begin to identify or cultivate successful We-Stories, we articulated the structural features of what constitutes a Good Enough We-Story—these were enumerated as a shared conscious expression of key events of the relationship in sequence; an agreed-upon consistency and coherence in the couple's narrative; a redemptive ending emerging from a story that includes struggle and/or obstacles; and a connection of the story to a lesson about the relationship

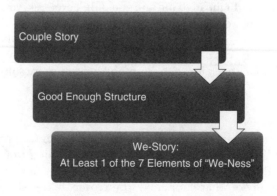

Figure 2.3. From Couple Story to We-Story

or relationships in general. These fundamental features are the groundwork for Good Enough stories that will support the couple in their quest to build a stronger and more resilient relationship (see Figure 2.3).

We now turn from our sketching out of a framework of We-ness and We-Stories to the implementation of these constructs in the work of couple therapy. The next chapter focuses in on how we assess couples' initial levels of We-ness. We then move on in the subsequent chapter to how we teach couples to find and cultivate their We-Stories.

References

Abbott, H. P. (2008). *The Cambridge introduction to narrative*. New York, NY: Cambridge University Press.

Agnew, C. R., Van Lange, P.A.M., Rusbult, C. E., & Langston, C.A. (1998). Cognitive interdependence: Commitment and the mental representation of close relationships. *Journal of Personality and Social Psychology, 74*(4), 939–954.

Alea, N., & Bluck, S. (2007). I'll keep you in mind: The intimacy function of autobiographical memory. *Applied Cognitive Psychology, 21*, 1091–1111.

Alea, N., Singer, J.A., & Labunko, B. (in press). "We-ness" in relationship-defining memories and marital satisfaction. In K. Skerrett and K. Fergus (Eds.), *Couple resilience across the lifespan: Emerging perspectives*. New York, NY: Springer.

Alea, N., & Vick, S.C. (2010). The first sight of love: Relationship-defining memories and marital satisfaction across adulthood. *Memory, 18*(7), 730–742.

Angus, L. E., & Greenberg, L. S. (2011). *Working with narrative in emotion-focused therapy*. Washington, DC: American Psychological Association.

Aron, A., Aron, E. N., & Smollan, D. (1992). Inclusion of Other in the Self Scale and the structure of interpersonal closeness. *Journal of Personality and Social Psychology, 63*, 596–612.

Baddeley, J. L., & Singer, J.A. (2008). Telling losses: Personality correlates and functions of bereavement narratives. *Journal of Research in Personality, 42*, 421–438.

Bauer, J.J., McAdams, D. P., & Pals, J.L. (2008). Narrative identity and eudaimonic well-being. *Journal of Happiness Studies, 9*(1), 81–104.

Blagov, P.S., & Singer, J.A. (2004). Four dimensions of self-defining memories (specificity, meaning, content, and affect) and their relationships to self-restraint, distress, and repressive defensiveness. *Journal of Personality, 72*(3), 481–511.

Bluck, S. (2003). Autobiographical memory: Exploring its functions in everyday life. *Memory, 11*, 113–123.

Bonanno, G. (2005). Resilience in the face of potential trauma. *Current Directions in Psychological Science, 14*, 135–138.

Bruner, J. S. (1990). *Acts of meaning*. Cambridge, MA: Harvard University Press.

Buehlman, K.T., Gottman, J.M., & Katz, L.F. (1992). How a couple views their past predicts their future: Predicting divorce from an oral history interview. *Journal of Family Psychology, 5*(3–4), 295–318.

Connor, J. J., Robinson, B., & Wieling, E. (2008). Vulvar pain: A phenomenological study of couples in search of effective diagnosis and treatment. *Family Process, 47*(2), 139–155.

Conway, M.A., & Pleydell-Pearce, C.W. (2000). The construction of autobiographical memories in the self-memory system. *Psychological Review, 107*(2), 261–288.

Conway, M.A., Singer, J.A., & Tagini, A. (2004). The self and autobiographical memory: Correspondence and coherence. *Social Cognition, 22*(5), 491–529.

Csikszentmihalyi, M. (1990). *Flow: The psychology of optimal experience.* New York, NY: Harper and Row.

Damasio, A. (1999). *The feeling of what happens.* New York, NY: Houghton Mifflin Harcourt.

Fosha, D., Siegel, D., and Solomon, M. (Eds.). (2009). *The healing power of emotion: Affective neuroscience, development and clinical practice.* New York, NY: W.W. Norton & Co.

Fredrickson, B. (2006). The broaden-and-build theory of positive emotions. In M. Csikszentmihalyi and I. Csikszentmihalyi (Eds.), *A life worth living* (pp. 85–103). New York, NY: Oxford University Press.

Fredrickson, B. (2013). *Love 2.0: How our supreme emotion affects everything we feel, think, do, and become.* New York, NY: Hudson Street Press.

Fredrickson, B., & Branigan, C. (2005). Positive emotions broaden the scope of attention and thought-action repertoires. *Cognition and Emotion, 19,* 313–332.

Fredrickson, B., & Joiner, T. (2002). Positive emotions trigger upward spirals toward emotional well-being. *Psychological Science, 13,* 172–175.

Freedman, J., & Combs, G. (1996). *Narrative therapy: The social construction of preferred realities.* New York, NY: W.W. Norton & Co.

Gergen, K.J. (1991). *The saturated self: Dilemmas of identity in contemporary life.* New York, NY: Basic Books.

Gottman, J.M., & Gottman, J.S. (2008). *Gottman method couple therapy.* New York, NY: Guilford Press.

Gottman, J., & Silver, N. (2012). *What makes love last? How to build trust and avoid betrayal.* New York, NY: Simon & Schuster.

Gottschall, H. (2012). *The storytelling animal: How stories make us human.* New York, NY: Houghton Mifflin Harcourt.

Greenberg, L.S. (2010). *Emotion-focused therapy.* Washington, DC: American Psychological Association.

Habermas, T., & Bluck, S. (2000). Getting a life: The emergence of the life story in adolescence. *Psychological Bulletin, 126*(5), 748–769.

Holmes, J.G. (2012). *The future of relationship science: The science of the couple.* New York, NY: Psychology Press.

Honeycutt, W. (1999). Typological differences in predicting marital happiness from oral history behaviors and imagined interactions. *Communication Monographs, 66*(3), 276–291.

Ireland, M.E., & Pennebaker, J.W. (2010). Language style matching in writing: Synchrony in essays, correspondence, and poetry. *Journal of Personality and Social Psychology, 99*(3), 549–571.

Janoff-Bulman, R., & Yopyk, D. (2004). Random outcomes and valued commitments: Existential dilemmas and the paradox of meaning. In J. Greenberg, S. Koole, and T. Pyszcznski (Eds.), *Handbook of experimental existential psychology* (pp. 122–138). New York, NY: Guilford Press.

King, L.A., Hicks, J.A., Krull, J.L., & Del Gaiso, A.K. (2006). Positive affect and the experience of meaning in life. *Journal of Personality and Social Psychology, 90*(1), 179–196.

Lieblich, A., McAdams, D.P., & Josselson, R. (Eds.). (2004). *Healing plots: The narrative basis of psychotherapy*. Washington, DC: American Psychological Association.

Lyubomirsky, S. (2007). *The how of happiness: A scientific approach to getting the life you want*. New York, NY: Penguin Press.

Madsen, W.C. (2009). Collaborative helping: A practice framework for family-centered services. *Family Process, 48*(1), 103–116.

McAdams, D.P. (2001). The psychology of life stories. *Review of General Psychology, 5*(2), 100–122.

McAdams, D.P. (2013). *The redemptive self: Stories Americans live by* (Rev. & exp. ed.). New York, NY: Oxford University Press.

McLean, K.C. (2008). Stories of the young and the old: Personal continuity and narrative identity. *Developmental Psychology, 44*(1), 254–264.

McLean, K.C., & Mansfield, C.D. (2010). To reason or not to reason: Is autobiographical reasoning always beneficial? In T. Habermas (Ed.), The development of autobiographical reasoning in adolescence and beyond. *New Directions for Child and Adolescent Development, 131*, 85–97.

McLean, K.C., Pasupathi, M., & Pals, J.L. (2007). Selves creating stories creating selves: A process model of self-development. *Personality and Social Psychology Review, 11*(3), 262–278.

Randall, W., & McKim, A.E. (2008). *The poetics of growing old*. New York, NY: Oxford University Press.

Sacks, O. (2013, February 21). Speak, memory. *New York Review of Books*. Retrieved from www.nybooks.com/articles/archives/2013/feb/21/speak-memory

Sarbin, T.R. (1986). *Narrative psychology: The storied nature of human conduct*. Westport, CT: Praeger Publishers.

Schacter, D.L., & Addis, D.R. (2007). On the constructive episodic simulation of past and future events. *Behavioral & Brain Sciences, 30*, 299–351.

Seider, B.H., Hirschberger, G., Nelson, K.L., & Levenson, R.W. (2009). We can work it out: Age differences in relational pronouns, physiology, and behavior in marital conflict. *Psychology and Aging, 24*(3), 604–613.

Shotter, J., & Gergen, K.J. (1989). *Texts of identity. Inquiries in social construction: Vol. 2*. Thousand Oaks, CA: Sage Publications.

Siegel, D.J. (2012). *The developing mind: How relationships and the brain interact to shape who we are* (2nd ed.). New York, NY: Guilford Press.

Siegel, D., & Hartzell, M. (2003). *Parenting from the inside out*. New York, NY: Penguin Press.

Siegel, P., & Demorest, A. (2010). Affective scripts: A systematic case study of change in psychotherapy. *Psychotherapy Research, 20*(4), 369–387.

Simmons, R.A., Gordon, P.C., & Chambless, D.L. (2005). Pronouns in marital interaction: What do "you" and "I" say about marital health? *Psychological Science, 16*(12), 932–936.

Singer, J.A. (2004). Narrative identity and meaning making across the adult lifespan: An introduction. *Journal of Personality, 72*(3), 437–459.

Singer, J. A. (2005). *Memories that matter: How to use self-defining memories to understand and change your life.* Oakland, CA: New Harbinger.

Singer, J., Blagov, P., Berry, M., & Oost, K. (2013). Self-defining memories, scripts, and the life story: Narrative identity in personality and psychotherapy. *Journal of Personality, 81,* 569–582.

Singer, J. A., & Bonalume, L. (2010). Autobiographical memory narratives in psychotherapy: A coding system applied to the case of Cynthia. *Pragmatic Case Studies in Psychotherapy, 6*(3), 134–188 (Target Article for Issue).

Singer, J. A., Labunko, B., Alea, N., & Baddeley, J. L. (in press). Mutuality and the Marital Engagement—Type of Union Scale [ME (To US)]: Empirical support for a clinical instrument in couples therapy. In K. Skerrett and K. Fergus (Eds.), *Couple resilience across the lifespan: Emerging perspectives.* New York, NY: Springer.

Skerrett, K. (1998). The couple experience of breast cancer. *Families, Systems & Health, 16,* 281–298.

Skerrett, K. (2010). "Good enough stories": Helping couples invest in one another's growth. *Family Process, 49*(4), 503–516.

Skerrett, K. (2013). Resilient relationships: Cultivating the healing potential of couple stories. In J. Jordan and J. Carlson (Eds.), *Creating connection: A relational-cultural approach with couples* (pp. 45–60). New York, NY: Routledge.

Skerrett, K., & Fergus, K. (Eds.). (in press). *Couple resilience across the lifespan: Emerging perspectives.* New York, NY: Springer.

Slatcher, R. B., Vazire, S., & Pennebaker, J. W. (2008). Am "I" more important than "we"? Couples' word use in instant messages. *Personal Relationships, 15*(4), 407–424.

Spence, D. P. (1982). *Narrative truth and historical truth: Meaning and interpretation in psychoanalysis.* New York, NY: W. W. Norton & Co.

Staudinger, U. M., & Glueck, J. (2011). Psychological wisdom research: Commonalities and differences in a growing field. *Annual Review of Psychology, 62,* 215–241.

Thorne, A., McLean, K. C., & Lawrence, A. M. (2004). When remembering is not enough: Reflecting on self-defining memories in late adolescence. *Journal of Personality, 72*(3), 513–541.

Tomkins, S. S. (1979). Script theory: Differential magnification of affects. *Nebraska Symposium on Motivation, 26,* 201–236.

Tomkins, S. S. (1987). Script theory. In J. Aronoff, A. I. Rabin, and R. A. Zucker (Eds.), *The emergence of personality* (pp. 147–216). New York, NY: Springer.

Walsh, F. (2006). *Strengthening family resilience* (2nd ed.). New York, NY: Guilford Press.

White, M., & Epston, D. (1990). *Narrative means to therapeutic ends.* New York, NY: W. W. Norton & Co.

Williams-Baucom, K. J., Atkins, D. C., Sevier, M., Eldridge, K. A., & Christensen, A. (2010). "You" and "I" need to talk about "us": Linguistic patterns in marital interactions. *Personal Relationships, 17*(1), 41–56.

Winnicott, D. W. (1957). *Mother and child: A primer of first relationships.* New York, NY: Basic Books.

Zimmerman, J. L., & Dickerson, V. C. (1993). Separating couples from restraining patterns and the relationship discourses that support them. *Journal of Marital and Family Therapy, 19*(4), 403–413.

3

ASSESSING THE "WE" IN THERAPY

Having defined the essential elements of the "We" and laid out the fundamentals of the role of stories in individuals' and couples' lives, we now turn to the first step in a "We"-oriented therapy. Once the couple has agreed to work on their relationship and made an initial commitment of 12 focused sessions, we then conduct an assessment of each individual and the couple as a whole. For each partner's individual history, we use a standard genogram (McGoldrick, Gerson, & Petry, 2008), but we have developed our own unique instrument to track the degree of We-ness that the couple displays in their daily interactions and shared communications.

Over the years we have found the best way that we could help partners explore their current attention to the "We" was by asking them about the major life domains that they typically share as a couple. We would ask them what arrangements they had created for a particular domain (e.g., finances, domestic chores, work lives, childcare) and then explore how effectively they worked together or came to decisions regarding each responsibility. Eventually, these questions evolved into a brief scale that we called the **Marital Engagement–Type of Union Scale** or the **ME (To US)** (Singer & Labunko, 2005; see Figure 3.1).

The ME (To US) is a 10-item scale to be filled out separately by each partner in a marriage or long-term partnership. They are told to bring the scale home with them, fill it out, and return it in the next session without sharing their answers with their partner. The therapist collects the two completed scales from the partners and then takes some time to analyze the results before discussing them with the couple.

Looking back over the last six months of the relationship, each partner is asked to consider the degree of mutuality and communication they have achieved in the following life domains: (1) domestic duties, (2) time commitments, (3) financial matters, (4) child-rearing or the decision to have or not have children, (5) sexual intimacy, (6) independent activities, (7) communication of fears and vulnerabilities, (8) shared activities and conversation, (9) interactions with in-laws, and (10) future planning.

Marital Engagement—Type of Union Scale

This scale should be filled out by each partner separately. Try to rate each item with your most honest and realistic answer. Do not answer how you wish the relationship could be, or how it has been at previous times, but how it has been within the last **6 months.** Each item asks you to make a generalization, so do your best to think in overall terms from the last 6 months rather than about one or two specific instances. Please fill out all items and use the 1–7 rating scale provided below. Please circle the numerical rating that best applies to each item.

1 = not at all, 4 = somewhat, 7 = very much

1) We discuss domestic chores and make a fair division of duties.

1   2   3   4   5   6   7

2) We discuss and agree on major time commitments before making them (e.g., work schedules, business trips, social events, appointments, separate outings with friends, etc.).

1   2   3   4   5   6   7

3) We openly share and discuss **all** financial resources and decisions (e.g. joint checking, big ticket purchases, shared mortgage, pooled investment, mutual beneficiaries, etc.).

1   2   3   4   5   6   7

4) We discuss, reach agreement, and present a unified front about child-rearing decisions (e.g., discipline, privileges, academic goals, etc.).

1   2   3   4   5   6   7

(**NOTE:** If you have no children, then answer this question, using the same rating scale below item 4: We have discussed and are in agreement about our current stance toward having children.)

5) We communicate about and share a mutually satisfying sexual relationship.

1   2   3   4   5   6   7

6) We have achieved a balance between pursuing recreational activities together and also giving each other space to pursue independent activities.

1   2   3   4   5   6   7

7) We communicate about our deepest fears and vulnerabilities to each other.

1   2   3   4   5   6   7

8) We regularly (i.e., at least once a week) set aside time of 30 minutes or more that is exclusively for us as a couple, to talk, share an activity, or simply hang out together.

1   2   3   4   5   6   7

9) We discuss and continue to develop plans for how our life together might be over the next 10 years and beyond.

1   2   3   4   5   6   7

10) We discuss and reach agreement about how to relate to and interact with extended family (e.g., in-laws, uncles, aunts, cousins, etc.).

1   2   3   4   5   6   7

Figure 3.1. Marital Engagement—Type of Union Scale: ME (To US)

As the items on the scale make clear, the emphasis in the ME (To US) is on the degree of discussion that couples engage in as they navigate the difficult arenas of a committed life. Almost every item on the scale begins with the phrase, "We discuss . . ." The underlying assumption is that We-ness is cultivated through ongoing dialogue, "checking in," and careful efforts at building consensus. Consensus does not always mean compromise or finding a middle ground, but it does mean that both parties feel listened to and that they have each agreed to the ensuing course of action (even when it may not be one or the other partner's personal preference). **We-ness need not always be equated to relationship satisfaction or happiness; it is more importantly a measure of how much the couple feels a sense of mutual respect, trust, and validation in the relationship.** A couple might be struggling with the disruptive behavior of a meddling in-law; such badgering may cause distress in the couple but in their united front in the face of these intrusions, they are strong in We-ness.

In an initial study of the ME (To US), we looked at the ME (To US) scores of 289 married individuals (Singer, Labunko, Alea, & Baddeley, in press). This was a community sample with a mean age of 47.19 years and who had been married, on average, 20.44 years; 86% of the sample had children. In addition to filling out the ME (To US), participants rated their marital satisfaction, emotional quality of their marriage, physical health, and the health of their spouse. Although the participants' ME (To US) score was strongly linked to both marital satisfaction and the positive quality of the marriage, it ended up being the best predictor of female partners' self-reported health, outperforming the measures of marital satisfaction.

In a second study with 36 married couples from the New London, Connecticut, community, we found an even more powerful result (Singer et al., in press). The strongest predictor of the *wife*'s self-reported health complaints was the gap between her item ratings on the ME (To US) and her husband's ratings. We examined this gap by subtracting the difference in scores on each item between the husband and wife. If the husband's rating of We-ness was higher than his wife's rating, we gave this difference a positive sign, and if the wife was higher in her rating than her partner, we assigned a negative value; we then summed the score for the total items. In other words, the more the husband claimed a sense of We-ness and the less the wife did, the larger the overall discrepancy score. It was this gap that correlated strongly and significantly with the wife's overall health complaints. Put in more positive terms, the more that the wife's perception of the couple's mutuality matched her husband's view, the better health she reported. The connection between the wife's health status and distress in the marriage is one that has been found before in research on marriage (McCabe, Cummins, & Romeo, 1996), but our work is the first study to find this link between health complaints and a more objective measure of the degree of We-ness that exists between the two partners. In addition to these health findings, we were able to repeat our earlier results showing a strong link between the couple's sense of We-ness (or lack thereof) and their overall satisfaction and feelings of good will in the marriage. The results of the two studies together confirmed what we have seen for years in our clinical work. **Couples who discuss the important decisions of their lives and who structure their time and activities with their relationship in mind have happier marriages, less stress, and healthier lives.**

Based on these two studies and other data collected through our courses on couple therapy, we have found that couples who are feeling positively about their relationship tend to score in the 50s or 60s on the ME (To US), meaning that their average response to an item is a 5 or 6, indicating a strong sense of We-ness. Once we have looked over the totals and individual item scores for each partner, we then devote a session to the discussion of the findings. Feedback can come in several forms. The therapist can tell them how their overall totals relate to couples that are not in distress and have developed a reasonably strong "We." This provides a rough measure of what they might aspire to achieve in building a stronger "We." Perhaps, more importantly, the therapist reflects on the items that are low for both partners, high for both partners, and where there are discrepancies (one partner high, the other low; one partner low, the other high). We have found that discrepancies larger than 2 points on the rating scale (e.g., 1 vs. 4; 2 vs. 5; 3 vs. 6, etc.) are often valuable to discuss.

To get a better sense of how the ME (To US) works, let's look at one specific couple and the respective responses of each partner.

Will and Katie Owens

Will and Katie Owens had been married 17 years and were both in their early 40s. They had teen-aged twins, a boy and a girl, and lived in a renovated farmhouse in a picturesque Connecticut town. Will owned a highly successful landscaping and nursery business, and Katie was a former executive secretary, who left her career to raise the twins. Will was tall, lean, and tanned. Katie also glowed with a healthy tan, and her reddish shoulder-length hair framed a bright white smile. She was petite and fit, giving no sign of early middle age. With their good looks, short-sleeved shirts, and khaki shorts, you could imagine that they had been clipped from a J. Crew catalogue.

Despite their country club appearance, there was warmth and a lack of pretense in their manner. The more we talked, the more I (JAS) liked them. They had a sense of humor, and they appeared very respectful to each other. They spoke with absolute devotion about their twins. They were practicing Catholics and attended church on a fairly regular basis.

They even found a way to ask me a few questions about my work and what it was like to see couples. They seemed genuinely interested in my replies. I imagined that they would be ideal companions at a barbeque or chatting on the sidelines while our daughters played a soccer game.

Why were they so miserable? Katie spoke first and blamed it all on their boat. Will had loved working on boats ever since he was a boy. Now he had bought a large one, 52 feet, and it was both a money and time pit. He was either at work or at the boatyard. Will said that he knew that the time away was bothering her, but it had been a big investment, and they couldn't let it fall into disrepair. He said that she had agreed to let him get the boat. She said that he only told her after he had decided to get it. Although they were talking about a physical object, their anger reached a rapid boil and was barely suppressed. In fact, it bordered on a genuine hatred, and it seemed to go way beyond the dispute over the boat. Just as suddenly as they flared up, they both fell silent and sank back in their chairs, looking everywhere but at each other. They seemed exhausted and slightly embarrassed by this outburst.

I asked them their goals for the therapy; they both stated that they did not want the marriage to end, but they knew that they could not go on like this. Will pointed out that there was little love left in the relationship, and it was clear that he wanted me to understand that they were not having much physical intimacy. Even with her faith and her responsibility to their children, Katie admitted that she was at the end of her rope. She felt locked out of the decisions Will made about his business, their finances, and the way he spent his time. When I asked about fun or time together, they said that this kind of together time had dwindled over the last few years. They still kept the house and family functioning effectively, but they felt like they were drifting more and more apart. If necessary, they could persevere in parallel worlds until the twins were out of the house, but the fights and arguments had been escalating.

Measuring Will's and Katie's We-ness

Will and Katie filled out the ME (To US) separately and then brought in their scores on their next visit. Figure 3.2 shows Katie's responses and Figure 3.3 shows Will's answers. The first thing to notice is that if you look at each of their total scores (Katie's was a 32 and Will's was a 48), both of these scores are below those of more positive couples who feel connected to each other. Just as important, there is a large gap between their two totals, which means that Katie saw a lot less mutuality in their relationship than Will did. It is not surprising then that one of her persisting difficulties was that she had trouble sleeping at night. In the previously mentioned study of 36 couples (Singer et al., in press), we also found that wives who showed larger gaps between their scores and their husbands' scores on the ME (To US) showed higher levels of sleep

Marital Engagement—Type of Union Scale

This scale should be filled out by each partner separately. Try to rate each item with your most honest and realistic answer. Do not answer how you wish the relationship could be, or how it has been at previous times, but how it has been within the last **6 months**. Each item asks you to make a generalization, so do your best to think in overall terms from the last 6 months rather than about one or two specific instances. Please fill out all items and use the 1–7 rating scale provided below. Please circle the numerical rating that best applies to each item.

1 = not at all, 4 = somewhat, 7 = very much

1) We discuss domestic chores and make a fair division of duties.
1   2   3   4   ⑤   6   7

2) We discuss and agree on major time commitments before making them (e.g., work schedules, business trips, social events, appointments, separate outings with friends, etc.).
1   2   ③   4   5   6   7

3) We openly share and discuss all financial resources and decisions (e.g. joint checking, big ticket purchases, shared mortgage, pooled investment, mutual beneficiaries, etc.).
①   2   3   4   5   6   7

4) We discuss, reach agreement, and present a unified front about child-rearing decisions (e.g., discipline, privileges, academic goals, etc.).
1   2   3   4   5   ⑥   7
(**NOTE:** If you have no children, then answer this question, using the same rating scale below item 4: We have discussed and are in agreement about our current stance toward having children.)

5) We communicate about and share a mutually satisfying sexual relationship.
1   ②   3   4   5   6   7

6) We have achieved a balance between pursuing recreational activities together and also giving each other space to pursue independent activities.
1   2   ③   4   5   6   7

7) We communicate about our deepest fears and vulnerabilities to each other.
1   ②   3   4   5   6   7

8) We regularly (i.e., at least once a week) set aside time of 30 minutes or more that is exclusively for us as a couple, to talk, share an activity, or simply hang out together.
1   2   3   ④   5   6   7

9) We discuss and continue to develop plans for how our life together might be over the next 10 years and beyond.
1   ②   3   4   5   6   7

10) We discuss and reach agreement about how to relate to and interact with extended family (e.g., in-laws, uncles, aunts, cousins, etc.).
1   2   3   ④   5   6   7

Figure 3.2. Katie's ME (To US)

Marital Engagement—Type of Union Scale

This scale should be filled out by each partner separately. Try to rate each item with your most honest and realistic answer. Do not answer how you wish the relationship could be, or how it has been at previous times, but how it has been within the last **6 months**. Each item asks you to make a generalization, so do your best to think in overall terms from the last 6 months rather than about one or two specific instances. Please fill out all items and use the 1–7 rating scale provided below. Please circle the numerical rating that best applies to each item.

1 = not at all, 4 = somewhat, 7 = very much

1) We discuss domestic chores and make a fair division of duties.
1   2   3   4   5   **(6)**   7

2) We discuss and agree on major time commitments before making them (e.g., work schedules, business trips, social events, appointments, separate outings with friends, etc.).
1   2   3   4   **(5)**   6   7

3) We openly share and discuss all financial resources and decisions (e.g. joint checking, big ticket purchases, shared mortgage, pooled investment, mutual beneficiaries, etc.).
1   2   3   4   **(5)**   6   7

4) We discuss, reach agreement, and present a unified front about child-rearing decisions (e.g., discipline, privileges, academic goals, etc.).
1   2   3   4   5   **(6)**   7
(**NOTE:** If you have no children, then answer this question, using the same rating scale below item 4: We have discussed and are in agreement about our current stance toward having children.)

5) We communicate about and share a mutually satisfying sexual relationship.
(1)   2   3   4   5   6   7

6) We have achieved a balance between pursuing recreational activities together and also giving each other space to pursue independent activities.
1   2   3   4   5   **(6)**   7

7) We communicate about our deepest fears and vulnerabilities to each other.
1   2   **(3)**   4   5   6   7

8) We regularly (i.e., at least once a week) set aside time of 30 minutes or more that is exclusively for us as a couple, to talk, share an activity, or simply hang out together.
1   2   3   4   **(5)**   6   7

9) We discuss and continue to develop plans for how our life together might be over the next 10 years and beyond.
1   2   3   4   **(5)**   6   7

10) We discuss and reach agreement about how to relate to and interact with extended family (e.g., in-laws, uncles, aunts, cousins, etc.).
1   2   3   4   5   **(6)**   7

Figure 3.3. Will's ME (To US)

disturbance. The strong difference in Will's and Katie's sense of We-ness tells us that they were indeed feeling separate, alienated, and frustrated in their communication. Given how low Katie's score is, the experience of disconnection was most profound for her.

Unpacking Will's and Katie's Problems With We-ness

Let us now look more closely at each of the individual items from the ME (To US). Examining individual items can tell us both about areas of the relationship where Will and Katie were succeeding in We-ness as well as the points where they radically diverged. Looking at the first item, "Domestic Chores," we can see that they were both pretty comfortable with how they handled the division of labor around the house. When talking about this part of their marriage, Katie felt that the household tasks were shared fairly, given that she was a stay-at-home mom and that Will worked full-time. They had a rather traditional arrangement in which she took care of everything inside the house and Will handled the outside along with general repairs. They both liked to garden and each was handy with a paintbrush. Katie complimented Will for his willingness to ferry the twins around town and get them to various athletic and social commitments. Will was also the "King of Home Depot" and very helpful in running errands or getting the extra item on the way home from work.

Their discussion of this first item set a trend that we found very important in our subsequent work with Katie and Will. In many respects, this couple was an effective partnership. They kept their beautiful home in tip-top shape and made sure their children's lives were structured, stable, and enriched. They agreed on décor, adored their dogs, and shared the same vacation preference (low-key Caribbean trips). Skipping down to item 4, "Child-Rearing," we see the same strong pattern of agreement—both put 6s. Will's constant refrain in discussing this item was that their kids could not have a better mother. He talked with pride about Katie's attentiveness to their needs, but also how she set good expectations for them. She was involved in their lives without spoiling or coddling them. Katie also felt that Will was very good with the twins and that each child relished the time spent with their dad. Her only regret was that Will's long work hours and time spent on fixing the boat was not allowing him enough opportunities to hang out with them.

There was also a good sense of unity in their replies to item 8, "Time Together." Unlike some couples who have not gone out on a date since their children were born or who seem to have no activity or hobby in common, Will and Katie still found time to do things together. They could watch a TV show, go out to dinner, take a walk with the dogs, or even play a little golf together. Their ability to spend time with each other and the easy companionship that they found in each other's company also boded well for the possibility of building a better relationship. In emphasizing these positives to the couple, I explained to them how many couples I see in which these basic points of contact and connection either never existed or have broken down. Will said to me, "That's what is so crazy. I really do think the world of Katie, but somehow we always end up angry and frustrated. I can be driving home excited to see her, but more times than not, I'll get a call from her on the cell, and before you know it, we are pissed off at each other. That's when I feel like turning the car around and going right down to the boatyard or else finding one of the guys from work and having a beer. In other words, going anywhere but home!"

The answer to where all that anger came from may indeed lie in the large differences that were reflected in some of the other items where Will's and Katie's scores were both very low or else where they wildly diverged. Starting with item 7, "Communicate Fears," we can see that Katie gave this a "2" and Will, a "3." These are both rather low scores for such an important sign of mutuality and trust. When we probed further about their ability to talk deeply with each other, Katie said that Will stuffs his worries and gets defensive and angry when she tries to learn more about them. Will shot back immediately with the comment that if Katie were not so critical of him, he would feel more able to open up to her. Katie smiled back at Will, but there was no pleasure in her eyes. She said, "I think that I try to be very understanding, but I am not going to just say, 'Yes, dear,' and accept everything that you say."

Despite the different ways that Katie and Will were able to get along, this exchange again highlighted that neither partner felt a sense of mutual good will or full trust in the best intentions of the partner. At the deepest level of sharing their fears, hurts, and vulnerabilities, they wondered if their partner would be there for them, if they were really safe to speak from the heart without being judged and criticized. Hovering behind this uneasiness with disclosure was an almost primal fear of rejection and/or abandonment (Johnson, 2004). How difficult it is to feel a true sense of We-ness with your mate if this door to honest disclosure does not seem open!

We were recently working with a couple, Glen and Sasha, who had lived together for 10 years and were now finally considering getting married. In the first session, they both began to talk about some of the frustrations they had endured in the relationship. At one point, Glen mentioned that he had not liked the fact that her son, who had briefly lived with them, came home at all hours of the night. Sasha looked incredulous and said, "He hasn't lived with us for 7 years and this is the first time I have ever heard you mention that this bothered you. Have you been holding on to this resentment all this time?" Glen looked at her with a kind of sheepish smile and said, "Yup." Sasha then immediately explained to him why this accusation about her son's behavior was not fair and how the son had been going through a difficult period at that time, and how she wished Glen could have felt more empathy and patience. We could see Glen sinking deeper into the couch and the thought right below the surface was clearly, "And she better believe that it will be another 7 years before I tell her what's on my mind." This exchange had the frightening potential to generate a negative story in Glen's mind, a stone of resentment that would get bigger and shinier over time. Finally, Glen might explode one day and say, "Remember that time at the therapist's office when I finally got the courage up to tell you about my problems with your son staying out all night? You shot me right down in front of the therapist and I felt like crawling under the couch. What's the point of telling you what's bothering me when you're going to treat me like that?" The stone becomes a boulder that blocks the way back to positive relations between the two partners.

Many times in couples when a fundamental sense of belief in the good will of the other is not in place, doubts and suspicions get played out in one of the other domains of the relationship (e.g., the in-laws, children, domestic duties, money). For Will and Katie, one of their clear battlegrounds was money. Take a look at the discrepancy between their scores on item 3, "Financial Decisions." Katie gave it a "1," the worst possible score and Will, a "5." These scores were "statements" that were meant to signal where the battle lines were drawn for each other.

This struggle became clear when we had them look at their scores together in session. Will said that he gave a high score to let Katie know that he was well aware of her complaints about his so-called secrecy regarding his business. He felt that he had done a good job of keeping her in the loop. She had the phone number of his business manager/accountant and could call it any time. All of the accounts were on their shared computer and he had given her the passwords multiple times. She was free to look at anything and everything that she wanted; he had nothing to hide.

Katie's "1" was a virtual scream to get Will's attention. With a controlled smile on her face, which seemed to be her familiar fragile seal against her rage, she answered him.

KATIE: I only found out from you the night before you signed the business loan that we had put our house as collateral for the loan! You bought that huge yacht, which we now can't sell, except at a loss, and you had promised we would put away money for the twins' college fund. Whenever I bring up saving for college, you tell me it's all under control—that the money will be there when we need it. I don't work like that. I like to have a plan. I want to have a handle on the future. Every time I try to get you to sit down and plot this all out with me, you find an excuse to leave the house or we end up in a big fight. Whenever I try to caution you about the risks that you are taking with our financial security, you tell me that I don't know what I am talking about. You tell me that I am too conservative—that if you followed my advice, you would still be planting rhododendrons and mowing lawns at the country club. Well, it was terrifying when we almost went under before. Do you know what it was like to feel like I could not write out a check for the kids' dentist or even be sure the check I had written for the groceries would clear?

Will thundered in, almost ready to jump up out of his chair and leave the room.

WILL: You never let me forget that. Always rub that in. How about giving me credit for where we have come from since then? I don't see you complaining about the Beamer you drive or the 4,000 square feet that you call home. Where do you think that all comes from? Am I just pulling it out of my hat? I must be so stupid that all of that is just going to disappear tomorrow.

Katie kept her smile fixed on her face and slowly began to nod her head. If you were watching her without hearing her words, you would think she was giving a tentative child reassurance in climbing a difficult step. What she said, however, reflected a different state of mind.

KATIE: You still don't see it, do you? I could easily live in a smaller house. I've driven much cheaper cars and been just as happy. What I can't live with is the roller-coaster ride and uncertainty you put us through. What drives me crazy is that I have no voice in my own security or the security of the children. You thrust your business plans on me and I don't feel like I can catch my breath or grab a chance to give an opinion. You get to speaking so fast and get so worked up that I feel like I am talking to a wild man. If I try to raise some legitimate questions or doubts, you say there I go again with my gloom and doom, destroying your dreams. All I see is the huge amounts we owe the bank, and I think about how we don't have 529 plans set up for the twins and they are getting closer to high school all the time. I can't sleep worrying about this, and then I see you head off to play with the boat engine or varnish the hull, and I want to tear my hair out.

WILL: Right! Just wind Will up and send him to work. Works his 12 hours, comes home and mows the lawn, drives the kids to their games, comes home again, writes out checks and then goes to bed. God help me that I should have something in my life—one thing—that might be for me. I certainly am not going to find any consolation in your arms.

Katie's smile stretched even a bit more and she continued to nod her head.

KATIE: You can bet that's true. Not when you treat me like an idiot.

The last comments certainly corresponded to one of the items in which they were closely matched in scores, item 5, "Sexual Intimacy." Not surprisingly, Will logged in at a "1" and Katie followed suit with a "2." They both indicated that their sexual relationship had badly deteriorated in the last few years. They might make love every couple of months, if even that much. Will had virtually given up making overtures to Katie. He said for the most part that he had just about accepted that this was no longer going to be part of his life, which he pointed out was "pretty pathetic for a healthy guy in his 40s." Katie said that she simply could not find the desire as long as she did not feel a sense of trust and true intimacy with Will.

Over the years we have found that the particular items on the ME (To US) that identify strong differences between partners are of less importance than the fact that major differences emerge. Acknowledging differences can be challenging for many couples, especially if the difference registers as a "threat." Almost always behind these differences are well-rehearsed stories of resentment that repeat the same old dance of conflict and argument that the couple knows so well (see Chapter 5 of this volume for an in-depth discussion of these "stuck stories," including Will's and Katie's). Once the resentment stories start to fly back and forth, each partner is literally fighting for his or her **individual life**, feeling that their supposed life mate is hell-bent on humiliating, rejecting, and abandoning them. Standing back from these "dances of death," we register the great sorrow that an unhappy marriage brings and are reminded acutely of all the plays and films that depict marriage as a suffocating trap or a living hell. Any reader who has seen a production of Edward Albee's *Whose Afraid of Virginia Wolff?* (a relentless account of an older couple who sadistically battle each other and play on the vulnerabilities of a younger couple whom they have invited to their home) or watched the more recent film, *Blue Valentine* (the poignant depiction of the breakdown of a young marriage) should know exactly what we mean. Where in such savage moments is the sense of one's partner as a soul mate, the one sure place of comfort in a world that is often indifferent to our longing for consolation?

Making Sense of the ME (To US)

Using the ME (To US) makes concrete our lofty pronouncements about finding the "We" and why it is important to learn how much day-to-day We-ness there might be in the couple. It also demonstrates to couples that their familiar stories of resentment have origins in their failure to trust in the relationship and pursue dialogue and mutual resolutions to conflict. Their answers to the questions are very revealing, but it is the discussion that the therapists and couples have about their replies that moves us to the next level of understanding about what may be missing from the relationship. The scale allows us to get at the misperceptions, assumptions, resentments, and frustrations that are born from the couple operating as two separate individuals who want to be together but have not yet formed a united and functioning "We."

For clients who are resistant to scales and/or assigning numbers to the nuances of their relationship, there is another technique that we use to assess We-ness that gets at the same questions in the couple. We simply ask each member of the couple to describe a typical day, week, and weekend, starting from the moment they wake up to the moment they go to sleep. As they run through the routine of breakfast, getting kids to school, work hours, appointments, shopping, errands, exercise, church, and so on, it becomes very obvious how duties within the relationship are allocated, how much time the partners actually spend together, and what the priorities are for each member of the couple.

One couple, Liam and Jenny, came to see us with the strong determination to improve the quality of their relationship within the marriage. As we had each partner go through their weekly routines, it became clear that they had structured every way possible to avoid intimate time with each other. Their work schedules assured them that Liam was out of the house before Jenny got out of bed. By the time Liam came home, Jenny was giving the baby dinner and getting her ready for sleep. When Jenny finished putting the baby down, she would often find Liam under the covers in their bedroom fast asleep.

Of course the weekends would be an alternative to this weekly whirlwind. Not at all! Liam had taken up skydiving and needed to travel long distances to the skydiving rallies that were held on weekends. Jenny supported his hobby, but by the time he returned in the evening, she would often be out with her friends, while her mother watched the baby, or she would be exhausted from a long day of cleaning up and childcare. Sundays, Jenny went to church while Liam spent time with the baby. In the afternoon, Jenny would do the grocery shopping for the week, while Liam caught up on all the household repairs and yard work. Sunday evening was dinner with Jenny's family, and Monday everything started all over again. In many respects, it was a rich and positive life that they had constructed, but where was the "We" in all of this?

This simple exercise of asking the couple to give a careful account of their time reveals much about how they have set up the actual priorities of their lives. It tells us to what degree the couple comes first and how much care and cultivation is going into growing the "We." When we ask couples about the space in their routine for the "We," many times they will ask how that could be possible given the demands and rigors of the schedule they have described. What is hard for them to see is that buried in the seeming inevitability of their routine is a series of choices that express the relative amount of attention and commitment to their own relationship. How they structure their time reflects what needs they are putting first—the needs of the couple or the needs of employers, children, in-laws, and so on.

When couples do not communicate clearly and openly about "What is best for us" with regard to their time allocations and priorities, they often end up misfiring and alienating each other, even when they have the best of intentions. Take Donna and Phil as an example. Phil is determined to be a better provider than his father who had rather low-paying factory jobs. He works long hours at the automobile dealership and agrees to take on the Thursday night shift in hopes of increasing his sales. He thinks that Donna will be pleased to see extra money coming in and decreased pressure at the first of the month. Donna is at her wits' end with taking care of their three children, working part-time at the elementary school, and running one of the Sunday school classes. Her best friend, Lynda, has asked her to sign up for a free Pilates class on Thursday nights at the local community center. Donna is thinking that this class will reduce some of her stress and help her gain greater patience around the children. She is also hoping that the exercise will help her tone up and feel a little more youthful and attractive around Phil.

Now Phil comes home with the news that he has agreed to work the extra Thursday night each week. Donna had been prepared to ask Phil to watch the children so that she could have the one night out. She starts to tell Phil about the class with Lynda, and he says it's too late for him to change his mind. His boss has already circulated the schedule for the coming month. He mentions the possibility of a babysitter. She says it's almost impossible to find a teenager on a school night and besides what's the point of spending cash on the same night that he is supposed to be making money for the family. Donna and Phil are not the yelling type, so this conflict does not degenerate into a shouting match or fight. Instead, Donna gives in to Phil and goes to put the youngest one to bed. That night, when Phil reaches over to Donna in their bed, she is fast asleep, withdrawn into her own separate world. Phil turns away, brooding to himself that he has taken on this new burden at work to help the family but finds no gratitude or love in return. Since they do not talk out this dispute the following day, it slowly hardens into a story of a mutual lack of appreciation in which each partner sees the other as an indifferent perpetrator and oneself as the misunderstood martyr.

Why does this happen with couples? What has gone wrong with Phil and Donna? They are two well-meaning partners who work each day to do the best for each other and their family. When asked about their commitment to and love for each other, they do not question it. Yet why are they so often silently angry at each other? Why do they frequently feel unappreciated and lonely in their efforts to help the family? The problem is not that Phil may need to work some additional hours to make up shortfalls in their budget or that Donna may need to get out of the house from time to time to clear her head of all of the family's demands. The problem is the process of how Phil and Donna go about doing what is "best" for their marriage. Each is still starting from the position of what "I" need to do to help my partner or the family.

The goal of the ME (To US) assessment is to help couples begin to shift their thinking away from this individual orientation. It encourages them to see the gaps in their communication and understanding of each other. It can serve as a springboard to a new set of questions about what they need to do that is best for their relationship—what steps might they take to function more as a team and to rediscover ways to prioritize their connection with each other.

However, even in the face of the evidence we can provide with the ME (To US), distressed couples often resist the shift to this We-consciousness. They quickly revert to the negative relational cycles highlighted by emotion-focused therapists and tracked so carefully by Gottman's methods. We saw this regression in action in the above argument between Katie and Will, as well as the exchange between Glen and Sasha about her son living with them. To develop effective We-ness, we have to get couples "unstuck" and loosen the hold of their negative stories over them. This can happen in two significant ways that we shall discuss in the next two chapters. First, couples can reframe negative stories in order to find redemptive meaning, compassion, and/or resolution of their enduring tensions. Second, they can counteract their rumination over these negative episodes with new attention to more positive shared stories that allow for deeper connection and empathy between the partners. To demonstrate how therapists can aid couples in these reparative efforts, we shall return to our work with Katie and Will in Chapter 5 after we have outlined the ways in which couples can find their positive We-Stories in Chapter 4. Building on the steps described in the next chapter, Chapter 5 illustrates how Will and Katie overcame their resentment to locate a story of compassion that broke an impasse for them and uncovered a stronger sense of "We."

References

Johnson, S. (2004). *The practice of emotionally focused couple therapy* (2nd ed.). New York, NY: Brunner-Routledge.

McCabe, M. P., Cummins, R. A., & Romeo, Y. (1996). Relationship status, relationship quality, and health. *Journal of Family Studies, 2*(2), 109–120.

McGoldrick, M., Gerson, R., & Petry, S. (2008). *Genograms: Assessment and intervention* (3rd ed.). New York, NY: W. W. Norton & Co.

Singer, J. A., & Labunko, B. (2005). Marital Engagement—(Type of Union) Scale—ME (To US). Department of Psychology, Connecticut College, New London, CT.

Singer, J. A., Labunko, B., Alea, N., & Baddeley, J. L. (in press). Mutuality and the Marital Engagement—Type of Union Scale [ME (To US)]: Empirical support for a clinical instrument in couples therapy. In K. Skerrett and K. Fergus (Eds.), *Couple resilience across the lifespan: Emerging perspectives.* New York, NY: Springer.

4

HELPING COUPLES CULTIVATE THEIR WE-STORIES

> We should not feel embarrassed by our difficulties, only by our failure to grow anything beautiful from them.
>
> —Alain DeBotton

Several years ago, I (KS) was supervising a group of therapists who were in the process of learning to work with couples. It had been a particularly arduous meeting with repeated expressions of puzzlement and frustration around the question of why this work felt so much "harder" than seeing individuals. Tales were told of "hanging out in stuck spots with couples—not knowing what to do" and mutual commiseration offered for—"I find myself hoping they'll cancel" or "I hate the one step forward and three back." One supervisee tearfully revealed how painful it is to coach couples toward positive repair while remembering that she hasn't said a positive thing to her own partner in weeks.

The common theme, certainly the most familiar one in our 30-plus years of teaching and supervising couple therapists, reflects the difficulty of helping couples and their therapists identify nuggets of positivity, appreciation, and hope in the midst of disconnection and despair. To attempt to help partners remember why it was that they got together in the first place is just as often met with eye rolls or "you've got to be kidding" as with softening and curiosity.

This supervision session set me on a path of reflection around the daunting challenges involved in helping partners shift their focus from their own distress and blaming stance to a curiosity about the other more positive direction. Despite the mounting evidence on the critical role of positivity in the promotion of change and maintenance of well-being (Diener, Sandvik, & Pavot, 2009; Fredrickson, 2009; Fredrickson, Tugade, Waugh & Larkin, 2003), the override from our critical, competitive, individualistic culture is formidable. Self-change is hard enough; stimulating partners' investment in one another's change and then simultaneously promoting individual and relational growth seemed near impossible.

76

These questions became the impetus for a series of qualitative studies, designed to explore ways that couples can develop positive, life-affirming relational stories, particularly narratives that reflect the essence of their partnership, the lifeblood of their generativity. The goal behind this work was to help couples see that the best way to de-escalate their conflicts was to reframe their struggles as mutual problems that they can solve together. The best way for them to learn how to reach this place of mutuality was to remember the positive elements of their relationship and to draw them to mind in the effort to down-regulate their negative emotion during conflict. And the best way to find these positive elements was through past stories of their caring behaviors and love-affirming experiences. The studies we are about to describe detail how We-Stories can be developed and worked with in couple treatment. Finally, we share some of the best methods we have found to enhance and cultivate an overall climate of relational positivity, especially how to promote positive dialogues that lead to positive stories.

Story Projects

In order to pursue these questions, I (KS) initially studied storytelling in nonclinical couples (Skerrett, 2010). I reasoned that it would be useful to explore the stories of couples before they came in to treatment to get a view of the landscape before focusing on the stories of those seeking help for their relationship. These couples, primarily white and with some college education, were all in first marriages from 30–43 years in length. By virtue of their marital longevity, they offered more experience with meaning-making and relational wisdom. Unlike early married couples who are just bringing together their individual histories, hopes, and dreams, these couples had had time to develop their shared narratives. They were interviewed at length using the Life Story Protocol of McAdams (2001) and then asked to identify a salient issue they wanted to change in their current lives. As a next step, couples were asked to write a two-page summary based on the interview questions and call it their "Life Story." Couples read these story protocols aloud to one another in a follow-up meeting and were then taught to blend their life stories into a "Couple Story."

Since that initial project, I have continued to collect couple stories, expanding the number of years married from 15 to 55 years. They now include African American, Indian, Asian, and partnered but unmarried LGBT pairs. The protocol has been altered to include an autobiographical memory, as well as a life theme in developing the Couple Story, as it seemed an easier concept for partners to grasp.

One of the unanticipated take-aways from the project was witnessing the powerful impact of reading stories aloud to one another.

Almost everyone described the experience as moving, surprising, meaningful, and poignant. The experience of sharing something so personally significant was emotionally compelling, triggering tears in many partners.

> There was something about just talking out my story all at once and having him listen that really got to me. A lot of this stuff I never think about anymore and to share it all at once . . . it was very overwhelming.

The experience of the listener, whether partner or investigator/therapist, was equally powerful as the storytelling.

> I remember that I started out this marriage wanting to be the best man and husband I could be. Over the years, I've felt like a failure at both. It was so good to hear her say she remembered me that way—that somehow buried under all these years is the guy who just wanted to do his best.

The structure of each partner reading while the other made no comment appeared to encourage emotion in the speaker and reflection and empathy in the listener. Several partners said that learning the sustaining importance of some life goal, dream, or longing in their partner's story made them want to be more of a helpmate. The following comment suggests the genesis of a budding compassion:

> I was always somewhat put off by her perfectionism—everything always had to be just so. I never realized she's been that way since she's been a little girl, her father was so critical and mean that I can see how that was her reaction—never make a mistake. I can have a little more patience with her now . . . she doesn't have to be perfect for me.

His partner said:

> That makes me feel so good—It helped me to share all that but to know you get my so-called quirks is such a relief—like you might help me let go of some of that.

Crafting We-Stories

The majority of our couples were able to develop a Good Enough We-Story and even name their stories. For example: "Caring and Sharing," "The Dream Team," "The Resilient Duo," and "Every day a Little Better."

The couples who had difficulty creating a We-Story from the directions given and struggled most to identify what they wanted to change told stories with considerably less evidence of reflection. They gave a more superficial reporting of life events, with less complexity, coherence, or thoughtful interpretation of their experiences. For example, one husband commented, "I gotta tell you, I really tried to think about these questions but I can't come up with much, I'm a guy that just tries to do what needs doing—I guess I'm not a deep thinker about much of anything."

What was most memorable were the ways in which the task of creating a We-Story, complete with title, helped couples expand their awareness of the relationship—their We-consciousness. It became clear to both couples and investigators that the process of co-creating and then sharing their Couple Stories significantly enhanced relational processing. As Reid, Dalton, Laderoute, Doell, and Nguyen (2006) elaborated, relational processing is growth in the ability to think about self in relation to other, to take perspective or empathize, and then use that knowledge to relate to one another. Individuals then begin to feel more a part of a relationship, a feeling that increases when each experiences the relationship as also a part of who he or she is. Interestingly, the majority of our couples commented that the shared vision (the We-ness of their partnership) was the quality that helped them not only adjust to life's challenges, but also helped them develop as individuals. Most couples remarked that becoming more aware of their partner's life story and, particularly, the patterns and overall continuity to their concerns, had the effect of wanting them to be more available to their partners to help, support, or to continue achieving their goals. As one woman said: "This just really helped us get back to the big picture. I can get so caught up in the minutia—in the everyday stuff, I lose track of where we've been together. It's comforting to know we're still headed in the same direction and that we can help each other get there."

It has been affirming to learn that by expanding partner perspectives regarding the meaning, continuity, and importance of each other's abiding concerns (expressed through themes, stories, and autobiographical memories), partners are better able to understand and invest in one another's change process. Watching the linkages develop between the partners' appreciation of mutual vulnerability and increased interest in compassionate caretaking was exciting and suggested promise for therapeutic applications.

We-Stories in Therapy

Before translating these ideas to the therapeutic encounter, several caveats require mention. As we've said earlier, most couples present for therapy hurt, disappointed, angry, disconnected, and with a litany of complaints about the other. One or both may also be experiencing what Roos and Neimeyer (2007) call "narrative disruption." There are several ways such disruptions can occur. Their individual stories may be shattered by a tragic event, such as serious illness or loss resulting in narrative disorganization, and the sense that there is no longer coherence and meaning in life. If the trauma is not named—lacking both voice and audience—one's story becomes thinned, resulting in "narrative dissociation" and silence. Another form of narrative disruption—"narrative domination"—is all too familiar to therapists. It occurs when one narrative takes over and crowds out all other versions. For example, the "mean, selfish withholding" story that becomes the lens through which all behavior is interpreted and understood. As Weingarten (2013) aptly describes, the challenge for the therapist under these circumstances is often unclear. Do we assist in the development of a coherent narrative that takes into account the current circumstances, or validate the incoherence of the narrative and thus help increase tolerance for the fragmentation, or some combination of the two? Perhaps seeking to locate the Good Enough We-Story—good enough for this moment in time, given the couple's circumstances and resources, is precisely what may be called for.

We have developed a clinical sequence that can be applied alone, or in conjunction with the Me (To US) Inventory, that has proved useful in the initial assessment phase of therapy. Since story creation is dynamic, this sequence (or parts of it) can also be used as therapy progresses, as well as a way to reconnect, when couples return to treatment in future years. Later in the chapter, we will describe ways to amplify the positive ingredients of We-Stories at any point along the course of therapy.

Mark and Jenn's Story

We illustrate this process with the story of Mark and Jenn. Married for 22 years, they came for a first experience in couple's treatment "immobilized by stress." They had four children, ages 17, 13, 11, and 5. The youngest suffered from severe cerebral palsy, resulting from complications during a birth that almost killed Jenn. Mark managed a car dealership, and Jenn, once a successful court reporter, had quit her job to take care of their disabled son. Describing themselves as "disconnected robots," they told a story of beginning each day focused on what needed to be done, who needed to do it, and ending the day "totally depleted" and disempowered. After spending time gathering information and getting better acquainted, I asked them to do the following series of assignments.

Part 1. Each partner writes a brief version of his or her life story to bring to a meeting and read aloud to one another. The story was to include but not be limited to personal concerns, life goals, and hopes and dreams for the future. Finally, they were each to give their story a title they felt summarized an overall theme or pattern in their lives.

As has been the case with most couples, they responded positively to being able to "have something to do" and not have to focus immediately on the issues they felt so "frustrated and stuck with." Here is a condensed version of the stories written by each.

Jenn

I was the baby in a big family of five kids, born in Champaign. We moved every five or six years—always in the Midwest, following my Father's promise of a better paying job. My siblings hated moving, but it never really bothered me. I liked the idea of going to a new school, putting my stuff up in a different bedroom, meeting new kids in the neighborhood . . . starting over. It always seemed kind of exciting to me. I was a good student, got along well with my classmates, and pretty much did what was expected. No wild teenage years—my brother and sisters would have ratted on me anyway. I was ready to go off to junior college for the independence. I met Mark second semester and that was pretty much that. We were a couple from day one. We were pretty sure this was it, but my parents were really opposed to us getting married. We hung in there for another year, but once Mark graduated, we got married. A friend who was a court reporter really loved her job and talked me into trying it. Once I started, I was hooked. I didn't see the need for more college, so I quit. I liked the money I was making because we were trying to save for a house. Mark started doing pretty well by the time I got pregnant for the first time. I really loved being a mother—it got pretty crazy by the time number 3 came along and I dropped to part-time. Everything changed when Adam was born. I almost died and then learning how to take care of him with his condition was like a nightmare I couldn't wake up from. I never sit down, I never stop. We've tried different caregivers and nurses' aides but they never last. Mark and I decided it would be better if we just take care of him ourselves. But it's killing us. I never thought this was where I'd be at this point in my life. I'm losing myself and really hope this counseling can help us figure out a better way.

TITLE: *NEVER GIVE UP*

Several features are noteworthy in Jenn's story. It is clearly sequential, highlighting Jenn's progress from point A to point B in her life. It is striking that the story thins and stalls following Adam's birth, and how she no longer writes of any dreams or wishes for the future. She read her story in a neutral monotone, looking up only when she came to the part about Adam's birth, her eyes reflecting a sad wistfulness. In McAdams's terms, it is very much a "Contamination" story that starts out in a positive direction ("We were a couple from day one"), but ends on a note of distress and frustrated expectations ("I never thought that this was where I'd be at this point in my life").

Mark

I'm a can-do guy. My parents always taught my brother and I—if you work hard enough, you can get anywhere. I'm proud of where I got to, growing up on the west side of the city next door to all the other city workers, scraping to get by and now I've got my own dealership. My parents really sacrificed for us to go to school, Catholic schools, then junior college, and I wanted to make it worth their while. I try to give our kids that same thing—if you apply yourself, you can tackle what life throws at you. When I met Jenn, I thought I'd died and gone to heaven. I never thought I'd find anybody like her. I've tried to do my best by her, but I know I'm not making her happy and that's what I want from this—to figure out how to make her happy. She's my future; I don't want to lose her and I got to figure out how to make life better. Adam is gonna be Adam, but I don't want to go down with the ship trying to raise him.

TITLE: *ALWAYS DO YOUR BEST*

Mark's story is less sequential than Jenn's, moving fluidly among past to present, present to past, then to future. It is coherent and emphasizes a goal for the future. He read his story in an animated fashion, sitting forward in his seat, making efforts to engage us both. He starts out by defining himself as the "can-do" guy, but ends with a little more uncertainty and a little less bravado. He has not given up by any means, but his narrative conveys a more shaky confidence; he is not as sure that his best will always be enough.

It is important to notice the reactions each partner has to the other's story—what each hears and interprets and how each chooses to respond. Mark was close to tears listening to Jenn's story and commented that he felt sad that her "life sorta stopped with Adam" and that she felt like she "had no self." He expressed frustration that she couldn't seem to see how hard he was working and how much better he wanted life to be for her; "All she saw were problems." Jenn said that the part of Mark's story that surprised her was how much he wanted to please her and make a difference for her. She said she tended to see him as only focused on Adam, and that she felt invisible in his eyes most of the time.

I felt quite moved by both of their stories, touched by the challenges they had taken on in their journey, as well as by their mutual desire for something better. I shared my reactions with them emphasizing the inherent personal strengths each story expressed, identifying the aspects of resilience they showed, and applauding their courage in coming for help. I normalized their dilemma in the following way:

> The stress you both experience is a natural byproduct of how hard you're working to do the very best you can—for your son, for one another, and for your whole family. Your efforts and

perseverance are remarkable. I also hear commitment and concern for one another and that is a powerful and treasured resource that we will draw on as we work together.

They both paused after this feedback and with an almost puzzled look on her face, Jenn remarked:

I never think of myself as having strength but when you put it that way, I can kinda see what you mean. Makes me feel better.

Giving couples feedback on their strengths or what we hear to be working well in their lives is typically responded to with surprise and even amazement, as if entirely uncommon and unexpected. The feedback sows the first seeds of hope in the treatment, counterbalancing the pessimism and negativity each felt.

It is also a useful bridge to moving forward to:

Part 2. Each partner helps to identify the relationship of the presenting issue (as they see it) to a recurring pattern in their personal development. Jenn required little coaching here and made this linkage quite spontaneously in her life story. She had built a personal identity around a pattern of accomplishment and success and got derailed with the shock and trauma of Adam's birth and the multiple stressors attendant to raising him. Once that pattern was broken, she experienced a loss of her sense of self and sought out therapy, in part, to restore both her identity and the support of Mark's loving partnership.

The pinnacle of Mark's "can-do" approach was meeting and marrying Jenn, and he frames his derailment as linked to her chronic unhappiness. He sought therapy to learn how to have more success in making her happy again. He identified that a primary way he felt good about himself was "being the kind of husband and father that makes my wife happy."

Part 3. The therapist teaches a variety of life and relationship skills that are utilized in the ongoing treatment as well. They include simple relaxation techniques, breath work, body awareness exercises, and loving kindness meditations (Hanson, 2013; Kabat-Zinn, 2003, 2009). All are designed to "turn on" the social engagement system (Porges, 2011)—priming the brain for neuroplastic change. We are working toward brain states of greater integration, involving harmony, flexibility, compassion, and connectivity inside and outside. These exercises focus on cultivating safer, more approachable, receptive states and a climate of "YES" vs. "NO." We have included two examples at the end of this chapter of exercises that couples can do that encourage expressing vulnerability and compassion with each other (see "Dialogue Guides for Couple Conversations" and "Love Letters"). Jenn, Mark, and I discussed another of these techniques, what I call the 3R process (Skerrett, 2010), and they were told to practice it as homework. The process is:

Reflect: Spend time in quiet meditation in which they each reflect on their life theme or autobiographical memory and how it is manifesting in their current life

Reorganize: Consider the components of the theme/memory in light of the problem they want to change

Recreate: Rewrite the problem in the direction of a positive outcome(s).

When both have completed this process, they are to share the experience with one another.

Jenn and Mark returned to our next meeting looking somewhat more energized and reported they had carved out two periods of time to work on their homework—a first time alone in many months. As a bonus, they had found a new high schooler in the neighborhood who did well with Adam and had agreed to come back on a regular basis. They each described having benefitted from the quiet reflection time, finding it both restful and supportive of their ability to do some creative, "big-picture" thinking. Jenn said:

> I got clear on how important it's always been to me to be able to roll with the punches—I even liked it growing up. But I guess Adam was just too big a punch. By expecting myself to just keep pushing forward, I actually made it harder on myself and everyone around me.
>
> I rewrote my title to be *Give up when you need to.*

Mark said:

> This was hard for me. I liked the R & R part but I think I got stuck on what's more positive than "always do your best"? Then Jenn and I got into a fight where she accused me of not listening to her, just runnin' my own agenda and trying to look good. That's when I think I started to get it—like trying to get her to be happy was just my way of feeling like I was the good guy. Checking her off my list.
>
> I rewrote my title: *Always do your best except when you can't.*

We continued and expanded the conversation they had had at home about the commonalities in their individual issues. They were each desperately trying to move forward in patterned and historically conscientious ways. However, they were trying to make this progress under very challenging circumstances with minimal external support and minus the regular nourishing connection of their relationship. Their respective body language became more open and engaged; Jenn in particular offered several empathic comments to Mark around his frustrated efforts to help her. One of the benefits of this exercise was to energize some of the key SERAPHS elements, specifically—**Empathy, Respect**, and **Acceptance**. In hearing each other's story, they could access their partner's pain and also grasp the effort each other was making to keep the family and the relationship afloat. Perhaps most important, they could hear the vulnerability expressed in each narrative and convey to their partner an acknowledgment of each other's very human flaws, as well as the impossibility of fixing their current dilemma with a perfect resolution. No wonder their life story themes changed to more qualified statements rather than definitive answers.

After processing these new insights, they were then sent home with the next exercise in the sequence.

Part 4. The therapist helps the couple blend their new individual stories into a We-Story, utilizing the themes/titles of each and the relevant individual issues that are related to ways in which each partner wants to change or grow. They are asked to incorporate an image or metaphor that they both feel characterizes their relationship, one that epitomizes the essence of what is loving and hopeful and makes their relationship unique.

This step took several weeks and required some coaching around the meaning of metaphor as well as fruitful dialogue on the different styles each brought to engaging in conversation. I emphasized questions that explored how they decided what they uniquely wanted for their relationship rather than assuming their wants needed to reflect the dominant and "accepted" cultural ideas around gender and power.

They prefaced their story by sharing an anecdote that occurred one evening during the time they were working on their We-Story.

MARK: So I'm coming in from the garage loaded down with groceries, I remember whistling I guess 'cause I thought she'd be happy to see that I shopped. Jenn's standing at the sink and when she turns around, she's crying.

JENN: I could tell he had no idea what he was whistling or what it meant—he was probably thinking he did something wrong. So I tell him—you're whistling "You Are My Sunshine." I haven't heard you whistle that since forever. When we were dating, he played in this grunge band that used to practice the only night I didn't have class, when we could have gone out. We'd been fighting about that off and on for weeks and trying to make up when I cut class one night and surprised him at practice. He told me later, practice was going horribly and they'd been playing stupid stuff. When I walked in, they were playing "You Are My Sunshine." They tried to make it look intentional—like just for me. Mark and I always laughed about that and for years he called me "Sunshine."

Following from this, here is their We-Story:

> We're alike in all the big ways, the ways that count. We've both had different problems and challenges in our lives, but we've tried to tackle them and move on in productive ways. There were lots of points where each of us could have given up, saying it's too hard, woe is me, whatever. But we believed it was best to keep on the right path and we were a great team doing that together. The hardest thing we've faced is almost losing Jenn and then parenting Adam. We got to a point where the stress was just too much. Nothing was working. We didn't have a plan for what to do when we couldn't do it anymore. Do your best was getting in the way. We were doing what needed to be done separately, but we forgot that we're each other's sunshine. We need that light and warmth every day, but especially on the hard days. That sunshine is bigger and better than all the problems— we have to have it! We're grateful that we didn't let things get too far without remembering the sunshine.

Their We-Story beautifully illustrates a sequence of events, coherence, a challenge to be mastered, and an image that points them toward a redemptive solution. The image became a touchstone (an "emotional handle") to ground their work and to guide them toward relational healing. The story also chronicles a re-emergence and re-emphasis on the "We," an active shifting from functioning in their separate spheres to a mutual interdependence. Where before they had been working furiously, but **in parallel**, to solve the problems that Adam posed for their family, their We-Story reminded them that they could work in unison—that by giving to each other, they could strengthen each of their individual efforts to keep the family afloat. Their together time, their reaffirmation of the "We" would not suck energy from what needed to be done independently. To the contrary, it would refuel them (and in their case with solar energy!) for the tasks that each of them needed to accomplish on their own.

Over time, we have found that the We-Story co-creation is more impactful in building We-consciousness than direct relationship education. Watching the "We" emerge organically through a process of dialogue provides partners a vivid, often moving, experience of the relationship in action—of dialoguing about an entity larger than themselves for whom they are responsible.

Jenn and Mark were able to recognize that the biggest challenge for the relationship was in learning how to develop a plan that would allow them to tackle the daily stresses of family life while staying connected to one another. We were then nicely positioned to collaborate on a plan of action to meet their goal and identify the ongoing practices that would keep the "We" nourished and bright (keeping the sunshine out and about).

Box 4.1 We-Story Interventions

Part 1. Have each partner write a brief version of their life story. This should include but not be limited to personal concerns and challenges, life goals, hopes and dreams for the future.

Give the story a title that summarizes an overall pattern or theme in the life story.

Read these stories aloud to one another in a session.

Part 2. Assist each partner to identify the relationship of the presenting issue to a recurring pattern in their personal development. For example, someone may say that they are stressed in their current life and that it is (may be) related to their lifelong habit of taking on too much responsibility.

Part 3. Teaching life and relationship skills.

The 3-R Process

Reflect: Spend time in quiet meditation in which each partner reflects on their life theme or autobiographical memory and how it is manifesting in their current life.

Reorganize: Consider the components of the theme/memory in light of the problem they want to change.

Recreate: Rewrite the problem in the direction of a positive outcome(s).

When both have completed this process, they are to share the experience with one another.

Part 4. Blend the new individual stories into a We-Story, utilizing the themes/titles of each and the relevant individual issues that are related to what each wants to change/how each wants to grow. Incorporate an image or metaphor both partners feel characterizes their relationship, one that epitomizes the essence of what is loving and hopeful and makes their relationship unique.

Cultivating a Climate of Positivity

At the beginning of the Couple Story projects, I was hopeful that I might be able to classify the stories into neat categories of positivity—like hope, curiosity, or joy. It soon became apparent that this wasn't going to happen, and I learned something very critical in the process. Positive states are innately amplifying—broadening one's view of self and other (Fredrickson, 2009). Positivity and openness reinforce and catalyze one another, generating upward spirals that nourish trust as we hear in the following exchange between Mark and Jenn:

M: I love it when you smile at me like that.

J: (blushing and moving closer). Like what?

M: Like you're interested in what I'm saying, like I'm the smartest guy in the room.

J: I am interested in what you're saying. I've wanted to know more about that new guy you hired and how he's working out. I have a lot of questions about how work is going.

M: Really? (face animated, color flushed, with a look of excitement on his face) I wasn't sure you were interested. I know how much you have on your mind, but I've missed getting your input on work stuff.

J: I've missed that too—I like when you confide in me and ask my opinion—even if it isn't the one you want to hear (both laugh). It feels so good to laugh again and be happy together.

M: Yeah.

J: So are you ready for those questions?

M: Shoot!

The positive states of curiosity, interest, pride, excitement, hope, and happiness are all contained in this brief exchange and the synergism between them cannot be untangled. It is also striking how one partner's appreciation and interest are expanded upon by the other, which in turn triggers greater sharing and exploration. It is precisely this synergy that creates the motivation in each partner to reinvest in the other's well-being. Similarly, it is this positive energy that enables positive repair efforts during periods of conflict and helps the couple down-regulate negative emotion and not escalate or prolong their dispute.

Guiding couples through an exercise in developing a We-Story is one way to begin to tip the scales in favor of relational positivity; there are many others. At the foundation of all of these are several skills critical for the couple therapist. The most essential is for us to hone our own capacity to be open, receptive, and willing to listen for signs of positive possibility in Couple Stories; to fine-tune our ability to resonate with and embellish the upward spiral in a story. When I (KS) hear or sense these positive emotions in the room, I often will ask the partner to identify the feeling (e.g., joy, interest, amusement, inspiration, awe, wonder), then amplify and expand with the following questions:

> When was the last time you felt that with _____?
> Where were you? What were you doing? What else gives you that feeling when you're together?
> What can you do right now to savor this feeling?

Fortunately, these therapeutic skills improve with practice but it is nevertheless a fine line to walk since positivity is a fleeting state and doesn't lend itself well to overanalysis.

In addition to guiding couples to engage around the positive qualities in their stories, expanding and amplifying them, we often need to raise or activate positivity where none seems to exist—turning on the "positivity levers" (Fredrickson, 2009, p. 51). These levers can be activated with thought or actions, and we've found the following questions to be particularly useful in this regard.

> What's going right in this relationship right now?
> What do you most celebrate about each other?
> What would you miss most if _____ were no longer here?
> What does your relationship look like at its very best?
> What are the key strengths of your relationship?
> What are you most grateful for about _____?
> What are you most grateful for about the relationship?

Interestingly, recent research suggests that supporting a partner when things are going well might be more valuable than support during tough times (Gable, Gosnell, Maisel, & Strachman, 2012). Study participants who felt supported when they got a high rating at work, or during another time they thought of as positive, reported feeling better about themselves and their relationships than participants who did not receive comparable acknowledgments of the good times in their lives.

"Bonds Last, Love Doesn't"

Mark and Jenn came in to one of our meetings with complaints that reminded me of the ones raised by the novice couple therapists described at the beginning of this chapter.

J: Yuk . . . it's been such a lousy week. I don't feeling very loving toward you right now.

M: Yeah, please don't tell me we need to work on this relationship—I already have too much work to do as it is and that doesn't exactly make me feel more loving.

One of the most common myths we all bring to our relationships—couples and therapists alike, is the belief that if we have to work at it, there is something wrong with us, the relationship, or both. Hence, the common complaint—"If you really cared about me, you'd know." Here is where some relationship education from the new science of love can be helpful. Although the cultivation of positive emotion we've been talking about is important—stretching our minds and triggering resilience and growth—love only happens in connection; "bonds last, love doesn't" (Fredrickson, 2013, p. 36). According to Fredrickson, a good description of the experience of love is "positivity resonance." It requires the momentary upsurge of three interwoven events: a sharing of one or more positive emotions between partners, a synchrony between one partner's and the other's biochemistry and behavior, and mutual caretaking by both members of the couple. In this particular moment of connection, partners respective feelings, actions, and impulses align and come into sync. In that moment, each becomes something larger than oneself. Such connections are far from random and require the perception of safety to occur. True connection is also physical, and unfolds in real time, explaining why eye contact is such a potent trigger. When partners lock gazes, the positivity and attunement of each become part of the other. When Jenn told Mark she had questions about his work, his internal state began to buzz with her enthusiasm and appreciation, and as he expressed that through his voice and gestures, a parallel process occurred for Jenn. A mutual reverberation went on between them.

Jenn gets this essential idea about love when at another time she tells Mark she doesn't feel very loving toward him. They had had virtually no contact other than household maintenance that week and no opportunities for positivity resonance. Yet what brought them back to sessions and kept them on relational task was their deep bond, the commitment they made to one another to be loyal and trusting to the end. We hope this knowledge about the difference between positive emotions and love will remove their complacency and get them moving every day to reach for a hug, share a funny story over breakfast, pop a loving note in their partner's lunch bag, or offer an after-work pick-up at the train station. Men seem to need these affirmations the most. Recent research (Veroff & Orbuch, 2012) postulates that because women get more positive affirmations from others on a daily basis, men are particularly dependent on their wives for this validation.

Foundational to any ongoing positive interaction in the couple, however, is the capacity for dialogue, and we turn next to helping couples learn how to have a "Good Enough Talk." We have found that often before we can work with the couple to build a strong and sustaining We-Story, we have to shift their manner of discussing conflicts and provide them with basic tools for communication. As Gottman's work has amply demonstrated, all the communication skill building in the world will not work if the couple refuses to extend some basic trust and good will toward each other. Our procedure for how to create the "Good Enough Talk" is premised on an initial commitment of the couple to accept at the very least a "cease fire" in their negativity and make an honest effort to explore working together. We take great pains to explain the "four horsemen of the apocalypse" that Gottman (Gottman & Silver, 1999) found in his research (criticism, contempt, defensiveness, and stonewalling) and ask that each partner take responsibility for minimizing these behaviors. Of course, these requests are not easy and there are definite flare-ups, but in general, the couples embrace and adhere to this welcome structure in what had often been frustrating and unproductive conversations in the past.

The "Good Enough Talk"

"I hate it when you watch TV when I am trying to talk to you."
"If you had anything useful to say, I would turn the set off."
"How would you ever know if you don't listen?"
"I am listening now."
"Fine—Forget it. I don't want to talk any more."
"See, what's the point of even trying?"

Every night in households all over this land exchanges like this spring up and die their unsightly deaths. In the aftermath the two partners sit in separate zones of despair, staring blandly at the television, surfing the Net, nursing a beer, or falling asleep over a half-read magazine.

Why do so many couples have such trouble talking to each other? Is it due to the gender gap as authors like John Gray, Deborah Tannen, and Samuel Shem and Janet Surrey might suggest? Is it due to childhood patterns and early wounds as Harville Hendrix might conclude? Does it have to do with couples' defensive maneuvers as documented by John Gottman in his research? Of course, the answer is all of this matters and much more.

We have not had good role models to teach us how to talk to each other. In a society where divorce and single-parenting are rampant, many of us have simply not been exposed to models of calm and constructive adult conversation about difficult topics. Unfortunately, for many people in our society, the template for conversation between partners is the situation comedy or the reality show in which people rely on put-downs, snappy retorts, or just plain profanity to make their points. To make matters worse, our highly competitive society is always pushing that "come out on top" attitude that fosters "being No. 1" rather than cooperation. The point is to show that we are right, isn't it? The point is to make sure that we are not the *loser*, isn't it? The point is to make sure we get what is due to us, or else we are shortchanging ourselves, isn't that true? Who wants to feel like the lesser person, the chump, the pushover, the fool?

On the other hand, while we don't want to be the fool, we are even more desperate not to be the bad guy, the villain, a different kind of loser in the game of who is the "better" person. Just as much as we battle to get what we want, we battle for the higher moral ground. Who wants to be king of the hill unless all who surround us are able to say we are a good king, fair and square? In fact, we would rather say, "You are right," or "I don't need this that much," or "You can do that, if you really want to," than feel that we have gotten our way unfairly and autocratically. All our lives we are taught not only to be good at things, but to be a *good person*—to do the right thing. Now in talking with our partners, we are told that we are selfish—that we are only concerned for our own needs—that we do not put the family or our partner first. We are thoughtless, self-centered, exploitative, and manipulative.

Wait a second! This is not the child our mother raised. We deny all of these attacks on our integrity, fight to regain higher ground, and make it clear how (if we are really being honest) it is our partner who suffers from all of these character defects and immoralities. In the game of being both right and righteous, we can take no prisoners. The key is to prove to our partner that we are the better person, the one with the best intentions, the one who loves the most and receives the least. And these battles are waged over the most trivial of concerns. How indeed do our simple efforts to determine who will unload the dishwasher or what we want to do this weekend or who will drive Jason to his clarinet lesson devolve into a moral battle reminiscent of Richard the Lion Heart's crusade into Palestine?

In order to explore these questions in depth, let's look at the ideals of **Good Talk**. How can a couple's dialogue be structured to maximize a sense of connection and mutuality? What are the concrete steps to follow that might improve the chances of reaching a constructive action plan rather than simply descending into finger pointing and a pissing contest? Before we can get couples to buy in to an "ongoing sense of We-ness" that can guide their storytelling, consensus-building, and independent behaviors, how might we teach them to talk to each other and talk through difficult conversations?

In clinical training when we were learning to be patient about allowing the other person to finish, we would pass a tennis ball around the circle and only the person with the ball in hand was allowed to talk. During heated discussions at home, we often feel like that tennis ball would go bouncing off each other's head if we tried this technique. Yet, and here is the critical point, despite the intensity of emotion generated by the family drama, we need to cling to the basic principles of listening and dialogue like a life raft in the midst of stormy seas. And this is what we ask of all the couples with whom we work—learn these steps and practice them over and over. They will not be a panacea that cures all yelling and agitation when the couple discusses difficult topics, but they provide a structure to ground dialogues in mutual respect and empathy. By adhering to this structure, couples will consistently pull themselves back from the brink of invective and personal attack. In other words, the following steps are the lifeline of the "We" and couples are well advised to hold to them with all their might.

How to Have a Good Talk

There are many names for the steps that we are about to detail—Active Listening, Constructive Dialogue, The Couple's Dialogue (Hendrix's term), but for most couples with whom we have worked, the partners end up describing what happens between them as a "Good Talk." What emerges from a Good Talk or the "Good Enough Talk" is that the couple feels closer and more connected than they did before the conversation. This outcome can result even when the conversation ends with an agreement to disagree or a decision that does not give either partner exactly what he or she wants. In a sense there is the same purpose for every talk and that is to strengthen the couple and to achieve the objectives that reinforce their We-consciousness—the rest of what happens are just details and logistics. So here is Step 1.

Step 1: The Talk Should Lead to a Stronger "We"

In order to achieve this objective, each partner must recognize that the purpose of sitting down and having a serious discussion about some dimension of the relationship is not to win the partner over or convince the partner of the rightness of one's own point of view. It is always to open up the exploration of what is best for the relationship. As we have seen in previous chapters, there are many factors that enhance successful We-ness; some of them include active pursuit of each person's personal goals and ambitions; financial security and prosperity of the family; physical and mental well-being of one's offspring; equity and justice in the distribution of wage-earning and domestic duties; respect for and attention to extended family and especially in-laws; and a number of other concerns. Whichever of these topics might become the focus of the dialogue across the kitchen table, the fundamental point is the same. The partner must vet any plan of action against this question: Will this choice reinforce each partner's feeling of being loved and respected by their partner? Will this choice help us to feel that the relationship will ultimately grow stronger by taking this course of action? Put simply—"Is this best for Us?" not for you or for me, but for "Us"?

To make sure this first step is clear, let's look at how Ali and Fatima handled her decision to move her medical practice to a new city. Fatima had taken a position with a cardiovascular surgery group right out of residency. The group had promised her big salary increases and an eventual partnership that would lead to profit-sharing. In the meantime Ali had taken on a position as a history and government teacher in a nearby boarding school. They had two children, and Ali was the primary care-taker for the children due to Fatima's long hours in surgery. Now five years into this arrangement it was becoming clear to Fatima that the senior partners had little intention of cutting her in on the group's over-all earnings. They preferred to keep her in a junior position and placate her with increased salary and occasional bonuses. Even with these efforts to meet her financial demands, the partners continued to impose a more arduous call schedule on her and relegated her to the more mundane and least interesting cases and procedures. Fatima saw little future in staying in the practice and felt that she had to move or else she would feel both exploited and stagnant in her career. She also sensed under-tones of sexism and ethnic discrimination in some of her social interac-tions with the most senior partners.

In contrast, Ali had flourished at his school; he had started a model UN club and his students had received multiple honors at statewide and regional competitions. He very much liked their children's preschool and loved the updated colonial home that he had painstakingly reno-vated. Through the school and the local Mosque, they had cultivated a warm and supportive Islamic community of friends and families. The problem was that there were no other comparable cardiovascular surgery practices in the local community. Fatima's group dominated the local hospital and there simply were no realistic competitors. For Fatima to take a new and more rewarding position, she had to cast her net wide and find a new practice that would recognize her need to grow both profes-sionally and financially. The situation was clearly taking a toll on her; she often felt depressed and angry, while her sleep had become horribly dis-rupted. She would lie in bed at night, playing over slights and patronizing remarks made by one or another of the partners in the course of the day.

Finally, she received word that a position had opened up in a group associated with her old residency hospital. One of her beloved mentors had emailed her and told her the job was hers if she wanted it. It was time for Fatima and Ali to sit down and talk. How could they discuss this decision effectively? How could Fatima ask Ali to move and give up his teaching post and the rich community network they had developed? How could he give up the house where he had scraped, primed, and painted virtually every square inch?

The only effective way to have this difficult conversation is to begin with Step 1—the goal that this talk should bring them closer. They agreed to this premise before they began. They agreed that they loved each other and wanted what would be best for the health of their relationship and for the strengthening of their love. The conversation did not end in one session but extended over the next few days. When they felt that they had reached an impasse or were growing strained and angry with each other, they agreed to resume it at a later point. They looked at every option under the sun—how Fatima might start her own practice in their current town, how she might sue her partners, how she might switch out of her specialty, how she might take a break from medicine altogether. Yet over and over they asked the question of what would bring her happiness and fulfillment— what would allow her to be the best partner in the marriage from an emotional and psychological standpoint? What course of action would break her depression and sense of tightening suffocation? At the same time, they asked, what positives could they identify in the community where the new position would be? Could Ali find another rewarding teaching job? Would they be able to recreate the welcoming Islamic community that they had found in their current home? Were they willing to accept buying a much smaller house that was in great shape, or could they bring themselves to start again with fixing up and thoroughly updating an older larger home?

In the end there were no simple answers to these questions, but there was one compelling fact—until Fatima could regain a way to find happiness in her work the integrity and harmony of the "We" was going to suffer. Knowing that they needed to put their sense of connection before all other choices, they continually reaffirmed their loyalty to each other and to the "We." This vital commitment led them finally to accept the new position and move the family to the new city. Fatima struggled with tremendous guilt over this decision, but also took seriously Ali's reassurances that this was the right choice for the relationship. In turn, no one worked harder than Fatima in making contacts that would help Ali to find a new teaching post and that would connect her family to the small but solid Islamic community in the neighborhoods near the hospital. Fatima's sense of Ali's love and devotion to their marriage was catapulted to a new level of trust, while Ali's pleasure in seeing Fatima's renewed energy and enthusiasm deepened with each new month in their new home. Their ability to have good talks based in the "We" had allowed them to make a painful but necessary decision—a decision that addressed the pressing needs of one partner more than another, but that ultimately strengthened the bond of love and mutuality that defined the best aspirations of the couple.

Their ability to keep an assumption of love for each other as the guiding force behind all of their discussions and ultimate decisions teaches us about the second step in all Good Talks.

Step 2: Assumption That "Love Is in the Room"

One of the hardest challenges that partners will face in having a dialogue about a conflict or a difficulty that has arisen within the couple is the sense that each person is under attack. We inevitably experience "constructive feedback" or "helpful suggestions" as personal attacks. How might we carry on a Good Talk about some aspect of the relationship without taking it as a judgment on our character or worth as a partner, lover, parent, provider, and so on? Once again, our proposal is to release our egos in the service of the "We." If we assume that what is about to be said is expressed in a context of love rather than performance evaluation, in a desire to be closer rather than in the spirit of a progress report, we might be able to step back from the extreme personalization that we tend to apply to any request for change from our partners.

For example, Lisa told Joseph that she wished he would not pressure her so much to make love at night when they would get into bed together. Joseph felt that they were not making love enough and Lisa's statement was just a further rejection of him. Yet when we explored this in their couple therapy, Lisa expressed an honest enjoyment of her sexual relationship with Joseph. The problem was simply that she often felt too tired after a day of work and taking care of kids to be able to get into the emotional space that the intensity of love-making required. She resented that Joseph would pout when she turned away from his advances. He seemed not to get the message that it was not about him, but more about her own physical limits and emotional reserves.

Through our couple work and its emphasis on building a loving "We" in their relationship, Joseph tried to approach this situation with a different attitude. He focused in on the assumption that **LOVE IS IN THE ROOM** and her turning away from intimacy at those moments was not a repudiation of him, but something Lisa needed for her own well-being. He trusted that her "no" was not a commentary on his performance or desirability. By having faith in Lisa's love, Joseph let go of the self-doubt that had been building up in him (Acceptance). He also began to see that part of the urgency he had felt about making love more often was tied up in his own desire to prove to himself that Lisa still found him exciting as a sexual partner. Now drawing on her reassurance, he actually relaxed and began to find more enjoyment in the nights that they simply snuggled together and went to sleep without love-making. In turn, Lisa felt so appreciative that these episodes of pressure and frustration had subsided that she looked for ways that they could be intimate with each other more often during the daytime and weekends. Assuming love had allowed them to avoid turning their conflict into mutual judgments of their respective worth. It had shifted their dialogue and ultimately their actions toward ways of building a deeper connection with each other.

If Steps 1 and 2 are the most important underlying frameworks for helping couples generate Good Talks, then what are the actual tactics and techniques that couples might apply to be effective listeners and communicators during the talk? Let's turn to Step 3.

Step 3: Choose a Time and Place

To have a dialogue is to make a commitment to asking questions. An open and constructive dialogue is based in the working premise that each member of the couple does not know each other as well as they might think; they must relearn who their partner is and not assume telepathy or intuition that enables them to understand their partner's feelings and needs without asking. How do partners begin to learn what their partner truly wants or needs? How do they learn about their partner's bottled-up frustration or long withheld desire? They only learn by asking, but even more by learning to listen carefully—to their words, but also to their faces and their bodies.

To begin this process, partners must be able to select a time of day and a place when and where effective talk can take place. To make a good choice about a location and time, here are some alternatives that we teach the couple to rule out:

- **Do not try to have a dialogue after you have just spent 2 hours putting your rambunctious 3-year-old to bed.**
- **Do not try to talk when it is 8:00 A.M. and you need to be at work by 8:30.** (We remember the anger one wife felt when her husband, with his briefcase in hand, said to her that he had felt she was being distant and they needed to talk about what was going on in their relationship. She was outraged that he could raise such a deep and wrenching topic while halfway out the door.)
- **Do not carry on serious conversations by cell phone, email, or text message.**
- **Do not talk when there are children in the room or in earshot.**
- **Do not attempt a thoughtful conversation if either of you has had too much to drink.**
- **Do not engage in a serious conversation during a time that has been previously agreed upon as a chance to have fun or relax.**

When and where **should** couples talk? They should reserve a time when there will be enough time to talk. This may be a morning when the kids are at Sunday school or an evening when they are off in their bedrooms doing their homework. It may be over a quiet dinner or during a long walk. Although some couples try to have constructive dialogues while having dinner at a restaurant, we see some serious obstacles to this approach. They are likely to be interrupted periodically by the wait staff; one or both of them may be having alcohol; both partners may censor the depth of their feelings due to being in a public place; and finally why not use a night out to eat for fun and romance rather than what may be a difficult and painful conversation? We believe the best places to talk (assuming the children are out of the way) are in the kitchen, living room, study, or else in a calm and soothing place in nature. We do not recommend the bedroom due to the thoughtful words one of our clients said to us, "We agreed never to have our most serious and painful discussions in our bedroom. We want to keep this room as a place of refuge and romance. We'd hate to connect it with arguments or discord."

Wherever a couple chooses, we strongly recommend that the couple sit face to face and that there be no media present. In other words, the television, radio, computer, and cell phone must be turned off. Books, newspapers, and magazines must be closed. The couple should be fully present to each other and be able to take in each other's faces and bodies as they speak.

Step 4: "I Feel . . ." "You Feel . . ."

Once the time and place are set, then the talk can begin. Both partners should have many opportunities to initiate these talks, so there need be no rule about who is going to state their feelings first, but it should be understood that the person who is going first is the focus of this talk. In other words, the initial goal is to recognize that one person in the relationship is feeling a difficulty or distress and that the couple is going to work on addressing this concern. If the talk begins to divert to the problems and complaints of the other partner, the couple needs to reorient the conversation back to the partner who has brought up the initial concern. There will be plenty of opportunities for the other partner to have their worries addressed. This is part of where the trust and assumption of love come in. "If I give you the floor this time, then you will surely give me an opportunity as well."

The partner who is going to express his or her concern begins by saying **"I want you to know that something is bothering me. When you do . . . , I feel . . ."**

For example, Claire tells Paul that, "When you talk to another woman for too long at a dinner party, I feel ignored and humiliated." After stating this initial connection of Paul's action to her feeling, Claire goes on to explain further. "I feel this way because you don't seem to notice that I may be looking your way or hoping that you will return to my side."

Having heard Claire's initial statement of her concern, Paul's responsibility (as any form of active listening would require) is to **restate** what Claire has said to him and to receive confirmation from her that he has gotten it right. So Paul needs to say back to Claire,

"So what you are telling me is that when I spend too much time talking to another woman at a party, you feel ignored and humiliated. **Do I have this right?"**

Claire needs to confirm that Paul has heard her correctly and that his restatement has captured the essence of what she is trying to communicate, both in content and feeling. If his restatement is accurate, she responds by saying, **"Yes, that's it. You have it right."** It is often helpful for Paul to take this a step further and ask, "Is there anything more about this that I need to know?"

Claire might then add, "I suppose there is. Sometimes I feel like you see me trying to make eye contact with you and you consciously ignore me and go on with your conversation. When that happens, I feel like sinking into the floor or running straight to the car and going home without you. I feel like you don't respect me or even want me to be there with you."

Once again, Paul needs to restate this additional information about his perceived actions and Claire's feelings. Claire will need to confirm once more that he has heard her correctly.

So, let's stop and regroup at this point. Anyone who has taken a beginning psychology or counseling course should recognize the practice of Carl Rogers's "client-centered" reflective listening. When teaching this unit in my Intro Psychology course, I (JS) will demonstrate this technique with a student volunteer from the class. By the second time that I have started up my "So what you are telling me . . .," there are already titters and stifled laughter from the class. It all sounds so phony and mechanical. How could repeating what someone has said back to them be of any particular value? These days we are able to program a computer to accomplish the same feat. What is either person gaining from this?

Having watched how couples that get the hang of this exercise realize extraordinary gains in their communication, we are all too willing to endure the cynical guffaws of our undergraduate students. Why indeed does it work? The answer is first and foremost that many of us are painfully aware that we are rarely listened to with the kind of patience and respect that are conveyed by these empathetic and caring restatements. When someone finally slows down (and especially when that someone is our partner) and hears what is truly hurting or troubling us, the experience is more than just relief and connection, it is a validation of our sense of reality—we are finally having someone reflect back attentively what it feels like for us to be in this world. Think of the alternative that so many of us have faced in conversations with our partners.

> "I feel left out when you talk to another woman at a party."
> "I can't believe how jealous you get. How ridiculous! Last Saturday, I
>   must have talked to Pam for no more than 5 minutes."
> "I still felt like you were ignoring me."
> "You don't trust me. Didn't I spend all of the next day hanging out
>   with you? I can't believe we are talking about this again. O.K., I
>   promise not to talk to any other woman at any party we go to ever
>   again. Would that make you happy?"

Too often, our efforts to express our difficulties and our pain to our partners are met with these kinds of denials or stampedes to solutions. What does not happen and what reflective listening demands is that we sit with the difficulty for a while—that as a couple we explore it and look more deeply into what might be causing this painful dynamic. Patient listening and restatement allow the couple to hold the concern together and to examine it not as an accusation against one partner, but as a challenging problem that both can work together to solve.

Another advantage of calm restatement is physiological. It buys the couple time to slow down their arousal and short-circuit the "fight or flight" response. In lowering the emotional volume by taking the time to register and repeat the partner's concern, both partners' physiological systems are taking a short breather and heading off an impulsive or panicky response.

One more step that is often included after the initial restatement is a **validating statement** offered by the listening partner (see Hendrix, 1988). So in this case after Paul has received confirmation of his restatement from Claire, he can then say, "It makes sense to me that if you feel I am ignoring you to flirt with other women at the party, it would hurt you and make you feel unimportant." This validation goes beyond a simple restatement to give assurance to Claire that her feelings are reasonable and understandable to Paul. We should be clear, however, that a validation is not a blanket acceptance of the truth of Claire's assertion about Paul's behavior or intention. Paul may not agree that he is disregarding Claire or that he is actually flirting with the women at the party. His statement validates Claire's feeling, but not necessarily the interpretation that has led to that feeling. Letting her know that he can see why she would feel this way at least allows Claire to know that Paul is following her explanation of her distress and its cause. They still must discuss and come to a clearer mutual understanding of the intentions and meanings of Paul's actions.

Box 4.2 The Keys to Good Listening

At the center of the Good Talk is the ability to keep your emotions under control in order that you can make sense of and understand what your partner is saying to you. Partners employ the following techniques for two powerful reasons. Obviously, feeling statements and restatements make sure that the content of the message is conveyed and received as unambiguously as possible. Yet equally important is the role of these tactics in slowing the couple down from the potential for emotional escalation that would block meaningful dialogue. Despite their aspects of artificiality and 1970s "California speak," they are introducing an opportunity for *mindfulness* that allows each partner a little breathing room to step back from a precipice of conflict, accusation, and defensiveness. They can offer a placeholder that allows both partners to remind themselves of their own and their partner's good intentions. The belief in these good intentions—(Commitment to a Stronger "We") and

---

(Assumption of Love in the Room) is the calming voice that pulls us back from the dangerous edge. Without it, the phrases, "I want to make sure I understand" or "Do I have this right?" can certainly be turned by irony or intonation into tools of mockery or counterattack ("Just so I understand—you plan to continue to humiliate me at parties by flirting and ignoring me while I stand in a corner looking pathetic. Do I have this right?"). The mistake that many couples *and* couple therapists make is thinking that practicing these listening techniques will build trust and good faith. In reality, couples must have already committed to a strong reserve of good will for the power of the phrases and questions to take hold.

1. **Statement of the Problem** ("I feel that you are spending too much time at work. When you come home, you can barely keep your eyes open.")
2. **Restatement of the Problem by Partner** ("You feel like I am working too much and that I tend to fall asleep at home when I am not working. Do I have this right?")
3. **Confirmation** ("Yes, that's it. You have it right.")
4. **Validating Statement** ("I can understand that this would make you feel lonely and that I am unavailable.")
5. **Gratitude for Validation** ("It feels really good that you are truly getting what I mean.")
6. **Movement Toward the "We"** ("Do you think we can talk together about ways to make this different?")

In this last phrase, we see how the couple allows this initial good listening to be the platform for constructive dialogue that will yield a concrete plan of action.

With the statement of the problem, the restatement, the confirmation of the restatement, and the validation of the distressed partner's feelings all accomplished, we come to a critical point in a Good Talk. Sticking with Claire and Paul, we can see that Paul (if he has done his reflective listening well) has demonstrated an empathetic understanding of Claire's perception of his actions and validated her feeling about them. Still, he may not in fact agree with her perception of his interactions with women at parties. Suppose he feels that his conversations at dinner parties with women are quite circumscribed and respectful of Claire. Suppose he sees her as exaggerating their length and intensity? Does he just concede to her view and accept what he sees as her "distorted" view of his behavior? These questions go beyond the issue of who is right or wrong about this particular situation. They go to Paul's sense of how Claire looks at his moral integrity. If she thinks that he is a person who flirts and disregards her, then he does not feel loved and respected by her. These questions simultaneously speak to how Paul perceives Claire. If she inflates his perfectly well-meaning conversations with other women out of all proportion, then she must be an insecure and overly sensitive person.

Both his critical view of himself through Claire's eyes and his perception of Claire's fragility take the relationship to a negative place. In other words, he could even be "right" that Claire's perception is exaggerated, but his rightness would not bring them closer or lead both partners to feel better about themselves. Attention to mutuality and We-ness encourages Paul to ask a different question that is not concerned with the respective "rightness" or moral/psychological superiority of either partner.

Step 5: "What Could We Do to Make This Better?"

When Paul asks this of Claire, he is acknowledging that she is suffering and that he wants to change this. He has shifted the focus of their dialogue from assignment of blame to the proposal that **they work on a mutual solution.** His asking her to be his partner in problem solving holds the implicit assumption that both will need to contribute to the solution. As we have emphasized throughout this book, this is the critical pivot from individual thinking to We-consciousness. How Claire chooses to respond sets the tone for where the talk might next take them. If Claire says, "You can stop your excessive flirting with women at parties and pay more attention to me," Paul could simply say, "I promise to do that." Ostensibly, the matter would be settled—Claire's feeling about Paul's action would be validated. Paul would change his behavior. Claire would thank Paul. End of problem.

We have seen many couples (and many counselors) "solve" problems this way over the years. Unfortunately, it is a superficial fix that may in fact be aggravating the deeper tensions and resentments that exist between the partners. Paul gives in, but he still feels wounded. He has not felt trusted, and he has also given up something that he enjoys. Claire now feels that she has won Paul's compliance, but has she also lost a bit of his respect? Does she feel guilty for confining him? Does she worry that he might resent her for reining in his natural impulse to chat and socialize? Has he put a "pebble in his pocket" that will grow to a boulder over time? In other words, they may leave the conversation with the matter resolved, but with the critical message of Step 1 not achieved—the outcome has not brought them to a stronger sense of "We."

The question, "What Can We Do to Make This Better?" takes their dialogue in a different direction. In order for the "We" to work together, they need to know what each person needs or wants from the other.

So, the crucial follow-up question to "What Can We Do to Make This Better?" is:

"What Do You Need From Me?"

And here is the most essential part of the Good Talk:

THIS QUESTION MUST BE ASKED BY EACH PARTNER, NOT ONLY THE LISTENING PARTNER.

Let's see how this works with Claire and Paul. Having confirmed that he has captured Claire's complaint about his behavior at dinner parties accurately, Paul now asks her, "What do you need from me?"

Claire responds,

"I want you to make me feel important throughout the night. I don't want you to show excessive attention to other women. I want you to reconnect with me throughout the night, so I feel that I am remaining in your thoughts."

Paul restates this to be sure he is clear on what she is asking.

Claire then asks, "What do you need from me?"

This is perhaps the most important turn in the conversation. By asking what she might do for Paul, she has removed the notion of offender and victim—of perpetrator and wronged party. It opens the possibility that both might make adjustments and that both might contribute to the solution.

Paul responds,

"I suppose I need to know that I can relax and have fun at the party without worrying that you are watching me from the corner of the room or disapproving of what I'm doing. I'd like to know that we are both having a good time without micro-managing it. But it's obvious from what you've said to me that if I don't give some thought to what I'm doing, I may hurt your feelings. So, how can I have a little fun and make sure you are O.K. too?"

At this point in their conversation, we can't help but interject and point out how wonderful a question Paul just asked. The beauty of this query is that it proposes a potential solution that respects both partners and seeks to honor their feelings without passing judgment on their differing perspectives. Claire picked up immediately on the proactive spirit of Paul's proposal. She thought for a bit and proceeded like this:

> "Suppose we made more effort to make eye contact over the course of the evening. If we are consciously trying to see where the other person is at more, I don't think I would feel so at sea. I don't really need to talk with you or be with you at every moment, I just need to know that you are conscious of what I'm feeling and where my head is at."
>
> "I can definitely do that more than I have been. I could also make a real effort to pull you into conversations I am having. You should also feel free to come over to me."

"I have always thought that you would think I am being too clingy."
"Not at all—It would actually help me because sometimes I don't know how to end some of the conversations I get into."
"O.K., I didn't think you wanted this, but I can try that."
"So do we have a plan?"

Step 6: Signing Off on the Plan

Once the couple has reached the point of the conversation at which they have developed a plan of action, they are ready to move the talk to its closing stages. Once concrete steps have been assigned to each partner, it is vital that they review exactly what they have agreed to do. Paul lays this out clearly for Claire,

> "Our goal here is to feel closer to each other by the end of the nights when we go to dinner parties. To accomplish this, we are going to change our ways of interacting over the course of the night. We are going to try to be more in each other's presence over the evening, but when we are not close by, we will make a conscious effort to make eye contact and keep track of how we are both doing. I will try to bring you into more of my conversations and you will also feel free to join in more."

Claire confirms this plan,

> "Yes, if we do this, you should be able to feel that you are still working the crowd the way you like to do, but I will also feel that I am not getting lost in it. If we work together on making eye contact and reconnecting more, I think I'll feel much closer to you. So we have a plan."
> "We have a plan."

Step 7: Expressing Gratitude

A Good Talk ends with gratitude for many blessings (Emmons, 2008, 2013). There is the blessing of being able to give voice to one's pain—of knowing that there is a space and time created with one's partner that allows this expression to take place. When we think of the many silenced victims of physical, sexual, and emotional abuse or of oppressed minorities and ethnic groups in our own country or of citizens trapped in foreign countries dominated by militaries or dictatorships, we realize what a gift it is when another person gives us the freedom to speak openly and honestly about a more private suffering. To step back from our busy worlds and to let go of our self-absorption in order to create room for the feelings and needs of another person, this is a conscious effort to acknowledge and show respect for the humanity of our partner. When this happens, we should not treat it as something expected, "part of the drill," or fulfillment of a clause in the marriage contract. We should see it, as Martin Buber would have seen it, as an *I-Thou* moment that affirms the most sacred and transcendent of relations—the meeting of two open minds and hearts in a spirit of mutuality.

There is the further blessing of being trusted enough that your partner believes you can help them with their suffering. When we despair of change, we often give in to silence and withdraw. When we believe in the possibility of growth, we reach out and allow hope to fill the space in which we meet the other. To be offered the chance to learn about what your partner needs from you is already to be engaging in the process of repair and renewal. To talk and to listen affirms the commitment each holds to the relationship, and this, in and of itself, is a blessing.

Finally, the mutual contract to act in support of the "We" takes the couple to the highest plane of gratitude. Knowing that each member of the couple has committed to action that will strengthen the relationship is to experience in real time the dynamic energy of what the couple can accomplish as a unit larger than either individual self. To have faced a difficulty and emerged with greater unity is indeed a shared accomplishment worthy of the deepest gratitude.

So a Good Talk ends on these words:

> Claire says, "**Thank you.**"
> And Paul responds, "**Thank You.**"

It is funny how self-conscious partners often feel saying these words to each other, especially when we have requested that they do so. Yet it is not uncommon that when they must look their partner in the eyes and say these two simple words loud enough to be heard across the couch, tears soon follow. To be grateful is to admit that a need has been fulfilled. To admit a need has been fulfilled is to admit that one was vulnerable enough to need something from one's partner. To be vulnerable is to open oneself up for disappointment, rejection, hurt. So within the words of thanks are always both a risk and a relief. They are saying simply—I admit I have a need and that you have helped me answer it. By implication, a thank you is a ligature—a tangible bond between two people. To experience an ongoing sense of gratitude with one's partner may be the strongest embodiment of love that we can imagine. It is like carrying a blessing inside oneself every day. It is the Hibiscus manifest in all its resplendent glory. It is the feeling of warmth, safety, and familiarity of "home."

Even though people argue and fight, it does not mean that they cannot stay together or even that they do not have a stable marriage. Yet returning to the themes of the Introduction, staying together in an atmosphere

---

Box 4.3 The Seven Steps of Good Talk

1. **Commitment That the Talk Will Lead to a Stronger We**
2. **Assumption That Love Is in the Room**
3. **Choose a Time and Place**
4. **"I Feel . . ." "You Feel . . ."**
5. **"What Can We Do to Make This Better?"**
6. **Signing Off on the Plan**
7. **Expressing Gratitude**

---

of periodic skirmishes and lingering resentments is not the realization of the loving We-ness that our work and this book aspire to build. The central role of Good Talk in a We-based partnership is a belief in each other's better selves—it links to a vision of how working together can release a more loving nature in each other.

If individuals remain wedded to a worldview that places their individual needs first, that champions ambition over connection, that equates success with material prosperity, and happiness with "fun," then it is likely that adults will continue to act like children—that they will rant and rave to get their own ways, that they will put each other down to gain competitive advantage, and they will endlessly ask inwardly and of their partners—"What is in it for me?" In other words, if each individual doesn't consciously stop himself or herself from treating their partnership as an extension of the marketplace, they should expect its climate to be just as harsh and unforgiving. If individuals see the "goods" of their marriage as just another way to please themselves and fill their wants, then they will render any well-meaning technique to build relationship ultimately irrelevant to their desires. Because deep down if partners bring a consumer mentality to their dialogue, they will view their partner as a competitor for the same scarce goods (of happiness, affection, children's love, career success) as they are seeking. In this model, each partner can't help but be perennial adversaries, and active listening and empathy only sugarcoat the facts of "dog-eat-dog."

On the other hand, if we work with couples to expand their vision of their relationship to encompass an alternative model—a model based in building something larger than the self—a model that puts a premium on loving relationship and mutual respect rather than getting one's due, we might find that strategies of listening and problem solving would be much more likely to take hold. In this model, the "I feel" statements are not attacks on the other person. They are problems for the couple to solve by both taking responsibility and accountability for what is causing distress in one or both of the partners.

By putting the raising of a difficulty in the context of an effort to improve and strengthen the relationship rather than to deflate or tear down the other person, the therapist is helping the couple to reinforce the assumption that love is in the room. This lets each partner know that the other partner is strongly committed to the relationship and its continued growth. When this thought is kept foremost in the minds of both partners, neither one has to be the "Dalai Lama," as Gottman and Silver (1999, p. 11) put it, in order to engage in active listening and the talking through of conflicts. Both simply need to be consciously holding to a common faith in the good will and loving foundation of their particular We-Story. This goes back again to the two first assumptions of the Good Talk: (1) Its purpose is to bring each other closer, and (2) The underlying assumption for each partner is that he or she is loved by his partner. The implication of these assumptions is that feedback is offered to help, not to hurt, to build rather than to tear down.

We have seen the ways that years of pain, disconnection, disappointment, focus on personal gratification, habit, boredom, and a myriad of other factors can result in partners losing sight of the fact that they are together for some purpose. Or perhaps they have always had a vision of the "We" but it has never been voiced. To bring that vision forward, we frequently recommend that partners coauthor a relational purpose statement (what are we together *for?*) to establish (or re-establish) that vision and to unite their sights toward a future goal. We close this chapter with Mark and Jenn's relational vision:

> We intend to be like a big sun—full of warmth, heat, and light that burns brightest when we're together. We will remind each other of this when we forget and think we can do it better alone. We will help each other by taking care of ourselves and by letting each other know what we need without waiting too long. We will shine our warmth and light on all of our kids, letting them know how much we love them and how much better life is when you share your Sunshine with one another.

References

Diener, E., Sandvik, E., & Pavot, W. (2009). Happiness is the frequency, not the intensity, of positive versus negative affect. In E. Diener (Ed.) *Assessing well-being: The collected works of Ed Diener* (pp. 213–231). New York, NY: Springer.

Emmons, R.A. (2008). Gratitude, subjective well-being, and the brain. In R.J. Larsen and M. Eid (Eds.), *The science of subjective well-being* (pp. 469–489). New York, NY: Guilford Press.

Emmons, R.A. (2013). Humility: Humility, the modest strength. *Activities for teaching positive psychology: A guide for instructors* (pp. 19–22). Washington, DC: American Psychological Association.

Fredrickson, B. (2009). *Positivity: Groundbreaking research reveals how to embrace the hidden strength of positive emotions, overcome negativity, and thrive.* New York, NY: Crown Publishers/Random House.

Fredrickson, B. L. (2013). *Love 2.0: How our supreme emotion affects everything we feel, think, do, and become.* New York, NY: Hudson St. Press-Penguin Group.

Fredrickson, B. L., Tugade, M. M., Waugh, C. E., & Larkin, G. R. (2003). What good are positive emotions in crisis? A prospective study of resilience and emotions following the terrorist attacks on the United States on September 11th, 2001. *Journal of Personality and Social Psychology, 84*(2), 365–376.

Gable, S. L., Gosnell, C. L., Maisel, N. C., & Strachman, A. (2012). Safely testing the alarm: Close others' responses to personal positive events. *Journal of Personality and Social Psychology, 103*(6), 963–981.

Gottman, J. M., & Silver, N. (1999). *The seven principles for making marriage work: A practical guide from the country's foremost relationship expert.* New York, NY: Three Rivers Press.

Hanson, R. (2013). *Hardwiring happiness: The new brain science of contentment, calm and confidence.* New York, NY: Harmony.

Hendrix, H. (1988). *Getting the love you want: A guide for couples.* New York, NY: Henry Holt & Co.

Kabat-Zinn, J. (2003). Mindfulness-based stress reduction (MBSR). *Constructivism in the Human Sciences, 8*(2), 73–107.

Kabat-Zinn, J. (2009). *Full catastrophe living: Using the wisdom of your body and mind to face stress, pain, and illness.* New York, NY: Random House.

McAdams, D. P. (2001). The psychology of life stories. *Review of General Psychology, 5*(2), 100–122.

Porges, S. (2011). *The polyvagal theory: Neurophysiological foundations of emotion, attachment, communication and self regulation.* New York, NY: W. W. Norton & Co.

Reid, D. W., Dalton, E. J., Laderoute, K., Doell, F. K., & Nguyen, T. (2006). Therapeutically induced changes in couple identity: The role of we-ness and interpersonal processing in relationship satisfaction. *Genetic, Social, and General Psychology Monographs, 132*(3), 241–284.

Roos, S., & Neimeyer, R. (2007). Reauthoring the self: Chronic sorrow and post traumatic stress following the onset of CID. In E. Martz and H. Livneh (Eds.), *Coping with chronic illness and disability: Theoretical, empirical and clinical aspects* (pp. 89–106). New York, NY: Springer.

Skerrett, K. (2010). "Good enough stories": Helping couples invest in one another's growth. *Family Process, 49*(4), 503–516.

Veroff, J., & Orbuch, T. L. (2012). Studying marital relationships. In J. S. Jackson, C. H. Caldwell, and S. L. Sellers (Eds.), *Researching black communities: A methodological guide* (pp. 114–134). Ann Arbor, MI: University of Michigan Press.

Weingarten, K. (2013). Sorrow: A therapist's reflection on the inevitable and the unknowable. *Family Process, 52*(1), 83–101.

DIALOGUE GUIDES FOR COUPLE CONVERSATIONS

Sort out the three common conversations.

A. **"What Happened" Conversation**

   1. Where does each of your stories come from?
      a. Different information, different past experiences, different rules and cultures
      b. Disentangle intent from impact
      c. Abandon blame

B. **"Feelings" Conversation**

   1. Own feelings
   2. Identify underlying and hidden feelings
   3. Describe your feelings (as opposed to venting)
   4. Acknowledge yours and your partners' feelings

C. **"Identity" Conversation**

   1. Identify what's at stake for you
      (am I competent? a good person? worthy of love?)
   2. Complexify your identity: Adopt the both/and stance
      (I am frightened and competent)

Adapted from Stone, D., Patton, B., Heen, S., & Fisher, R. (2010). *Difficult conversations: How to discuss what matters most.* New York, NY: Penguin Books.

LOVE LETTERS

In the years to come, there will be much to write and talk about. Some starter statements are provided here for your use in the future. Feel free to develop your own, though. The two of you know what you ought to be talking and writing about!

The greatest gift that you bring to our relationship is . . .
The fears that I have about relationships are . . .
My relationship with you has changed me in this way . . .
The greatest gift that I bring to our relationship is . . .
The feeling that I have the hardest time expressing is . . .
What I hope to gain most from our relationship is . . .
What I hope most to give to our relationship is . . .

5

STUCK STORIES

Helping Couples Confront and
Move Beyond Them

If only every story had a happy ending . . . if only we could always step back from painful episodes with our partners and find a helpful lesson just as Mark and Jenn were able to do; yet even for the healthiest couples, it does not necessarily work this way. All partners have their individual stories of hurt, betrayal, and misunderstanding; all couples can recall moments from their relationship when they were far from their best selves. What distinguishes the most troubled couples that we see in therapy is that they gravitate over and over to these same distressing stories—moths to flames that immolate the trust that they might build together.

Susan Johnson (2008) in her book on emotion-focused couples therapy, *Hold Me Tight*, calls these self-destructive cycles in relationships—*demon dialogues*. There is the "Find the Bad Guy," an exercise in the Gottman Apocalypse of "finger-pointing," where each partner's purpose is to tell the more horrifying story of the other partner's malfeasance. There is the "Protest Polka" in which partners alternate pursuing and withdrawing, angering and hurting, nagging and shutting down. These stories are like a bad ride at the amusement park that disorients and sickens, but goes on and on. Finally, there is the "Freeze and Flee," in which each partner checks out and gives up. Here you have two separate people who placate each other with "Fine," "Whatever you say," "Let's just drop the matter," and "What's the point?" Their stories describe isolation; separate rooms and activities; the conviction that what they say, do, and feel is of little import to their partners. They may tell narratives of "truce" and "cease fire," but there is still a lethal war of attrition being waged that is destroying good will and any lingering faith in each partner's love for and commitment to the other.

In EFCT, couples are encouraged to engage in seven productive conversations that move them back to a healthier connection and intimacy. The conversations first highlight (1) the recognition of demon dialogues, and (2) the underlying emotional concerns behind these repetitive conflicts. Once these concerns are out in the open, the couple can (3) revisit a dispute and reframe it in a healthier manner. They then proceed (4) to build compassion and emotional responsiveness so that they engage with

111

rather than draw away from each other. Drawing closer allows for (5) the forgiving of injuries, which leads to renewed commitment to a stronger connection. This connection opens up (6) the possibility of greater sexual intimacy and a rejuvenated love life. Last, the couple is urged to (7) keep love alive by pursuing daily practices that reinforce connectedness and prioritize the relationship.

We heartily embrace these EFCT conversation steps, but we often find that the demon dialogues and their underlying emotional concerns are traceable to distinct and evocative stories that block each partner's ability to take a risk in the present. For example, whenever we would ask Allie and Trey to talk about their struggle with trusting each other, Allie would return to the following story:

> You're asking me to trust that Trey will be there for me—that he really cares about our relationship and not his own needs. But where was he the day I was in labor, screaming in pain and fear in my hospital bed? He was on his fucking cell phone in the hallway, talking to "his people" in St. Louis about a sale going through. Why wasn't he beside me? And if he couldn't be with me at the moment that I needed him most—when our baby who was about to enter the world needed him the most—how the hell can I ever let go and trust him? I hear the right words coming from his mouth, but I don't connect the feeling to it. I know he means well, but somehow I don't trust that his heart is there.

Sometimes Trey would protest and justify his actions ("It was only one call over a 12-hour labor and only for 5 minutes."). Sometimes he would concede his mistake and claim full repentance ("I am so sorry, Allie. I learned my lesson and I would never put my work first like that again."). Sometimes he would just hang his head in despair.

In other cases, both members of the couple may share the same story, but both see themselves as wounded victims within a relational breakdown. My (JAS) most compelling example of this shared defeat is of an older couple who had built up powerful walls against any kind of emotional or physical intimacy. Within the first few sessions of our work together, they must have told the same story five times. It referred to a time nearly two decades earlier when after a year of in-patient work to overcome his alcoholism, the husband was discharged and driving home with his wife. The past year of recovery had also been a year of slowly repairing the painful rift between the partners caused by the addiction—they had even used the last months of hospitalization to take tentative steps toward a revival of their sexual relationship during weekend visits home. However, on this fateful ride, the wife reached out to the husband's hand, and he pulled back due to lingering frustration about how she had sided with the

112

treatment team to keep him in the hospital longer than he desired. And for the next 17 years they never held hands, kissed each other, or made love again. They each knew every nuance of this story and as long as they clung to its tale of disconnection ("Flee and Freeze"), they had a firm touchstone for staying apart, each in their lonely space.

What we have suggested throughout this volume is that stories are central to how individuals and couples define their respective personal and collective identities. To help move partners to a place where they can be receptive to the techniques of EFCT or the acceptance therapy of IBCT, we have to dislodge their adherence to stories that speak to resentment and disconnection. There's the expression—"That's my story and I'm sticking to it." Partners get hardened in their view of the other partner and use these **stuck stories** to reinforce their familiar perceptions and forestall any momentum to change (Angus & Greenberg, 2011) have identified similar stories in individual therapy and call them "*same old stories*"—defined as "repetitive, unproductive experience[s] based on core maladaptive emotion schemes," p. 59). On the surface, the couple's rigidity does not make sense. Why stay mired in the past—especially when you are paying a professional for the explicit purpose of moving you away from these previous negative experiences?

The answer can be found in risk and fear; to reach the emotional vulnerability that effective couple therapy requires of our clients, they have to expose themselves to the renewed possibility of disappointment, rejection, and hurt. They have to say that they are willing to believe in their partner and the relationship at the risk of being wrong again(!) and made to feel "less-than" or fooled (and foolish). In attachment terms, the therapy asks them to test out their attachment bond and to see if it will hold with their partners. Once out on this limb, fear is a primary emotion and the unknown future is the primary threat. Stories take us out of this terrifying present and take us back to the *terra firma* of the known. However disillusioning or disappointing a stuck story may be, it is a familiar quantity and therefore not a risk. It may be frustrating and unpleasant ground, but it is safe, certain, and predictable.

Any couple therapist can tell you about the "same old dance" or the "well-worn groove" to which either one member or both members of the couple retreat. If couples are going to do the real work of building We-consciousness and make the emotional connection that is at the heart of EFCT and other couple treatments, we have to employ therapeutic techniques to unstick these stories and help the couple find their way to the more positive, trust-building narratives described in the previous chapter. Once they can let go of the power of these stories, they will be ready to do the present-based work that can build new success stories for their relationship.

In order to demonstrate our We-Story approach to shifting couples from these destructive stories into more positive directions, we return to the Owens from Chapter 3 and look at how each member of this partnership relied on past stories to avoid present intimacy. We then show how we used techniques of imagery, We-consciousness, and new We-Story construction to open up possibilities of greater trust and intimacy.

The Owens's Stuck Stories

As we worked with the Owens, we talked about our findings with the ME (To US) and ways in which they could enhance a sense of We-ness in their marriage. Yet, repeatedly, as we discussed changes in their lifestyle or activities that could build trust, they would return to familiar suspicions about each other and the old stories would resurface. In one session, as we discussed a way in which Will could be more transparent about his business dealings, Katie returned once again to the earlier period of their marriage where Will had hidden their near bankruptcy from her.

KATIE: You tell me that you can be more open, but look at how you held back information from me when we were on the brink of collapse. How can I explain what it felt like to get a call from the accountant and be told not to write any more checks? And then, when I am shaking and not able to sleep, I find out that you had used our house to secure your loan? Where were our children going to sleep if we lost everything? How can you expect me to believe you now?

WILL: It never got to the point where our house was in jeopardy. There was plenty of good will with the loan officers and we were solid again long before anything as dire as you imagined would have happened. Why do you think I kept stuff from you—because I knew that you would not be able to handle it—that you would freak out and panic, when it wasn't necessary.

KATIE: Well, I can't live like this. I can't be in the dark—how can I trust that you will tell me the truth about where things stand? I am not a child and I was right to be upset.

WILL: But that's the whole point—you blew a gasket and didn't have faith in me. You still don't. You think that I am a wild gambler—some kind of loose cannon. You don't understand that business is based on risk and that you finance with debt.

KATIE: It wasn't just me in tears at that time. You came to me, crying, telling me that you were scared that you had screwed things up. Didn't I hold you and stroke your head and try to comfort you?

WILL (VISIBLY WINCING): You always throw that moment back at me—that I showed a moment of uncertainty—that I let you in on my worry. You are so hypocritical—you want me to open up and then you rub my face in the fact that I showed some fear.

KATIE: If you just could have been more honest from the beginning.

WILL (ANGRY WITHDRAWAL): What's the point? I can never win. Strong or weak—nothing I do is good enough for you. I can open up all my books for you—show you every transaction, but it won't make you have any more faith in me. I'm done.

KATIE (SEEKING TO CONCILIATE): Please, Will. You're going to have to trust me.

WILL (LOOKING OUT THE WINDOW, IN A FLAT MONOTONE): Fine. I'll do whatever you say.

KATIE: Fine, Will. I can see there's no point in ever trying to talk seriously with you.

Step 1: Identifying the Script in the Stuck Story

This stuck story for the Owens has numerous variations, but it returned multiple times in our work. Stuck stories contain *narrative scripts* (Siegel & Demorest, 2010; Singer, Blagov, Berry, & Oost, 2013; Tomkins, 1979, 1987)—sequences of events and emotional responses that are repeated so frequently in individuals' lives that they form a schema or template for how current experiences are received and organized by their thought process and memory. In this particular story, we see a sequence of Katie feeling that actions of Will's are out of her control and this loss of control is very threatening to her. She then expresses this strong concern to Will, often in a highly critical and rigid manner. Will takes the full impact of this criticism and feels both judged and unsupported. Katie in turn defends her efforts to support him, but he is already too wounded to acknowledge these efforts and feels that she is shaming him. Katie may then try to patch up the rupture with a "repair effort," but by this time Will's anger has led him to withdraw and stonewall. Katie responds with an equally cold and dismissive reaction. They then both pull into sullen "neutral corners" and go on with their separate activities. As Johnson (2004, p. 67) writes,

> Eventually the toxic patterns can become so ingrained and permanent that they totally undermine the relationship, blocking all attempts at repair and reconnection.

Here is the basic template of the Owens's script:

Katie feels a loss of control in the relationship.
↓
Criticizes Will's unilateral actions.
↓
Will feels put down and unsupported.
↓

Katie reminds Will of all the support she supplies.
↓
Will, experiencing this as "rubbing in" his inadequacy, grows angrier.
↓
Katie seeks to conciliate.
↓
Will withdraws and stonewalls.
↓
Katie withdraws.

Step 2: Connecting the Script to Individual Stuck Stories From the Partners' Past

Once we have identified this repetitive pattern across multiple stuck stories that the couple tells about their relationship, we look for links in their individual stories from their past relationships or families of origins that are likely to be contributing to these frozen versions of their partners that they continually recruit. Why does Katie struggle with themes of control and autonomy in relation to Will? Why does Will go back time and again to Katie as a "critical" and "unsupportive" figure bent on outing his inadequacy? Is it possible that they are recruiting earlier attachment patterns with caregivers that have created "wounds" or expectations of hurt or disappointment. In the parlance of couple therapy, we refer to these persisting influences as "ghosts in the room" who often make our sessions very crowded. Our job is to see how these specters from the past still haunt our clients' present interactions.

Katie's History

Katie came from a middle-class family that struggled at times with money concerns. Her father had worked in the real estate title business and had made a reasonable living while her mother had stayed at home with Katie and her two younger siblings, a sister and a brother. Her father had always been a drinker and one day suffered a bad fall down a staircase while drinking. After the accident he went on disability due to back injuries and traumatic brain injury (TBI) from the fall. His memory became faulty and his mood often ornery. Katie's mother had always been a tight-lipped unemotional person, and she became even more shutdown and businesslike after the accident.

As the oldest child, Katie seemed to feel that her mother was toughest with her. When it was time for Katie to go to college, her parents let her know that they had no savings and that she would have to work first. Katie managed to get a secretarial job, but soon found that she got caught up in paying bills and rent without finding a way to save much on her own for college.

Shortly before she had met Will, Katie had begun working in a more prestigious corporate setting. She continued to work in this office after her marriage and only quit after the twins were born. More recently, Katie had learned that her father had been diagnosed with cancer, and his health was rapidly declining. She took on the main responsibility for helping her mother during this time. Even in her adult relationships with her parents and siblings, Katie had continued to feel like the "oldest child," the one with the biggest shoulders for bearing all the stress and worry in the family.

In exploring this history with Katie, she talked about the unpredictability of her father and her family's constant money worries during her childhood. She highlighted her mother's stoicism and emphasis on practicality. In her oldest child role, Katie modeled herself after this tight-lipped style and recalled her determination to keep their family life in order despite the chaotic environment created by her father's drinking and volatility.

Will's History

Will's father was a retired naval officer. Will's mom came from a close family that had started off modestly but through real estate investments had become increasingly well-off. Although Will's dad was a very competent man, he had not been overly ambitious after he left the Navy. He had worked in middle-management positions and put more focus into his hobbies of sports, carpentry, and hanging out with his buddies.

Will's mom had thoroughly enjoyed the pomp and circumstance that she had experienced during her early years as an officer's wife. She found the retirement years a significant let-down and constantly harped at Will's dad to show more ambition and to make more money. Her family had climbed out of near poverty into a certain level of social prominence in their small town, and she wanted her husband to keep ascending the ladder. As Will and Katie observed his parents' marriage, his mother seemed to dominate and constantly criticize his father, while his father did his best to hide out in the basement and amuse himself by tinkering or watching sporting events on the television.

As the oldest son, Will took on the weight of his mother's ambition and his father's love of sports. He quickly seemed to fulfill neither of their hopes. He was not a diligent student. He preferred being outside and running down to the boatyards to sail or work on boats. He also was not inclined to sports, showing no aptitude on any of the athletic teams his father pushed him to join. Will's status in the family was not helped by the fact that his two younger brothers both excelled at school and played football for their high school teams. By the time Will graduated from high school he was already working almost 40 hours a week and had no intention to go to college. He had begun a pattern of "partying" with alcohol, pot, and cocaine. His parents were severely frustrated with him, and he felt the mantle of "black sheep" descend upon him. This identity became even more prominent for him as his brothers went on to universities and then landed fast-track positions with major corporations after college.

Very different from his brothers, rugged and down-to-earth, Will loved to be outside and work with his hands. From his initial job, cutting lawns and planting shrubs for a small landscaping firm, he managed to put together earnings to buy a truck and start his own company. Relying on his easy-going personality and an excellent head for business, within 10 years he had a fleet of trucks and a dozen men working for him. He then took a bold step and bought out his old employer and became the owner of the major nursery and garden center in the town. He subsequently added two more branches of his nursery business in two other towns in the state. He had met Katie over a discussion of hydrangeas in his center one spring day in 1992. She was working as an executive secretary at the time. They dated for more than a year and married in fall 1993. His efforts to build and expand his business had coincided with their years of married life together.

Ghosts in the Family Tree

With this background information laid out for both members of the couple, we had a rich set of questions that we asked ourselves about the "ghosts" that could climb out of this family tree and populate Will and Katie's own attachment stories. We wondered:

- Will Katie's sense of not being in control growing up due to her father's unpredictability and financial struggles lead her to feel particularly anxious about Will's business ventures and expansions?
- How will Katie's role as the "responsible" child mesh with Will's reluctance to include her in some of his major financial decisions?
- How did Will's mother's frustration with his father get repeated in her disapproval of Will's unconventional path?
- How might Katie's criticisms of Will echo his mother's disapproval?
- How might Will's siblings' success affect his own ambition and determination to be a financial success?
- How will the fact that both Will and Katie grew up in families where neither of the parents modeled affectionate relationships affect their own ability to accept intimacy and warmth from each other?

Some of the answers to these questions emerged when we asked Katie and Will to share some of their most important "self-defining memories" from their earlier years. Of relevance to their stuck story, Katie shared the following story,

I could never feel safe having friends over to my house because I never knew what state my father would be in. He could have had too much to drink or even just be in an angry nasty mood when he was cold sober. One time I took a chance and a few girlfriends came over to watch some videos together. I thought maybe he would just go to sleep upstairs and I would be fine. But, of course, he came out to the top of stairs and starting yelling to turn the sound down, then he slipped and stumbled down half the stairs. I was so embarrassed that I just had the girls leave.

We can hear how haunted Katie is by the inability to control her environment and the fear that the caretakers on whom she counts will disappoint and humiliate her. It is not surprising then that Will's financial risks and earlier secretiveness made her feel more free-floating and out of control. In her constant worries about money, she could feel herself "becoming her mother," and feared developing a similar hard edge. With these anxieties reverberating in her thoughts, she often seemed frustrated and bitter in her interactions with Will. Nervous and exhausted, she seldom felt a desire for physical intimacy or romance with him. Katie's ghosts were continually causing her to focus on self-protective and individualistic questions that took her away from the "We":

- Do I have control over my life?
- Am I financially secure?
- Am I respected and valued?
- Am I ever going to be truly safe with another person?

With these questions haunting her at present, it was very hard for her to look beyond her own important needs to see what Will's questions and needs appeared to be. These questions led her back to familiar defenses that would block their terrifying threat to her. She would become detail-oriented and rigid with Will. She would make lists and point out the places he overlooked. She would seek to control whatever areas of their shared lives that were available to her. She would defend herself against hurt and disappointment in their intimate life by withdrawing and shutting down—going to bed earlier, complaining of headaches and fatigue. Most of all, she put her focus on the children and the management of their lives, given how little ability she had felt to manage the chaos Will seemed to bring to their marital relationship.

Turning to Will, his family ghosts equally haunted him. Raised in a home in which his mother had focused on social status, business success, and material wealth, he had felt a constant refrain of "not good enough." As his brothers had surpassed him by taking conventional paths, he had suffered internally with his "black sheep" status. This dynamic was no

119

more clearly exemplified than in his love-hate relationship to his family country club. He shared a memory from his adolescent years that still stung him to this day.

> I started in the grounds department, cutting the golf fairways and greens. I used to drive my dad's old beat-up truck to work and one day my mom gets a call from the club. "Willy," that's what they called me, "was driving his truck too fast in the cul-de-sac and kicking up dust into the club entrance." I worked my butt off there, 7 days a week, always doing something for the members, and I end up getting chewed out. The thing that puts me completely over the edge is that I've been a member there now for 10 years and about a month ago one of those same blue-blood old-timers complained that I drive my beamer too fast in the parking lot. I will always be "Willy, the groundskeeper" to those old bastards.

Will pushed himself to succeed with his business in part to show his family and the other members of his community that he was not the ne'er-do-well they made him out to be. His push to be economically well-off and to have a large home and a number of "toys," including his impressive yacht, was, in part, a way to answer the deepest insecurity that he felt about his status in the family and his own identity as a man, especially in relation to his brothers. He saw the way his father had retreated and shrunken in response to his mother's withering criticism over the years. Will was driven not to feel this way. Will's ghosts had led him to struggle with these individualistic questions:

- Am I able to be a financial success?
- Am I as good as my brothers?
- Am I another "disappointment" in my mother's eyes?
- Will "good society" accept me or will I always be the "black sheep"?
- Am I desirable as a man and lover?

Ironically, his anxiety about the demons from his family background led him into the exact courses of action that most alienated Katie. Will's ways of running from his ghosts (his "defenses") were based in the same ways he escaped his mother's "evil eye"—a dalliance in substance use, a preoccupation with material "toys," and occasional bursts of temper and tantrum to scare off any serious talk about what might be going awry. Confronted by Katie's questions and doubts about their financial picture, his insecurity would well up, leading him to be defensive and hostile in response to her. He would find endless ways to slip away to work on the boat or hang out with the guys he had hired to help with the re-varnishing of its hull. He would run errands or grab a beer and try to find a moment of peace away from the "nagging."

A chief result of these self-protective strategies was to estrange Katie further and shut down any interest she had in intimacy with him. This seemed the final and cruelest blow to him. He "worked his butt off" for the family, did everything he could to make money and give them a luxurious standard of living. Yet he found no love at home and no physical validation of himself as a desirable man. And even though he sought solace through his boat, Katie was angrier about the boat and the excessive expenditures and time spent on it than nearly anything else. What was supposed to be his refuge had become their battlefield.

Step 3: Generating Compassion From the Airing of the Individual Stories

Once we have defined a stuck story and the roots of its origins in individual stories, our next step is work with partners on *rediscovering their empathic concern* for what has been difficult for their partners. For example, when Katie told the story of her father during our session, we asked her to talk about what she felt at the time and what feelings it stirs up in the present. We then asked Will to ask Katie more about the memory—to explore it further with her. In this exercise, we often find that even highly alienated partners find rich veins of caring and compassion for the pain that their partner has suffered from this experience. We then use this delicate bridge of connection to remind the other partner how these same painful feelings are generated over and over in the script they share through their stuck stories. For example,

THERAPIST: Will, when you hear Katie's sense of not having any control, of being embarrassed and shamed by her father—can you see that this may be how she felt when she got the call from the accountant or many other times when she feels your financial picture is teetering and she has no way to influence it?

WILL: I know how hard it was for Katie with her dad—I don't want to recreate that for her. What's happened with us is not the same—but even still, I can see how it could set her off. I don't want to upset you, Katie.

Immediately, we see a shift toward We-ness in this bid for emotional connection. Will and Katie are suddenly united in their mutual understanding that Katie has had to bear an undue burden of chaos in her life and that her strong desire for control has been an antidote to this weight. In demonstrating compassion for this problem and her response, Will helps Katie feel less alone and gives her hope that they can make a constructive change in their own relationship. There is a small glimmer here that they just might be able to work together to move forward from this stuck place.

Another Compassion-Building Technique

Another technique that we use is a modified exercise from Harville Hendrix's (1988) Imago Therapy (see pp. 155–156). It is an imagery exercise in which the therapist asks each partner to imagine revisiting his or her childhood home. With eyes closed, the partner imagines walking through the rooms of the home and then confronting mother or father. For each parent, the partner first asks for something that he or she wanted and did not get, and then asks to have removed something that he or she received and did not want. The therapist records each of these items in a list on a whiteboard.

Here is Katie's list of what she did and did not get from her parents.

What I Wanted and Did Not Get	What I Received and Did Not Want
Stability	Chaos
Positive Attention	Overcontrol
Financial Security	Coldness
Fun and Laughter	Anger

Here is Will's list of what he did and did not get from his parents.

What I Wanted and Did Not Get	What I Received and Did Not Want
Acceptance	Criticism
Respect	Lack of Confidence
Warmth	Disappointment
Encouragement	Pressure to Prove Myself

In almost every case when we have done this exercise, the next step is the one that catches the couple's attention. We wipe away the word "parents" (or in some cases, it may be specifically "mother" or "father" or even "grandmother") and write in the partner's name (e.g., Katie's list of what she wants and does not get from *Will*; Will's list of what he wants and does not get from *Katie*). Immediately, each partner sees how alive the ghosts are in the current relationship and how powerful a role they play in shaping each partner's expectations of the other. Seeing the parallels allows for further compassion and cultivates that "We are in the same boat" spirit that is pivotal to building a powerful We-consciousness.

The next goal, as the great psychoanalyst Hans Loewald put it, is to turn "ghosts" into "ancestors." That is, to acknowledge their presence in our lives but not allow them to haunt our current interactions.

Step 4: Drawing Meaning From the Stuck Story

Once the couple can see their mutual contributions, based in their own individual life struggles, to their shared stuck story, they are more inclined to accept the challenge of working together to change it. With accumulated compassion, they can begin to ask the right questions:

- **What can we do to make this better?**
- **How can we be helpful to each other?**
- **How can each of us give more to the other of what they most want?**

There are a series of corollary acknowledgments that the couple is simultaneously able to make:

- If we continue to put each other in the same box, we will get the same results
- Getting unstuck means questioning our current positions and modifying our stances
- If we don't believe in the good will of our partner, we will go right back into stuck mode.

These are the critical lessons that every couple needs to extract from looking with new eyes at a stuck story. More specifically, in the case of Will and Katie, they needed to see that transparency and trust are the key ingredients to overcoming their impasse and rebuilding intimacy in their relationship. As long as Will could not be open with Katie, she would feel out of control and anxious—thrust back into the uncertainty of her growing up years. As long as Will felt that Katie would be critical and demeaning in her judgments of him, then he would be unlikely to allow that transparency to occur. Only through mitigating some of her sharp critiques, and only through his willingness to open up, were they likely to achieve substantial trust and share in intimacy again.

The meaning that their story teaches is that Katie cannot protect love and achieve security through rigid control, and Will cannot find acceptance through secrecy, avoidance, and a shelter of material wealth. Although they may have known these "truths" in the abstract, their work with their stories, individual and shared, is the emotional core behind these truths and what moves them to more positive action. The next step in this process is to replace the stuck story, the old script, with a new success story—a We-Story. In the language of Angus and Greenberg's narrative model of EFT, they were ready to find their "healing story."

Step 5: Building the We-Story to Replace a Stuck Story

Once we help couples to see the toxic patterns of their stuck stories, we work actively with them to recruit those "unique outcomes" or "sparkling events" in which they have worked together and experienced the We-ness that affirms their relationship (Madigan, 2011; White & Epston, 1990). These stories become the linchpins and "go-to" reminders that keep them grounded in a sense of trust with each other.

It should be clear that these stories cannot be artificially generated and that they are unlikely to occur without continued work on emotional vulnerability, communication, and acceptance that the best couple therapies demand of their clients (e.g., EFCT, IBCT, Gottman approach). However, too often these stories can be overlooked and not fully exploited for the therapeutic value they can provide. Once our clients bring to session an experience that illustrates an improved sense of We-ness, we go over it carefully with them and help them to see it as an explicit story that they can reference together, and individually, to sustain their best sense of relationship during periods of conflict and alienation.

To make this process concrete, let us show how we proceeded with the Owenses. As we know, one of their most pressing bones of contention was Will's time and money spent on their rather grand boat. Given some of their financial worries, Will knew that he had to sell it and was eventually successful in finding a buyer. However, ever since he was a young man he had always owned a boat and could not imagine living without one. Based on the work in therapy, he approached Katie and asked her how they might think about purchasing another boat. Katie knew how important this was to Will and also recognized how the twins loved the family outings to the local beaches. Will and Katie went over possibilities together and found a much smaller and more reasonably priced boat that required a minimum of work. It had none of the grandeur of the previous yacht, but it would meet all of their needs with a lot less fuss. Most important, Katie had been included on the decision and even helped to name it after the purchase. Although there were still many moments of contention in their relationship, the new boat and the story of its purchase was now a We-Story in which they took great pride and that they often referenced as a step forward in their marriage.

Equally important to these behavioral shifts were stories in which they could find evidence of compassion expressed between them. One of the most powerful occurred when they had been driving home from a visit to Will's mother. Katie recounted how Will had been sullen on the drive home and they had had one of their typical sour exchanges. As we talked about it in the session, Katie asked Will if he knew why he had behaved this way in the car. He said that he had no idea. This is how the following exchange played out:

KATIE: Don't you remember what your mother said at the table in front of your brothers and all of us?

WILL: I'm not sure. She says a lot of stuff that I try not to take in.

KATIE: You know, about you being the smartest one of the three . . .

WILL: Oh yeah. And how I could have done well in engineering in college and I never used all that potential.

KATIE: I watched your face—it just sank.

WILL: It's always the same. Since I didn't do the college thing, everything else that I've done . . . (trailing off)

KATIE (STARTING TO CRY): And then in the car, I could see how you just went into yourself. It's not fair to you.

THERAPIST: Do you see that Katie is crying? She's crying about you. You've been saying how cold she has become to you—that she doesn't care. What is this about?

WILL (WITH EMOTION): I didn't think this could hit you so hard. It's all right, Katie. She can just get under my skin.

KATIE: She should not put you down. Look at what you have done with your business. She should be so proud of you.

THERAPIST: Will, ask Katie why she has tears—why she is choked up.

WILL: Why are you crying, Katie?

KATIE (SMILING AND SNIFFLING): Because I care about you, you idiot.

WILL (SMILING): I haven't heard you say that in a long time.

THERAPIST (SMILING): So these tears, the caring—they're gifts, right, so you say . . .

WILL (SMILING AND LOOKING AT KATIE, IN A SLIGHTLY EXAGGERATED VOICE): Thank you!

KATIE (SMILING): You're welcome.

This exchange in therapy became known as "The Story of the Car Ride and Katie Crying," and it served as a critical reference point going forward in the couple's work together (contrast this car ride story with the older couple's car ride story at the beginning of this chapter). The critical lesson that Will took away from this We-Story is that Katie *does* care and does indeed have his back. During exchanges when he would start to go back to the dark place of doubting her love for him or her investment in the relationship, we would encourage him to remember the "Car ride" story and he would calm down and regain his composure. Similarly when Katie would revert back to saying that Will locked her out of all his decisions, we would highlight the purchase of this new boat and remind her of how different this experience had been from the previous boat.

As a final example, and connecting to Johnson's emphasis on the possibility of greater sexual intimacy and a rejuvenated love life, we were pleased to have the Owens come into session and acknowledge that over the holiday break there had been progress in this area as well. They alluded to a night in the hot tub and a much more free and fun intimacy than they had had in a long time. They dubbed this story, "The Hot Tub Night" and it became a code phrase for them to encourage and reaffirm their sexual connection with each other.

Other Techniques for Stuck Stories

Given the dynamic power of stories with their characters, visual images, and plot sequences, we often link them to classic Gestalt Therapy techniques in order to make full use of their transformative potential for deadlocked couples. Three techniques that we use regularly with couples are "reverse role play," "family sculpting," and "the empty chair."

Reverse Role Play

In a standard role play, the therapist might play the role of one of the partners and allow the other partner to experiment with a particular dialogue or discussion of an issue. This could be done in a couple session or in an individual session when the other partner is not present. The advantages of role playing are obvious in that they allow for the dress rehearsal of a conversation and also give the therapist an opportunity to model more effective responses for the client to employ during the exchange.

Reverse role play asks each partner to take over the role of the other partner in a particular exchange in order to experience this contrasting vantage point firsthand. Reverse role play is a technique that has been recently used with great effectiveness in helping men who have engaged in domestic violence grasp the experience of their partners and develop empathy for their difficult situation (Tonkin & Michell, 2010).

Let's look at an example of reverse role play from our practice with a couple named Lamar and Keisha. Keisha has felt unsupported during family gatherings at Lamar's house. She came into therapy with the following story:

> It was Superbowl night and we were all eating dinner before the game. Lamar knows that I couldn't care less about football and that all his family knows that he had to beg me to be there for the evening. He also knows how I hate to be embarrassed in front of his family. Well, his brother says to Lamar—"I'll bet 20 dollars that Keisha will be out of here before half time." And his other brother chimes in with "I'll take 50 for the same bet." I can feel my face turning red. Now what does Lamar do—does he stand up for me and say cut that nonsense out? No, he says, "I

126

can hold the money for the bets." You know what, they didn't get a chance to bet, because I left at that moment and went home.

Using this story as our guide, we asked Lamar to be Keisha and Keisha to be Lamar, while the therapist chimed in to play one of the brothers. We then played out the scenario with the therapist getting the scene started by teasing Lamar. Keisha joined in by making fun of Lamar. After a couple of rounds of our teasing, we could see Lamar starting to get a bit hot under the collar. He stopped the role play and said he could see what Keisha felt. He then apologized. Next, the therapist asked Keisha what she was feeling in the role of Lamar. She said that at first it was fun to bond with me playing her brother, but then she started to feel guilty when she saw Lamar getting pissed. The therapist then asked Lamar if that was right—had he felt guilty about setting Keisha up. He nodded and said, "Yes, I did—the minute the words came out of my lips at the dinner. I knew it went against what we had been working on in the therapy." Keisha was very pleased to hear this—it made her feel better to know that Lamar had some insight and remorse right after it happened. The reversal had allowed each partner to gain a slightly different perspective into the other partner's feelings and encouraged a deeper compassion for each other— the glue that binds the "We."

Family Sculpting

Reminiscent of the saying, "a picture is worth a thousand words," it may be useful to have partners create a wordless tableau that captures a particular couple or family stuck story. With this technique, we have one of the partners create a living sculpture that consists of himself or herself along with the other partner (and sometimes the therapist). The distance between the participants, the direction they are facing, the position of their arms, the gestures they are making—all of this can communicate intimacy, control, power, secrecy, conflict, and much more. Pausing and taking in the nonverbal postures of each participant can speak volumes about various emotions, feelings of connection, and coalitions within a family structure.

As an example, let us look at the newlyweds, Carl and Tiffany. Carl had often told Tiffany about how his mother had always made him feel a bit larger than life and as if he could accomplish anything. He shared a story in therapy about when he was coming home from school and could hear his mother speaking to their neighbor while he was outside the kitchen window. She was telling the neighbor that Carl was going to go to a fine college and maybe become a doctor (he was 8 or 9 at the time). He could feel himself filling up with pride and dedication to prove her right. He said to Tiffany that the contrast of her to his mother was powerful. She seldom made him feel that he did anything right, let alone that he had special talents or abilities. Tiffany scoffed at this and had trouble connecting to his theme of the difference between the two women's support of him. Carl insisted that this was a place at which they often got stuck. He told a story of how when he received his promotion to supervisor, his mother was on the phone to his siblings and posted a message on Facebook. In contrast, Tiffany pointed out that after taxes and pension contributions, the salary bump amounted to less than $1,000 for the whole year. Carl said that it was stories like that that made him feel hopeless about ever changing the dynamic of their relationship. To help them get unstuck, the therapist asked him to create a family sculpture without words that would get across his point.

Carl thought awhile and then explained that the therapist would be in the role of his mother and Tiffany would be herself. He would play himself as well. He first positioned himself between the therapist (mother) and Tiffany. He then stood up on his chair to rise above both of them. He brought the therapist/mother over to his side and instructed her to form a funnel with her hands over her mouth so that it would look like she was blowing air into the stem of a balloon. On his other side, he positioned Tiffany to look like she was reaching out with her long fingernail to prick him. He then puffed up his cheeks and made a big circle with his arms to convey the image of an inflated balloon. The tableau said it all—on one side his "mother" was giving her all to inflate Carl and on the other side was Tiffany, ready with a sharp fingernail to pop the balloon and deflate any sense of pride or puffery. Tiffany could see the sculpture as a three-dimensional expression of the dynamic that had been challenging their relationship for a while, and it helped her to make sense of Carl's frustration in a particularly evocative way. They laughed over the image of a popped Carl suddenly deflating and sputtering around the room like a shrunken balloon. In this laughter there was a sense of understanding and perhaps some seeds of what they needed to do to improve their relationship.

The Empty Chair

Not surprisingly, another hurdle that Carl and Tiffany faced in their relationship was that Carl's adoring mother also knew few boundaries in her desire to be everything that Carl could want. Tiffany had a bounty of Mother–Carl stories in which his mother had overstepped her role and intruded on their married life. There was the time after they were first married when she sent Carl one extra pillow in the mail because she was concerned that he would not be comfortable in his new bed. Or the first six months when she would send homemade cakes in the mail to make sure Carl was getting his favorite desserts. And then there were the letters addressed only to Carl and not his new bride. These stories coalesced into a perfect storm of enmeshment that needed to be addressed if Carl and Tiffany were to have any hope of building their own solid "We" without Mother–Carl in the middle.

To aid them in getting unstuck from this repetitive story of motherly love, the therapist asked Carl and Tiffany to imagine an empty chair in the office to be Carl's mother. Tiffany was now to coach Carl in speaking to this chair, as he told his "mother" about how much he appreciated her support, but how she also had to recognize his life was different now that he was married.

CARL (ADDRESSING THE EMPTY CHAIR): Mom, I know that you mean well, but you have to think of both of us now all the time, not just me.

TIFFANY (TO CARL): That's good, Carl, but tell her that she can't hurt my feelings all the time.

CARL (TO THE CHAIR): Mom, Tiffany sees the letters and packages and knows they're only for me. (pausing and with some effort) You can't do that any more, Mom. It is causing me more strain than comfort. I want Tiffany to know you love her too.

TIFFANY (TO THE THERAPIST): At this point, she will be crying and telling him that she only tries to be a good mother. It is the only thing that she has ever wanted to be. He would have to be strong now or else he would just back down and fall apart. Hang in there, Carl.

CARL (SCREWING UP HIS COURAGE): I know, Mom. You are a great mom, but I really need you to be one to Tiffany. You have to show her how great you can be. This is really important to me—could you do this for me?

THERAPIST: You guys are working well together here. A little more rehearsal and it will be time to "go live."

TIFFANY: I hope Carl can do it.

Couples in distress live in hamster-wheel cycles of stuck stories. They go round and round with only minor variations on the same themes of rejection, abandonment, silent alienation, and distrust. In this chapter we have presented a series of methods for identifying, challenging, and shifting couples away from these insidious narratives. The more one works with couples and learns to focus on the stories they tell, the quicker one becomes at rooting out these "demon dialogues" and short-circuiting their repetitive hold over the couple and their vision of a possible future. By pushing to counteract stuck stories with success stories and lessons of resilience, as well as dynamic Gestalt techniques, we help couples find greater compassion and move them closer to the discovery and cultivation of We-Stories. In the next chapter, we introduce a more explicit developmental approach and look at how couples vary in the kinds of stories they generate depending on where they are in the life cycle.

References

Angus, L. E., & Greenberg, L. S. (2011). *Working with narrative in emotion-focused therapy: Changing stories, healing lives.* Washington, DC: American Psychological Association.

Hendrix, H. (1988). *Getting the love you want: A guide for couples.* New York, NY: Henry Holt & Co.

Johnson, S. M. (2004). *The practice of emotionally focused couple therapy,* 2nd edition. New York, NY: Routledge.

Johnson, S. M. (2008). *Hold me tight: Seven conversations for a lifetime of love.* New York, NY: Little, Brown.

Madigan, S. (2011). *Narrative therapy.* Washington, DC: American Psychological Association.

Siegel, P., & Demorest, A. (2010). Affective scripts: A systematic case study of change in psychotherapy. *Psychotherapy Research, 20*(4), 369–387.

Singer, J., Blagov, P., Berry, M., & Oost, K. (2013). Self-defining memories, scripts, and the life story: Narrative identity in personality and psychotherapy. *Journal of Personality, 81,* 569–582.

Tomkins, S. S. (1979). Script theory: Differential magnification of affects. *Nebraska Symposium on Motivation, 26,* 201–236.

Tomkins, S. S. (1987). Script theory. In J. Aronoff, A. I. Rabin, and R. A. Zucker (Eds.), *The emergence of personality* (pp. 147–216). New York, NY: Springer.

Tonkin, T., & Michell, D. (2010). The reverse role play—An innovative way of confronting men. *Australian Social Work, 63*(4), 460–465.

White, M., & Epston, D. (1990). *Narrative means to therapeutic ends.* New York, NY: W. W. Norton & Co.

How Our Past Relationships Influence Our Current Relationships

The Unconscious Marriage

1. Emotionally, a romantic intimate relationship is the closest thing to the connection we felt as young children with our primary caretakers.
   a. All those same emotions of love, excitement, admiration, fear, insecurity, and anxiety are there.
2. We choose partners who:
   a. Have both positive and negative traits of our parents
   b. Have attributes we admire and feel that we wish we had
   c. Have disowned or unacknowledged parts of our selves
   d. Give us the opportunity to rework *unfinished business* from our primary relationships.

3. Certain conflicts and interactions in your current relationship push old buttons and activate old feelings.
4. The intimate relationship of marriage allows you to deal with unfinished business.
5. Key steps to keeping the past from limiting your present relationship
   a. Recognize when old buttons have been pushed
   b. Label these feelings to yourself and your partner
   c. Practice *containing* the feelings of your partner and not reacting defensively (Listen and Mirror when you find yourself reacting)
   d. Take responsibility for communicating your needs and desires to your partner (and value your partner's needs and desires)
   e. Search within yourself for the strengths and abilities you feel you are lacking
   f. Deal with unfinished business with the "original" people if possible.

6

BUILDING WE-STORIES ACROSS
THE LIFE CYCLE

One cannot live the afternoon of life according to the program of life's morning; for what was great in the morning
will be of little importance in the evening, and what in the
morning was true will at evening become a lie.

—Jung (1980)

I (KS) was recently at the wedding of a friend's son and listened to the
familiar words:

Love is patient, love is kind, love is not envious or boastful or
rude. It does not insist on its own way, it is not irritable or resentful. It does not rejoice in wrongdoing, but rejoices in the truth.
Love bears all things, hopes all things, endures all things. Love
never ends.

—1 Corinthians 13:4–8

Whatever the tradition, the imagery surrounding the occasion of marriage
is powerful—out of this vast universe we have found the presence and shelter of the beloved other who transfigures our loneliness. Love is held up
as the threshold where the divine and human presence ebb and flow into
each other. Such imagery taps into the universal longing in each of us to
belong, to love and be loved in a protective haven that collapses distance.

And yet, watching this pair, filled with optimism and passion on the
brink of making a lifelong commitment, I wondered if either of them
projected themselves forward into the future? Did they, or do any of us,
imagine ourselves in various states of "worse" as in for better or worse?
Is it even helpful? I was reminded of the lovely story of the 40-year marriage between the distinguished literary critic John Bayley and eminent
novelist and philosopher Iris Murdoch. Murdoch had been stricken
with Alzheimer's disease and Bayley was her sole caretaker. Bayley wrote
about their experience of taking a dip in a river where they had gone on
hot days for nearly half a century.

132

In her shabby old one-piece swimming suit, she was an awkward and anxious figure, her socks trailing round her ankles. She was obstinate about not taking these off, and I gave up the struggle. A pleasure barge chugged slowly past, an elegant girl in a bikini sunning herself on the deck, a young man in white shorts at the steering wheel. . . . We must have presented a comic spectacle— an elderly man struggling to remove the garments from an old lady, still with white skin and incongruously fair hair.

—(Bayley, 1999)

Few of us, with stars in our eyes, imagine ourselves in the future, let alone in a scene like the one Bayley describes so poignantly. And yet, change—the axiom of all development—is our steady companion. It is our least-considered assumption and our most certain fact. Few of us appreciate that for love to be redemptive, it must be reoriented, reconceived, and regularly made into something that can outlive flesh itself. The passage of time can be friend or foe; it can be a generative force or one that cools and causes atrophy—heart disease with no evidence of organic damage.

We have said how uncommon it is to find couples that come to a relationship with an awareness of the "We"—let alone the skill set to support it. An equally unusual perspective is the developmental one. No matter how uncommon, we believe a developmental lens to be a crucial part of the context for couple therapists. Given the standard medical model training of most practitioners, it is easy to look at a problem as a sign of pathology or deficit when what is needed is a normative view of development through which to filter daily experience. We have often seen couples and families with a depressed, acting up, or chronically ill member whose difficulties can be traced to a struggle to accept and integrate normal developmental change and reorganize the family system in response. We believe the couple relationship itself to be a developmental context for individual and relational growth, a "culture to grow in" (Kegan, 1982), as partners reach out to repair disjointed, dysfunctional, or foreclosed life stories. If we as clinicians can utilize a life span perspective, increase our sensitivity to gains and "necessary losses" (Viorst, 1986), we will be better able to help couples navigate through the rough waters of change.

In this chapter, we provide an overview of the new developmental realities triggered by changes in 21st-century demographics. We reframe the traditional individual model to a systemic and intergenerational one and highlight several key developmental processes unique to couples. Finally, we examine developmental We-Story possibilities associated with various couple stages and offer questions to help open those stage-linked stories to further change and growth.

Development: Then and Now

One of the things that attracted me (KS) to my doctoral studies in Human Development and Psychology was the opportunity to learn about the newly emerging field of "adult development." This was in the early 1980s when the common wisdom was that most of what was significant in development occurred by age 18. Eric Erikson's life cycle developmental stage model—the first to move psychology beyond childhood and adolescence—was beginning to generate greater attention to the final 3–4 stages, while there was also new interest in women's development. Since then, not only do we have considerable evidence that change and growth occur throughout the entire life cycle but a robust field of gerontology is taking center stage for scholarly attention and research funding.

The life span perspective places change and growth in a broad context and benefits from a complex, interdisciplinary approach. Understood as a process, development has many dimensions—biological, social, psychological, and spiritual. Change is considered multidirectional and reciprocal; gains and losses occur simultaneously, and change in one area influences change in another. Life span development is often roughly divided into two phases: early (childhood and adolescence) and later (young adult, adult, and old age). The early half is characterized by rapid age-related changes in people's size and abilities, while in the later half changes in size have slowed, but abilities continue to develop and adapt (Baltes, Lindenberger, & Staudinger, 2006). Paul Baltes (Baltes et al., 2006), a leading theoretician on life span development, identified four key features of this perspective:

1. Multidirectionality: Development involves both growth and decline; as people grow in one area, they may lose in another and at different rates.
2. Plasticity: One's capacity is not predetermined or set in stone. Many skills can be improved with practice, within certain limits.
3. Historical context: Each of us develops within a particular set of circumstances determined by the historical time in which we are born and the culture in which we grow up.
4. Multiple causation: how people develop results from a wide variety of forces.

This perspective emphasizes that human development takes a lifetime to complete, with no one part of life any more or less important than another; it is a dynamic interaction among growth, maintenance, and loss regulation. Baltes et al. (2006) point out that as people grow older, they show age-related decreases in the amount and quality of biologically based resources and an age-related increase in the amount and quality of culture needed to generate continuously higher growth. Usually this results in a net slowing of growth as people age.

One of the key drivers behind the emergence of a life span perspective is the changing demographics in the last quarter of the 20th century and the beginning of the 21st century. Individuals, families, and societies worldwide are rapidly aging. In the United States, life expectancy has increased from 47 years in 1900 to over 75 years currently, with women holding a 7-year advantage over men. Not only are people living longer, but they also stay healthy longer. In fact, the idea of retirement at age 65 has become more of a myth than a reality for most people. By 2030, the over-65 group will exceed 20% of the population, creating many challenges for our resources and for couple and intergenerational family relationships (Walsh, 2006). Adults over 85 are not only the fastest-growing segment in our population, but the most vulnerable age group with over half projected to develop dementia. For younger and midlife couples, economic shifts suggest that dual careers are now necessities to attain and sustain middle- and upper-middle-class lifestyles. There is more outsourcing of early childhood care and diminished capacity to create a nest egg for later life. Each generation is no longer wealthier and/or more accomplished than its predecessors, and we are witnessing greater numbers of couples struggling with fears of outliving their financial resources and their ability to take care of aging parents. Women are becoming more educated and accomplished than men, resulting in a different developmental arc for women who take time out to raise their children. For example, it is now more common than ever to see women peaking professionally in their 50s, 60s, and 70s. These economic shifts are also contributing to the extension of pre-adulthood in Western societies. The need for higher education extends into the mid- and late 20s and beyond, and marriage, especially for the highly educated, is being postponed until the 30s or indefinitely. More adult children need economic and social support from their parents, and aging parents often express ambivalence about their refilling nest.

Development now takes a highly variable course over the life cycle with a wide range of phases and transitions better suited to the diverse preferences and challenges of contemporary families. Some individuals become first-time parents at the age when others become grandparents. Others start second families at midlife or beyond, and some who remarry have children as young as their own grandchildren (Walsh, 2006).

The Landscape of Adult Development

Despite all the variability, or perhaps because of it, there are many models that attempt to organize and structure life span development. Almost all pay homage to Erikson's (1968) 8-stage theory of psychosocial development and his pivotal construction of identity. At the heart of his theory is the concept of epigenesis—the idea that development happens gradually over time and becomes increasingly complex. It implies an essentially organic process, one that works itself out according to its own unique story logic (Randall & McKim, 2008). It reminds us why the chambered nautilus has become a metaphor for personal growth; development proceeds by pressing past the stages we occupy at present— spiraling toward more inclusive, complex levels. Whether one is open to or even aware of it, the process takes place beneath the surface all life long.

The various stages of adulthood are sliced and diced in a variety of ways, depending on whom you read, but the current demographics do suggest new broad epochs. The most recent addition to the schema is "Emerging Adulthood"—the time period between adolescence and early adulthood. During this period young adults are often viewed as preparing for adulthood, utilizing parental economic and social support and preoccupied with defining their identity (who am I), intimacy (who do I love), and work (what do I do).

Adulthood is now generally thought of as comprising a set of time periods from the early 30s through the end of life. In early adulthood (roughly 30–45 years), the focus is on building a family, having and raising children, while differentiating from one's original family. Many are also tasked to integrate parents/grandparents as parental adjuncts due to economic or other necessities. This is also the time to build successful employment trajectories and consolidate a viable work identity.

In mid-adulthood (45–70 years), energy pivots around generative issues—caring for and helping aging parents in their final years, launching children, and assuming occupational authority and leadership, including mentoring younger people.

Older adulthood (70+) finds individuals shifting the balance of power both at work and in the family, moving to peer relationships with one's adult children and adjusting to altered status occupationally. Changes in physical health, energy levels, and stamina highlight an awareness of the fragility of life. Illness and loss are experienced, offering opportunities for deepened and expanded spiritual development. There may be a heightened generativity, with greater concern to pass on values, life lessons, and wisdom to those coming after. An increase in positive affect and perspective-taking (Carstensen, 2009; Sadler, 2000) may result in renewed zest for life and deeper appreciation for momentary satisfactions.

Those are far from invariant sequences but represent broad guidelines within which considerable variability, diversity, and richness play out.

Although these broad stages are useful to orient our thinking, it is critical to remember that developmental theory is based on an individual model. Just as couple therapy is designed to provide a context beyond the individual concerns of partners, couple development adds a more systemic, complex dimension to our understanding.

From Individual to Systemic/Intergenerational Development

> We're the Baxters . . . a long line of wannabe jocks. Some of us got farther than others. My grandfather and two uncles almost made it to the Olympics in track, my sister coaches D1 women's basketball; I played three sports in college. It's what we do . . . hell, it's who we are. I hope our kids carry that on.

This comment reflects the inherent sense of time passing—an awareness of the continual process of movement—both continuities and discontinuities across the generations. Well-functioning families display such knowledge, and members experience strong intergenerational connections with stories updated and modified into an ever-shifting mythology. At its best, the family is an intergenerational tale and testament that simultaneously facilitates the individual and social development of its members.

The formation of a new committed partnership is often misrepresented as the joining of two individuals when what it really represents is the joining of two entire family systems. Each partner brings to the new endeavor experiences from their own family about what it is possible to hope for in the way of relationships, and what it is possible to have. Over time, these past experiences, expectations, and dreams of two entire intergenerational constellations somehow meld into a new entity—the "We." The process of this melding also includes the effort to integrate their various intergenerational stories as the couple writes the first chapters of their own unique story.

Rather than being too complex, we have found the systemic/intergenerational orientation to be quickly embraced by couples in treatment. It not only normalizes their distress but also links it to larger processes outside of themselves. The seasons of family life, often framed as developmental tasks, are familiar to couples. They can identify with the phases of childrearing, launching, empty nest, and so on, if not from a personal perspective, then as witnesses to friends' or family members' experiences. They intuitively grasp that developmental transitions, while disruptive, can also be seen as milestones that encourage the reevaluation of assumptions about one's place in the world (Walsh, 2006). They can generally embrace the necessity of growth and change, the need, for example, to adjust parenting skills to fit adolescents versus younger children.

To aid couples in absorbing these developmental insights, we draw on our We-Stories perspective. We work with couples to help them find the particular story language and metaphors that crystallize the specific challenges that they are confronting. Sometimes these developmental challenges are normative issues—the result of life transitions or crises (e.g., aging, illness, job loss, "empty nest")—and sometimes they are signs of stagnation in a couple's dynamic as the relationship extends over time and each partner experiences life cycle–related changes. To illustrate our general We-Story approach, we first present two examples from our practice—the first case example focuses on helping a couple identify a helpful story frame in the context of a life-threatening illness. The second example highlights a couple that has stalled in their relationship development due to their clinging to their initial way of being together. Our story work allowed them to find an appropriate image to characterize this "stuckness" and then to find a new image that freed them from this impasse.

Finding the We-Story in a Life Transition

When partners and family members cannot accept the passage of time and the continuities among past, present, and future, we often see symptoms develop and stories become stuck. Problems also arise because family members perceive the same event in different ways and don't possess the resources necessary to bridge the gap. Additional challenges emerge when members further labor under the impact of illness, medical or psychiatric. These crises reverberate throughout a family system, leaving no one untouched. An illness experience acts like a magnifying glass for families, exaggerating and placing their dynamics in bold relief. Also, if the child of a couple is ill, particularly with a chronic or debilitating illness, there is an even greater need to acknowledge the presence of and/or history of that child's healthy self, as well as healthy and non-illness–related aspects of the couple's own relationship. Parents frequently remark about the relief they feel in being helped to remember and talk about non-illness–related issues, to recount stories of past developmental milestones, and to reengage with their wishes and fantasies for their child's future. In our experience, it has proven crucial to identify the issues a couple is dealing with in the normal developmental scheme of things to prevent a normative process from being perceived in a catastrophic and distorted manner.

For example, the Johnsons typify a family in which members became frozen in an adaptive structure that had outlived its utility. Bill, a housing contractor and the sole family financial provider, was diagnosed with liver cancer. Initially, he responded well to treatment and returned to work part-time. Linda was able to secure a job that helped maintain financial stability. Their four children, ages 15, 12, 11, and 7 were "relatively unaffected." When they arrived for therapy two years later, Bill had experienced a rapid progression of the cancer, leaving him very disabled. Initially responding to the first diagnosis with a "fighting spirit," they had now succumbed in quiet submission. Their Couple Story and manner of coping had become one of stoic determination. They expressed concern about their oldest son Ryan, now 17, who had planned to go away to college, but the specter of financial hardship and his perceived need to "man-up" for his mother and three sisters had stymied this choice. He had started to talk about not going away to school. Ryan took great pride in his ability to take care of his father and be a supportive resource for his family, but as the time drew closer to leaving for college, he had become angry and withdrawn. He had started picking fights at school, leading us to bring him in to the couple sessions. In that setting, Ryan began to talk about his frustration that his Dad "never seemed to get mad, that he just took all the setbacks in stony silence." He wondered if his father "gave a shit about sticking around." He asked his Dad if he ever got mad about the cancer or had he "given up already." He tearfully admitted to sometimes feeling so full of rage at his father's illness that he wanted "to fight *for* him." He claimed that when he started fights, he had flashes of being the "arms, legs and mouth for my Dad." Bill was able to share with Ryan that while he did feel angry at times and devastated by the fact that he was dying, that he had learned it was healthier for him to conserve his energy and focus on the positives. Bill reinforced that Ryan's job was to use his arms, legs, and voice on his own behalf and that that was what would help him (Bill) the most.

We all talked about the fundamental clash they were experiencing—between the developmental pull of Ryan's separation and growing individuation from the family and the ongoing demands of Bill's progressive disability and impending death. Literally "standing in and up for his father" was an expression of Ryan's grief and helplessness. In our couple dialogue, we now had a narrative theme and touchstone that we could use to focus our discussion. The image of Ryan "doing the fighting" and the question of "Who needs to be in the ring?" sparked Bill and Linda to show more active engagement regarding their current struggle with Bill's cancer. Rather than resent his brief period of outbursts at school, they were able to thank him for his fighting spirit. In turn, they started to talk about the need for a new, shared story about Bill's cancer that could inspire themselves and the rest of the family.

This new story began with Bill and Linda taking a more open and communicative stance with family members about Bill's illness and its status. Bill also renewed his efforts at actively overcoming or at least minimizing the effects of his illness. The new story also included an explicit recognition of Ryan's need to focus on himself and no longer spend so much time "fighting Dad's battles." Ryan could still help out, but the other children were also encouraged to voice their reactions and to explore ways they could step up and help Dad and Mom out. Gradually, Bill and Linda became less reactive to Ryan, as well as to one another, and began to appreciate the love and loss expressed by their son's combative efforts to get his Dad "back on his feet."

Bill and Linda felt more empowered and secure in the knowledge they could simultaneously launch and let go of both fighters, each to a different mission. Linda said that she liked having two men in the family with different strengths and so much love for one another. Ryan said he felt relieved to know he didn't have to battle for, but could stand *with* his father and support him in different ways as they shared their painful journey. As Bill became more open to sharing his experience and asking for help from the rest of the family, Bill and Linda began to pull in extended family resources. Once Ryan was able to see that his parents could enlist a wider network of "fighters," a "fighting team" as he liked to call them, Ryan agreed to begin his first semester of college as planned. Bill and Linda were then freer to carry on their own struggle with deeper recognition of the love and dedication that existed both between them and throughout all members of their family.

Finding and Revising the We-Story When the Couple's Development Stalls

Too often couple development is simplistically portrayed as a kind of multiple of individual development—two people going through the same tasks of identity: trust building, integrity, generativity—in different ways or at different rates. Several writers have come closer to categorizing change over time from a dyadic, rather than individual, perspective. Tamashiro (1979) proposed an invariant sequence for the evolution of committed partnerships and titled the sequence—magical, conventional, individualistic, and affirmational. The phases are not tied to time but rather to the inner logic of each partnership. Other theorists outline similarly themed sequences such as Cobb, Larson, & Watson's (2003) romance > disillusionment > companionate/altruistic, or DeMaria's and Harrar's (2007) seven stages of passion through completion. Bader and Pearson (1988) developed a schema and a treatment approach based on the developmental tasks of separation and individuation. The general typology seems to be that couples come together in mutual passion, enjoy a honeymoon period of varying lengths, become disillusioned when they realize their partner is not who they initially thought, then, if they stay together, work through that disillusionment into some degree of mutual understanding, compromise, and satisfaction.

Sheila Sharpe (2000) noted the paucity of work viewing the marital relationship with a distinct evolution all its own. In *The Ways We Love*, she described the couple relationship as a system that develops over time in a way that is different from, though related to, the development of individual partners. She views a couple relationship as consisting of multiple relationship patterns and claims that these patterns develop in an interwoven, interdependent fashion throughout the life of the relationship. Each pattern of intimate relating has its origin in the individuals' early relationship development: nurturing, merging, idealizing, devaluing, controlling, competing for superiority, and competing in love triangles. Each pattern also has its own developmental course and recapitulated childhood themes. Through all of the patterns, there are the contrasting urges for connection and independence, and these urges take on distinct and unique expressions for each partner. She claims that when any one of these relational patterns dominates and rigidifies into a primarily defensive form, the relationship will suffer.

In our framework of the couple's own story, these individual developmental patterns coalesce into the couple's unique pattern of interaction, a pattern that can often emerge in a series of similarly themed and plotted stories—the couple's "narrative script," which it is likely to revive precisely at developmental crossroads in the relationship (see the previous chapter, Chapter 5, for examples of this). If therapists are able to help the couple articulate a metaphor or key story trope for this script, the couple then has a shared language to address and work at overcoming a developmental blockage.

For example, Sandra and Marlene came to therapy for help in deciding whether to end their committed partnership of nine years. They described the deterioration of a once-vibrant, playful, affectionate relationship into a boring, sexless, habituated obligation they were "too passive to leave." Both nurturers by nature, they were also healthcare providers who took care of others for a living. Each had come from neglectful, abusive homes, and early in their relationship, basked in the comfort of being carefully tended to by the other. They described "loving" as knowing that they initially used to be able to read each other's minds and have unspoken desires met "perfectly" by the other. This way of loving was exemplified in the following story that illustrates how an early, idealized narrative was being carried forward when it could no longer effectively serve their current developmental needs:

> From day one, what attracted us to each other was this ability to just *get* each other, to feel this intense sense of understanding of one another. Our friends used to comment on how tuned in to each other we seemed. We could go to a party or event and just intuitively tell when the other one was ready to leave, our sense of timing was so perfectly matched.

However, as the years wore on and they found disagreements (both major and minor) were being squelched to preserve harmony, their understandable resentment was experienced as apathy and detachment. They had become locked in a pattern of merger that was not only inhibiting individual change but relational growth. In a sense they both knew that their story of seamless understanding was too fragile to be sustained. They therefore avoided any significant conflict that would inevitably cause its delicate structure to unravel. Still, both were highly dissatisfied and long overdue in learning how to take risks, voice their unique perspectives, and tolerate tension and uncertainty.

Effective couple therapy for Sandra and Marlene, as is true for all couples at any stage along the life course, depends upon understanding the protective meanings of their particular defensive patterns or

141

vulnerability cycles (Scheinkman & Fishbane, 2004; Sharpe, 2000), as well as the associated narrative scripts. Sandra and Marlene's current detachment in the relationship was based in an unexpressed longing to return to a blissful, seamless understanding of one another. They knew that this merged understanding was no longer possible to sustain, but they had no language or acceptable structure that could serve to replace it. As a result, they played out a narrative script of experiencing difference, withdrawing from potential conflict, and diffusing any potential passion by isolating or maintaining a bland façade.

Highlighting the stuck story in the therapy hour (see Chapter 5) captures a moment in which the couple appears to be frozen and creates a vivid opportunity to break through a developmental impasse. For Sandy and Marlene, we were able to key in on their "seamless garment" story and illustrate that this fragile structure was not the right framework for the more weighty issues they were now facing. Using some brainstorming, we asked them to envision a new metaphor—a new way of telling their story that could bear the demands of their more complex lives without being overwhelmed by inevitable conflict. This new metaphor, and the story that accompanied it, incorporated the concept of "messy seams" and "missed stitches" without fear that the basic covering would rend or incur permanent damage. Not only were they able to see that the life course of their relationship brings change, but that their We-Stories will often need to shift in response to these changes. They had gone from the couple of "seamless understanding" to a couple whose patchwork quilt could keep them warm, even through moments of chilly discord or frustration.

As useful as Sharpe's model is, it has an individual/attachment base and reminds us of the inherent challenge in building a truly systemic model without an explicit systemic variable built in. This is another reason why we find the concept of We-ness so important and are intent on building a model of the "We" that will be pertinent over time. The "We" clarifies that there is individual development, and there is couple development, and the development of the couple system (the "We") has its own distinct trajectory. Tension within and between these two trajectories is in itself normative, occurs across the life cycle, and is particularly acute during times of transition and/or crisis. We-Stories provide a language that each member of the couple can mutually embrace to give concrete expression to the joint challenges and solutions that they may share. From stuck stories that are often unarticulated, the couple can move to a We-Story that provides comfort and renewed energy to work through their blockage and overcome relational obstacles.

Studying change in the same couple over time—longitudinally—is the very best method to make a case for developmental change. But those studies are expensive and time consuming; thus few exist. The far more common approach—examining different couples at different points along the life cycle is exemplified by the work we share in this book. In the following sections we review the components of We-Stories in light of key life stages, discussing the developmental possibilities unique to couple processes, and offer suggestions for opening We-Stories to greater change and growth. The therapeutic goal in every case is to aid couples in restoring developmental progress and balance between relational and personal growth. The final goal is to help couples build mutuality in ways that also support individual development.

Early Adulthood (20–30 Years): The Balancing Act Begins

> You are young. So you know everything. You leap into the boat and
> begin rowing.
> but listen to me.
> Without fanfare, without embarrassment, without any doubt, I talk
> directly to your soul.
> Listen to me.
> Lift the oars from the water, let your arms rest, and your heart, and
> heart's little intelligence, and listen to me. There is life without
> love. It is not worth a bent penny, or a scuffed shoe.
> It is not worth the body of a dead dog nine days unburied. When
> you hear, a mile away and still out of sight, the churn of the water
> as it begins to swirl and roil, fretting around the sharp rocks—when
> you hear that unmistakable pounding—when you feel the mist
> on your mouth and sense ahead the embattlement, the long falls
> plunging and steaming—then row, row for your life toward it.
> —Mary Oliver (1998, "West Wind #2")

Novelists and philosophers often allude to this phase of the life cycle by borrowing images of nature . . . a time of setting down new buds, sowing young seeds, lush greenery. And yet it also usually encompasses the beginning of watching the failure of some seeds to germinate, of realizing some were misplanted, some were not right for the soil conditions, and acknowledging others never should have been planted at all.

This is usually a time of initiations and establishment—establishing physical, financial, social/emotional in(ter)dependence, and the first experiences of realizing the utter relativity of independence. This time of "getting a life" usually includes developing the courage to be oneself in the face of parental challenge or disapproval, resisting the urges to cut off or fuse in order to avoid conflict or anxiety. This also involves defusing the catastrophic expectations attendant to self-revelation—that

143

the other will not disappear if I express and reveal my true self. Tied up in this transition to full adulthood is relinquishing childhood fantasies and expectations, and seeing the other as separate with both positive and negative attributes. This sows the seeds for the establishment of compassion for the other and eventually the self.

Since this is also the time in which serious relationships are formed and long-term commitments made, the issues above also extend to the significant other. It is a time when passions are savored, love languages learned, a sexual vocabulary developed, and the new "We" is forged. All this occurs against the backdrop of major decision making around work, housing, lifestyle, and shifting friend and family networks.

Elisha and Carl

Elisha and Carl are a 31- and 30-year-old couple with four children who have been married for seven years. They met in college and had an intense, fast courtship. They each came from middle-class backgrounds; Carl was particularly proud of being raised by a single mother who went on to become a successful lawyer. His mother recently married a man with a successful packaging business, and Carl works for him. His stepfather is the "patriarch," and Carl admits to being afraid of him, yet feels tied by loyalty and financial perks to a resentful compliance. Carl travels a lot for work and is pushing for a nanny to reduce the daily burdens on Elisha. After years of heavy partying and drug use, Carl joined AA and has been sober for one year.

Elisha's parents divorced when she was four, and she and her two sisters are close to both parents as well as to her stepmother and two stepbrothers. She was hospitalized for "cutting" and bulimia at age 14 and has a long history of on/off alcohol abuse. She is trying to substitute her "bad addictions" for positive ones, like exercise, but still feels anxious and stressed out with parenting four children under 6 years of age. They are hoping to be able to move in to a larger apartment soon, but neither wants to overextend financially. She is dedicated to her family and committed to "not repeating my parents' mistakes."

Elisha and Carl's story typifies many of the challenges of this building phase of life—dealing with the remnants of earlier developmental individual issues, such as substance use and relationships with parents. There are numerous strengths as well—their recognition of stressors and their willingness to ask for help top the list.

Their key patterns of relating tended to alternate between idealizing one another ("I knew he was just the perfect guy for me") and devaluing ("I don't know how I ever found that nonstop energy so attractive"). They tended to be low on nurturing, both saying they gave what they had to their children, and high on competing for superiority. They said they treated one another as "unpaid employees."

144

The challenge for the development of their We-Story was to introduce, build, and nurture a sense of We-consciousness that expressed a larger relational purpose outside the routine tasks of life. The relationship and sense of who "We" are is often not a priority for couples at this phase; there are too many other competing agendas. One of the chief challenges of the therapist in the early sessions is to refute the couple's defensive conviction that they are too busy to put time into the relationship. The therapist must remind them (and certainly more than once) that the therapy does not work by their coming to sessions, but by changing their priorities or allocation of time outside of sessions. They cannot build a "We" if they do not devote time to this constructive process, and they will not allocate this time if they are not willing to agree and commit to making the building of the "We" an essential priority. It is often necessary to bring couples repeatedly back to this fundamental contract or else they will allow the momentum of their busy lives to dictate their priorities and the *status quo* will continue to make We-ness a lower-rung concern.

A key skill for the couple to learn once they commit to working on their We-Story is how to reframe their negative story outcomes into positive ones. For example, Elisha learned that shifting her constant complaints about the lack of help with childcare routines into a small specific request more often resulted in getting the help she needed. They practiced giving each other regular feedback on their accomplishments ("You had the kids dressed and fed early today—that is such a big help to me") and connecting twice each day via text or phone to check in on how the other was feeling (not what they had "done").

The keys for story development at this phase are to help partners link past, present, and future experiences and expectations in the interests of building a coherent storyline, to develop a redemptive outlook toward their challenges, and begin to frame a larger relational mission and purpose. These tasks, of course, are the establishment of the "Good Enough" structural features that are the minimal foundation of a strong We-Story (see Chapters 2 and 4). With these in place, the couple can begin to access their unique We-Story that places their relationship at the center of their universe. It truly is "Us" against the world, and the fierceness and spirit they bring to this commitment to each other is likely to support them through the perilous challenges that young couples face in establishing emotional and financial security for the years ahead.

QUESTIONS FOR EARLY ADULTHOOD

Imagine that your relationship is an infant. Describe that baby in terms of looks, temperament, energy level, engagement, growth, and so forth. What does that baby need right now?

How would you describe your partner's personality? In what ways do your personalities complement each other, in what ways do they collide?

How would your friends describe your relationship?

Are there ways in which each of you has shown respect for the other's goals and ambitions?

How are you working as a team to realize your individual and mutual dreams?

Where do you each see your relationship in 5 years? 10 years?

Adulthood (31–45 Years): Balance Revisited

I am plump with my husband's love, overfed by his kindness, yet still I treat our marriage like an all-you-can-eat buffet, returning to him over and over again to fill my plate, as if vows guaranteed me unlimited nourishment. During Ramadan, when he turns inward and has less to offer me, I feel indignant. I want to make a scene. I want to speak to whoever is in charge, to demand what I think was promised me when I entered this marriage. But now I wonder: Is love an endless feast, or is it what people manage to serve each other when their cupboards are bare?

—Bremer (2014)

Our clients usually describe this phase as an outright juggling act— juggling the multiple and competing inner psychological demands with external ones. Couplehood has inevitably brought disillusionment, disappointment, even despair when the idealized masks of early romance are replaced by "the real deal." This process, often extending into midlife, will have one of three general outcomes: the dissolution of the relationship, adjustment to the realities with resignation, and adjustment with contentment (Cobb, Larson, & Watson, 2003). Unfortunately, few couples have ever been educated about the inevitability and necessity of this process.

Cathy and Tom

Cathy and Tom, 34 and 44, respectively, had been married ten years. Cathy was a first-generation American whose parents brought her to the US from Lithuania at age 3. Her parents spoke Lithuanian at home while she was growing up, and she viewed them as "old world critics—no one

146

I'd ever want to be like." She described her father as distant and emotionally abusive and was drawn to Tom because he was "exactly the opposite." Tom, a hard-working, quiet electrician, was one of nine children in a Catholic, Czech family. He thrived in Cathy's early adoration and was mystified by her recent complaints that he was "too much of this, not enough of that." Once having wanted a big family, her chronic dissatisfaction and threats to leave had put off childbearing to a "critical point." Tom experienced Cathy as a "control freak," totally unaccepting of who he really was. Cathy agreed that if she'd realized who he was, she probably never would have married him.

The developmental opportunities here involved the reexamination of family of origin legacies in light of ongoing projections and expectations for one another. The fact that neither felt content suggested a potential to rework the interpretation of things "as they were in the past" and to see one another with fresh eyes. If Cathy could let go of her demands that Tom make up for the father she never had, and Tom could let go of his desire for unconditional acceptance, both might find new and authentic things to love and appreciate about one another. Opening the dialogue to the imagined role of children in their lives, what it meant to each of them and how they would see their current lives changing with the addition of a child, would be critical, especially in light of the fact that in both of their original families, children "weren't planned," they "just happened." Bridges to connection had to be built before a "We" could be forged.

Threats for "story foreclosure" are particularly high during this time because the pain of disapproval and the risk of reevaluation can be too intense and frightening for some couples. This is different from a natural foreclosure that comes with making choices in our lives—do I live in Seattle or Spokane, become a mechanic or pilot? By choosing one course, we close off other opportunities. The other kind of story foreclosure has to do with the way one experiences and interprets life events—like Cathy's interpretation that because Tom wasn't who she thought he was initially, she couldn't stay with him. The therapeutic, story-expanding challenge is to find ways to decrease the perception of threat and increase each other's curiosity to learn more about who the other genuinely is now and wants to become.

Their "Good Enough" Story challenges hinge a great deal on the future story that they might construct and in which they are willing to invest. The therapist's job is to help them to develop confidence in their capacity to write this story together with greater compassion and patience than they have displayed to each other previously. What is likely to open up this sensitivity, if it has not been widely evident in their recent interactions with each other? For Cathy and Tom, their We-Story begins with the metaphor of bringing a newborn "We" into the world. How might they begin to write a story of their kindness to this third entity in their lives, the infant and toddler "We"? In their daily interactions, how can they be attentive, nurturing, and respectful of their own relationship? In mastering this concept and enacting it, they will have already started writing their couple narrative that will include bringing an *actual* child into the world.

QUESTIONS FOR ADULTHOOD

How do you imagine that children would add (or have added) to your couple life? How would they (or have they) complicate your couple life?

How has your love for your partner evolved over the years? Think about levels of passion, intimacy, and commitment.

How are roles and chores divided between the two of you? How do you know that the balance you've got isn't working?

Which of your expectations about married life have been fulfilled and which have not?

What can the two of you do better together than apart?

In the midst of all the busy aspects of your lives, how do you cultivate your connection to each other?

How are you both supporting each other in keeping true to your goals and values for your relationship and your family?

Midlife (46–65 Years): Balance Is Abandoned

We are good at opening dialogue
It's our specialty
That and the goodbye scene
We could recite in our sleep.
It's the middle that defies us,
The substance, the ordinary progressions
That weave events into patterns,
Textures, the 3 dimensional . . .
   —Kate Braverman (1987, "Afterthoughts")

© Kate Braverman. Reprinted with
permission.

By this point most couples have faced many changes, accrued many losses, and come up against unimagined limitations. Many have faced experiences so traumatic they have not yet been storied in an intentional, let alone coherent, way. Some chapters have been so all-encompassing that identities are reconfigured in unexpected and debilitating ways. Partners may fear their present selves, and their Couple Story is not big enough or flexible enough to incorporate the affairs, secret addictions, career setbacks, premature deaths, and other generalized chaos, such that they cannot imagine "going there." It might feel safer to cling to the well worn and well known—once a tragic hero, always a tragic hero. The past may become frozen . . . we are forever the "Football legend," "Just a housewife," or other such master narratives. Gender plays a clear role here as Bateson (1989, 2010) reminds us that men have been culturally conditioned to story their life experiences into the image of a quest, while women's lives are composed from a more improvisatory score, given that their career and life paths tend to be more broken up and diversified than men.

Midlife couples, often referred to as the "Squeeze generation," are vulnerable to being the group most preoccupied by simultaneous losses. This is also the point at which the subjective sense of time shifts—from time since birth to time left to live. This recasting of one's relationship to mortality can have repercussions from the unsettling to the dramatic. Many of the issues are reflected in the story of Rhonda and Stan.

Rhonda and Stan

The Rogers, both in their late 50s, were launching two adolescents and overseeing the nursing home care of one set of aging parents and the retirement of the other. They came for help with their escalating conflict, which coincided with Stan's recent job change. It soon became apparent that they were reacting to the strain of multiple responsibilities, multiple transitions, and limited resources with which to manage the situation. Although there were pragmatic issues to attend to, such as negotiating with nursing home personnel, allocating time to children and each other, dealing with retired (and more demanding) parents, the couple thrived most when they worked on letting go of problems they could not control and adjusting more explicitly to their new generational status. As parentified children, both Rhonda and Stan were moving at midlife into an awareness of their own unmet needs for caretaking. At the same time, they were faced with parental dependency, death, and becoming the elder generation. As Stan commented, "Now that I know that I'd like someone to look after me, I find that the buck stops here, and everyone is counting on me to take care of them." They both identified their resentment at still being in the role of parental caretakers, especially as that diverted attention away from the needs of their maturing children, and from one another. Several sessions were spent refocusing on their nuclear family—milestones with each of the children, concerns and pleasures each parent felt in connection with each child, and the identification and appreciation of current parent–child issues. This appeared to help them reorient and reprioritize as well as solidify the dyadic partnership and sense of We-ness. Simultaneously, they described an awareness of one of the more subtle transformations involved in the maturation of children—"not knowing how they got from here to there." Rhonda tearfully commented, "I guess our children continually march away from us, a step at a time and into their own lives." She captured the process beautifully:

> I was standing in the bathroom and it suddenly dawned on me. I was surrounded by acne pads, thongs that weren't mine and athletic socks bigger than Stan's. I think the last conscious idea I had about our kids growing up was that we were going through a lot of diapers.

Stan replied:

> I'm actually thinking he's become sexually active. . . . How did I miss his first kiss? How did he get so confident with girls and know all this about relationships?

This is a time when parents address the question: Who is this person I've helped to shape? Intimately tied to that question is confronting and gradually letting go of the child they dreamed about and hoped for, and embracing the person who is. As Greer (1992) suggests, parents must grieve for their child's growing up and growing away.

This was more complex for Rhonda and Stan to absorb because talking about how much they had invested and given to their children brought up complicated feelings of grief tied to how each was neglected during their own childhoods, as well as their resentments around ongoing demands for parental care. While benefitting from an understanding of the meaning of their resentment, their Couple Story had become stuck; it was as if they could see no way to do what needed to be done and *not* feel resentful. The challenge/opportunity for the therapist was to help Stan and Rhonda build a more flexible narrative, one that could honor their needs to grow personally, uphold the values that continued to be important to them, and experience themselves as less burdened caregivers. Rhonda came up with the key. An avid gardener, one of her frustrations was not having enough time to tend to her flowers and vegetables. She decided she would "tend her garden first" and only devote time to others as it was available. She encouraged Stan to do the same and he chose "time in the basement woodworking."

Slowly they began practicing giving to themselves first, then others, while appreciating the ways they were "growing self, other, and the relationship." Over time, "growing themselves within the We" helped them transform their mutual resentments into a sense of appreciation for the generosity and the filial loyalty each showed toward their aging parents.

Being able to validate their individual needs for nurturance and support helped them find ways to make more time for one another. They came to value one another as a place to get support, comfort, and other necessities for growth when depleted, instead of seeing the other as just one more demand to be met. The larger challenge/opportunity for the midlife story involves the gradual letting go of parental expectations into acceptance of the adult child as he or she is, while moving out of the parent role into the person/peer role. Since parenting children together often helps open our hearts to truly being able to love a spouse, this is a period to expand the capacity to reveal vulnerabilities and practice forgiveness. Telling the necessary stories and listening with an open heart can lead to heightened acceptance of differences and the appreciation that respect does not always necessitate agreement.

This time also offers the opportunity to create a couple bond that is once again partner rather than child focused. It is a time that can greatly benefit from a re-visioning of the couple mission statement—to incorporate, consolidate, and integrate the many simultaneous renegotiations of this time of life. Slowly, the couple is shifting to again seeing the story of their relationship (rather than the story of their children growing up or their parents growing old) as the central narrative of their lives.

QUESTIONS FOR MIDLIFE

What are the two of you most proud of in your relationship at this point in time?

How have you each been able to support one another through the changes you have been going through?

If your children were suddenly out of the house, what would be different about your relationship?

What would you like your children to know about the ways you have helped your parents (their grandparents)?

How would you describe the way you are coping with the evolution of your family and the changes that you're experiencing?

What about your relationship at this point surprises you?

Where do you want your future to take you together?

How do you help each other reconnect with old wishes and dreams or pursue new goals and passions?

Late Adulthood (66–80 Years): Balance Is Redefined

Let me imagine that we will come again
when we want to and it will be spring
we will be no older than we ever were
the worn griefs will have eased like the early cloud
through which the morning slowly comes to itself
and the ancient defenses against the dead
will be done with and left to the dead at last
the light will be as it is now in the garden

151

that we have made here these years together
of our long evenings and astonishment
—W. S. Merwin (2013)

"To Paula in Late Spring" by W. S. Merwin. Copyright © 2008
by W. S. Merwin, used by permission of The Wylie Agency LLC.

Credit: W. S. Merwin, "To Paula in Late Spring" from
The Shadow of Sirius. Copyright © 2008 by W. S. Merwin. Reprinted
with the permission of The Permissions Company, Inc., on
behalf of Copper Canyon Press, www.coppercanyonpress.org.

As Morrie put it, "Aging is not just decay, you know. It's growth." (Albom, 2002). The enormous popularity of the book, *Tuesdays with Morrie,* was undoubtedly tied to Morrie's optimistic, glass-half-full view of the aging process. It is a perspective too seldom heard. This is the season in fact when couples reap the benefits of earlier compromises and adjustments, and enjoy the wisdom of time's passing. One woman put it so well:

> I've always loved to dance. Joe is a terrible dancer. Over the years I've tried everything—shaming him, dragging him to dance classes, refusing to dance with him. Why, I used to actually say to his face—"You stink, you have no rhythm, you are hopeless" . . . can you believe that? Now I wonder how I could be so cruel. These days, I'm grateful that he still wants to dance with me, that he tries and I don't care how we look when we get on the dance floor at weddings. I realize he asks me because he knows how much it means to me to dance and for that I'm very grateful.

This is precisely the kind of perspective we can offer as therapists; when it occurs organically, it is an example of the magic and mystery of human development. In late adulthood, couples have the opportunity to see their stories gain definition. What may have been hovering on the horizon, vaguely outlined and familiar in its basic form, is now called home from its liminal borders to a shape that carries dimension, heft, and meaning. It is the time of integrity and as Erikson (1950, pp. 268–269) put it: "Acceptance of one's one and only life cycle as something that had to be." It is the acceptance of one's relationship as the one and only relationship that one could have.

James and Beth

Youthful looking and fit at 71 and 70, James and Beth were six years into a retirement that was evolving just as they had planned. Living in one of the sunshine states for 3–4 month stints, they traveled back to the Midwest for visits with their three children and eight grandchildren. They described their 45-year marriage as full of the "usual ups and downs," most related to James's import/export business, which had been very volatile, putting them close to bankruptcy several times. James seemed particularly proud that he had pulled them back from the brink and had managed to return them to financial solvency and even stability, making a comfortable retirement possible.

Beth was more negative and feeling quite discouraged by the crisis that had brought them to therapy. She described feeling "totally disgusted" by James's request to open their relationship sexually to include encounters with a longtime friend and neighbor. He said he thought it would be good to "spice things up a bit." Beth had expected that at this point in their lives he'd be "almost done with that" and the fact that he not only wanted a sexual relationship, but also wanted it to involve "experimenting in ways they'd never once ever even talked about" left Beth feeling "stunned and sickened." She wondered what else he thought he was missing and what he'd "ask for next." James described having learned to keep his "kinkier" ideas to himself throughout their long marriage and thought he was way overdue to finally get some variety. Now that they were alone, without pressures of work and family, he thought it was just the time to "turn up the volume sexually." By the time they came for help, there was such a backlog of resentment and misunderstanding, they had almost stopped talking about anything. The story they shared of James's revelation of suppressed sexual desires tapped into a familiar narrative script that was often repeated in their frequent financial crisis talks in which James would make an announcement of impending catastrophe to Beth, Beth would complain she'd been kept in the dark until it was too late for her to help, followed by James retreating into defensive silence. Beth would either continue to push for more details or withdraw into her own stony silence.

In order to reengage them with one another, it was critical to help them develop a new story for their "We." Their stuck story was one in which James was the risk taker and Beth was the reactor. Beth never felt very good about her role, and James had picked up her resentment over the years, but didn't know the source. Building their new story started with education regarding the normative and even crucial role of novelty in a long-term relationship. Shaking up the status quo and the old patterns of relating was essential to craft a story that would better sustain them for the long haul. Beth softened with the recognition that James must have trusted her to make what he knew would be a risky request, and that his desire for new ways to "spice up" their sex life was normative, affirming, and hopeful. She could respond to his intention positively and still decline a specific activity. The risks may not be of the magnitude that James might envision, but by dialing back the level of risk, Beth could join him in the adventure and feel ownership of the fun rather than be cast as the spoilsport or naysayer. Their new story became that of a couple that can take risks together. This was another deepening layer to the spiral of differentiation—an expansion of the mutual capacity to hold more tension in the relationship. In the face of threat, both partners can remind themselves of a fundamental Security, Empathy, Respect, and Acceptance (SERA in SERAPH) in the relationship. Ultimately, they can see differences as opportunities to coauthor a more nuanced, deeper, truthful narrative that turns the negative to positive and reflects a larger relational purpose.

What evolved to be important for James and Beth was to develop the capacity to "talk about" the unspoken—to experience their relationship as something that could incorporate and tolerate different needs and wishes. There were many sessions in which we explored safer areas of dealing with the new and different—sampling spicy Thai food, taking a hiking trip to South America, deciding to live away from the family for bigger parts of the year. Each time that we circled back to their sexual relationship, it became easier for each partner to express their preferences authentically and negotiate for change in their moments of intimacy. Gradually, this had the effect of revitalizing other aspects of their relationship. Beth started taking watercolor classes; James started volunteering in a migratory bird counting program; and they planned a short cruise together—something they always said they'd "never, ever do." And they were also able to introduce new sexual fantasies and novel experiences into their intimate life without taking the more extreme risk of adding a new partner into their love life.

What is perhaps critical to take away from this late adulthood case example is that the story is never finished—there is always room for revision and growth—creativity and novelty have no age restrictions. What matters is for the couple to see their relationship as their mutual "masterpiece," a shared work they have uniquely created and that is coming into a mature focus as their individual lives draw closer to their natural ends.

QUESTIONS FOR LATE ADULTHOOD

How do changes in your health affect the way you think about yourself and your partner?

What is on your "bucket list" of things to do together?

What are the best things about your relationships with your children and grandchildren?

What are your relationships to the material world (money, possessions, status) and the spiritual world (membership in a religious or spiritual community, personal spiritual practices, the role of God or any other spiritual force in your life)?

Elderhood (80+): Balance Is Reclaimed

This thou percev'st, which makes thy love more strong,
To love that well, which thou must leave ere long.
                           —William Shakespeare, Sonnet 73

This time of life, soon to represent our largest segment of the population, is widely diverse, reflecting all the many faces of the aging process, the myriad ways the relentless force of gravity brings each of us down to earth.

Throughout this chapter we have described a view of the life cycle that expresses an intrinsic drive toward growth. Gerontologist Torns-tam (1996, p. 38) coined the term *gerotranscendence,* meaning a "shift in meta-perspective, from a materialistic and rational vision to a more cosmic one, accompanied by an increase in life satisfaction." The self is redefined. Fear of death decreases while our affinity with present, past, and coming generations increases. Just as any overarching construct of the life span should be viewed with skepticism and counterbalanced with an awareness of the contextual complexity of the experience of aging, as therapists, we have certainly been privy to many *moments* of transcendence. We have frequently witnessed midlife and later couples, in the middle of their stories, begin to glimpse its end. They want to see the big picture, to have the experience of having made as much sense of their relationship as they were able. They are then freer to live more fully in the moment. The lesson to be learned for the elder story is that precisely because life is so transitory, it is extraordinarily valuable.

One elder, rather philosophical client put it well: "I'm the only one who can see in my wife all the women she's been—the young girl, the new mother, the aging granny." He reminds us that lasting love is a history of different loves for one's partner at different periods of life; this multiplicity gives the relationship more dimension and depth, turning each partner into the one who keeps track, remembers, restores. As Weinstein (2011, p. 390) wrote, "This is the edifice we build by loving each other over time. The rich temporal awareness of shared experiences, of countless earlier days and nights, of an entire textured existence together, of a 'we story'."

As therapists, if we can develop and maintain a clear perspective on the outlines of normative developmental change, we can be of great value to our couples' capacity to mobilize their resources, adapt to whatever additional challenges they are facing, and move forward to future developmental tasks. We also provide a profound service to couples when we assist them to acknowledge the natural ambivalence of change and bear witness to their struggles on the path of creative transformation. In doing so, we can help them shape their lasting We-Story that may hint at an ending for them, but is also to serve as a legacy for the generations that follow them and sustain their memory.

We will not do justice to the full life cycle if we do not briefly touch upon the inevitable fact that most couples do not "die in bed together at 90 holding hands." The "We" ends in its corporeal form with the death of one member of the couple before the other. Yet its death in loving couples is only at this physical dimension. "We" made our first house a home; "We" raised our children together; "We" gave each other vital support in building careers and communities; "We" stood by each other as time slowly chipped away at our strength and health; and finally, it is the "We" that gives the surviving partner solace in the moment of supreme loss. If, over time, the process of caring for and loving a new partner begins to fill in the emptiness left by a longtime partner's death, this does not diminish the truth of what the former partnership had achieved. To borrow from another Shakespeare sonnet (#18) and alter its final word with good humored intent, we can indeed state what the remembered result of We-ness can be within the partner as well as those who have known and loved the couple, even in the face of death,

> So long as men can breathe, or eyes can see,
> So long lives this, and this gives life to "We."

The "this" in the poet's words is the sonnet he has created; the "this" in the lives of the couple is the We-Story that they have forged—a catalogue of remembered events that they have shared and endured together. *This* story lives on in the partner's heart and mind, even if another partnership emerges over time.

In closing, we offer several questions for elder couples. As in the ones that have gone before, they are intended to stimulate their creativity and deepen their appreciation for growth and change over time.

QUESTIONS FOR ELDERHOOD

What is some wisdom you have gained over the years, especially about being a couple?

What are the strengths of your relationship now?

In what areas of your relationship do you feel the greatest sense of accomplishment?

How might you approach being caretakers for each other?

What issues do you wish you could talk about together that you haven't been able to?

What would life be like without your partner?

What do you want your legacy as a couple to be?

References

Albom, M. (2002). *Tuesdays with Morrie: An old man, a young man, and life's greatest lesson.* Portland, OR: Broadway Books.

Bader, E., & Pearson, P. (1988). *In quest of the mythical mate.* New York, NY: Brunner/Mazel.

Baltes, P.B., Lindenberger, U., & Staudinger, U.M. (2006). *Life span theory in developmental psychology.* Hoboken, NJ: John Wiley & Sons.

Bateson, M. (1989). *Composing a life.* New York, NY: The Atlantic Monthly Press.

Bateson, M. (2010). *Composing a further life.* New York, NY: Knopf.

Bayley, J. (1999). *Elegy for Iris.* New York, NY: Picador Press.

Braverman, K. (1987). *Hurricane warnings.* Los Angeles, CA: Illuminati.

Bremer, K. (2014). *My accidental Jihad.* New York, NY: Algonquin Books.

Carstensen, L.L. (2009). *A long bright future: An action plan for a lifetime of happiness, health, and financial security.* New York, NY: Broadway Books.

Cobb, N., Larson, J., & Watson, W. (2003). Development of the attitudes about romance and mate selection scale. *Family Relations, 52*(3), 222–231.

DeMaria, R., & Harrar, S. (2007). *7 stages of marriage: Laughter, intimacy, and passion.* Pleasantville, NY: Readers Digest.

Erikson, E.H. (1950). *Childhood and society.* New York, NY: W.W. Norton & Co.

Erikson, E.H. (1968). *Identity: Youth and crisis.* Oxford, England: Norton & Co.

Greer, G. (1992). *The change.* New York, NY: Knopf.

Jung, C. (1980). *Collected works.* Princeton, NJ: Princeton University Press.

Kegan, R. (1982). *The evolving self: Problem and process in human development.* Cambridge, MA: Harvard University Press.

Merwin, W.S. (2013). *Collected poems of W. S. Merwin.* New York, NY: Library of America.

Oliver, M. (1998). *West wind: Poems and prose poems.* Boston, MA: Mariner Books.

Randall, W.L., & McKim, A.E. (2008). *Reading our lives: The poetics of growing old.* New York, NY: Oxford University Press.

Sadler, W. (2000). *The third age.* New York, NY: Perseus Books Group.

Scheinkman, M., & Fishbane, M.D. (2004). The vulnerability cycle: Working with impasses in couple therapy. *Family Process, 43*(3), 279–299.

Sharpe, S.A. (2000). *The ways we love: A developmental approach to treating couples.* New York, NY: Guilford Press.

Tamashiro, R. (1979). Adolescents' concepts of marriage: A structural-developmental analysis. *Journal of Youth and Adolescence, 8,* 443–452.

Tornstam, L. (1996). Caring for the elderly: Introducing the theory of gerotranscendence as a supplementary frame of reference for caring for the elderly. *Scandinavian Journal of Caring Sciences, 10*(3), 144–150.

Viorst, J. (1986). *Necessary losses: The loves, illusions, dependencies, and impossible expectations that all of us have to give up in order to grow.* New York, NY: Free Press.

Walsh, F. (2006). *Strengthening family resilience* (2nd ed.). New York, NY: Guilford Press.

Weinstein, A. (2011). *Morning, noon and night.* New York, NY: Random House.

7

LIVING AND TELLING THE "WE"

Giving Our Stories Away

> [There] is another tradition to politics, a tradition (of politics) that stretched from the days of the country's founding to the glory of the civil rights movement, a tradition based on the simple idea that we have a stake in one another, and that what binds us together is greater than what drives us apart, and that if enough people believe in the truth of that proposition and act on it, then we might not solve every problem, but we can get something meaningful done.
>
> —Obama (2006)

"Who Ate My Frigging Philly Cheesesteak?"

These were the fighting words that set Janet and Ray into a tailspin before they came to see me (JAS) for their Thursday night session. Janet was furious with Ray. They had been to lunch the day before, and she had put aside the rest of her meal and looked forward to it all during her brutal afternoon of work. Coming home starved and exhausted, she opened the fridge to find it gone and knew the pitiful answer to her rhetorical question—there was only one other mouth in their home and it belonged to Ray. She knew that she hadn't explicitly told him to save it for her, but even still . . .

It had been a long day for Ray as well, another one in which his boss played favorites and overlooked his efforts. Now his wife was screaming at him. He tried to tell Janet to calm down and that he would cook something up for her, but it was no use. Finally, he lost his temper and told her "to shut the hell up." Janet was boiling mad and still had not eaten; she thought that they might as well cancel their appointment with me. "What's the point?"

Luckily, she took a few breaths and told herself that she didn't want to give up totally and she also knew how disappointed I would be. Instead, she called a take-out place and ordered food to pick up after the session. Janet and Ray arrived late and were still in near open warfare with each

158

other. Both were close to despair about anything ever changing—about ever being able to work together.

I had seen Janet and Ray for a few months in couple therapy and grown to like them a great deal. They both had a good sense of humor; they were devoted to their jobs, and I could tell that they cared about and valued each other. However, they had little trust in the good will of their partner, and despite 7 years of being together, were still uncertain about the future of their relationship. They were unwilling to buy a house or have children, since either of these steps would represent a more permanent commitment and make them more vulnerable to each other. Despite their marriage contract, they were only a little bit in the "same boat" together and sometimes perhaps more out than in. They certainly had not developed a working sense of We-consciousness and seemed very far from knowing how to do this.

When we look a bit deeper at Janet's and Ray's history, we can see why this struggle over finding common ground was so pronounced for them. Janet is a second-generation Greek American; both her parents were born and raised in Greece before coming to the United States. Until they retired a few years ago, they ran a grocery and deli store in a small Connecticut city. Open 7 days a week, with coffee, hot buns, and newspapers on Sunday mornings, the store defined every aspect of Janet's family life. Her mom kept the books, did the ordering, and made the sandwiches. Her dad and older sister ran the registers, handled the Lotto tickets, and did all the maintenance. As the youngest, Janet helped out wherever she could, but also had strict marching orders to succeed in school.

She recalled her childhood as sitting at the table in the back of the store and doing her homework on her own. She had little time for friends, and her parents had little time to relate to her in any way that was not about school or the store. She never saw her parents express affection to each other, nor did they hug or kiss their children. Money worries and material aspirations preoccupied the mealtime conversations. Now with Janet an adult, they sometimes ask her why she is not more attentive or respectful to them. Such queries reinforce for Janet how little insight they have into their own behavior around generating emotional connections. She says that she wants to tell them that they taught her to be this way—to pursue her career ambitions, gauge her worth by money and possessions, and minimize the importance of relationships in her life. She bites her tongue, realizing that they would not immediately clue in to her sense of sorrow and neglect. With this profound disruption in attachment, Janet is a complicated mixture of super competitiveness and a powerful desire for connection.

Ray experienced more affection in his family, but military service and alcoholism across two generations disrupted family ties, leading to stoicism and angry frustration as dominant themes. Although not a heavy drinker, Ray's own participation in the War in Afghanistan perpetuated this dynamic and created a pivotal rift in his relationship with Janet.

Deployed twice in the first years of their relationship, Ray felt that Janet shut down; she both feared losing him and felt overwhelmed by how vulnerable his absence made her. Since his return, they have seemed to circle each other in repetitive conflicts, not allowing either partner to let their guard down and feel truly safe in the relationship.

We have introduced the reader to Janet and Ray not so much to discuss the subsequent work we did with them to build positive stories and a greater sense of We-ness. Our strategies with them were similar to the other couples we have discussed in this volume, and the work, although slow, generally moved in a direction toward greater mutuality and satisfaction in the relationship. Rather, we have talked about Janet and Ray as a way of moving into the topic of the larger world in which our couples often find themselves. Janet and Ray are strong examples, although sadly not even the most extreme, of the social disconnection that is rampant in our culture.

In 1968, Robert Kennedy said these words in a speech shortly before he was assassinated,

> For too long we seem to have surrendered personal excellence and community value in the mere accumulation of material things. Our gross national product now is over 800 billion dollars a year, but that gross national product, if we judge the United States of America by that, that gross national product counts air pollution, and cigarette advertising, and ambulances to clear our highways of carnage. It counts special locks for our doors and the jails for people who break them. It counts the destruction of the redwoods and the loss of our natural wonder in chaotic squall. It counts Napalm, and it counts nuclear warheads, and armored cars for the police to fight the riots in our city. It counts Whitman's rifle and Speck's knife and the television programs which glorify violence in order to sell toys to our children. Yet, the gross national product does not allow for the health of our children, the quality of their education, or the joy of their play; it does not include the beauty of our poetry, of the strength of our marriages, the intelligence of our public debate or the integrity of our public officials. It measures neither our wit nor our courage, neither our wisdom nor our learning, neither our compassion, nor our devotion to our country. It measures everything in short except that which makes life worthwhile. And it can tell us everything about America except why we are proud that we are Americans. (Kennedy, 1968)

In our view, teaching couples about the "We" has to be about more than their private psychological worlds or the small domestic arena of their home. Before readers jump to political conclusions, this is not about

160

championing a particular political agenda. Here is a quotation from Mitt Romney's Acceptance Speech at the 2012 Republican Convention.

> We look to our communities, our faiths, our families for our joy, our support, in good times and bad. It is both how we live our lives and why we live our lives. The strength and power and goodness of America has always been based on the strength and power and goodness of our communities, our families, our faiths. That is the bedrock of what makes America, America. In our best days, we can feel the vibrancy of America's communities, large and small. (Romney, 2012)

What these two representatives of different political parties and vastly different ideological viewpoints about government's role in our lives share in common is an understanding that a life worth living is a life that is lived for something larger than the self. To live only for oneself, and not for one's family or community or faith or country, is not enough. Of course, there is risk in giving oneself up to something that transcends the individual—there is always the possibility of losing autonomy, of sacrificing one's best interest, of no longer thinking for oneself. Yet as we have emphasized throughout this book, a true We-consciousness is always a relationship, not a surrender or total submission to the other. We both give and get back in connecting to a larger entity. In Judaism, there is the distinction between an "offering" and a "sacrifice"—the offering emphasizes what we gain by connection—what we *offer* makes a bridge to the other; what we *sacrifice* places the focus more on what we have given up—what we lose in propitiation rather than what we secure through affirmation.

Many social scientists and public intellectuals believe that the inability to find the "We" in our personal lives and in our larger community and political lives is one of the most serious problems in our society today. Robert Putnam, author of the celebrated book on the decline of community involvement, *Bowling Alone*, recently summed up the dilemma facing us in contemporary culture,

> The crumbling of the American dream is a purple problem, obscured by solely red or solely blue lenses. Its economic and cultural roots are entangled, a mixture of government, private sector, community and personal failings. But the deepest root is our radically shriveled sense of "we." (Putnam, 2013)

In contrast to this malaise, once couples are working actively toward the promotion of the "We" in their relationship, they tell us that they feel a greater sense of purpose in their daily lives. They point to the final "S" in SERAPHS—the **Shared Sense of Meaning and Vision**. This can often be

161

found in couples who embrace a spiritual faith, but this is by no means the only route to this greater meaning. Some couples find sufficient meaning in the building of a self-sustaining and joyful partnership—pride in an enduring and loving relationship is an end in and of itself.

Yet we would like to argue that the "We" and the couple's commitment does not live in a vacuum. It resonates to their immediate and extended family, as well as to friends and community. Here is a small example from our own lives. When one of our daughters (JAS's younger daughter, Chloe) turned 14, she began to increase her weekend sleepovers with friends. She might leave for school on Friday morning and beg for a sleepover that night and then try to roll it over into a second one on Saturday night, meaning we would not see her from Friday morning until Sunday. As you can imagine, we quickly enforced a policy of one sleepover per weekend. But even more, we realized that the Friday night *Shabbat* (Sabbath) dinners that Chloe had grown up with were now being compromised by the Friday night sleepover option.

Our solution was that Chloe might or might not have a sleepover on Friday night, but either way she had to be home for Shabbat dinner first. We stated that this dinner was a commitment to our family and our tradition. It was a way to catch our breath and regroup after a week of work and before a weekend of socializing and sports events took off full-blast. Not surprisingly, we met with great resistance, but holding firm to our vision of the "We," we did not back down. Then something unexpected happened, Chloe asked if one or two of her friends could come to dinner. We were delighted and shared the candle-lighting, prayers, and *challah* bread with them, not to mention the roast chicken and roasted potatoes. The next week one of the friends came back and a new one came as well. For the next four years until Chloe went off to college, we had Friday night dinners with her, her sister (until she left for college), and a steady crew of Chloe's buddies. Although no parent of a teenager is likely to know all (or even much) of what is going on in their volatile social worlds, these dinners helped us and Chloe to be more grounded with each other and to reinforce our family's We-ness on a weekly basis.

Couples have shared many similar stories with us over the years. They find that believing in something loving and positive in their lives has given them more patience at work and greater acceptance of coworkers who seem to be struggling or frustrated. The emphasis on finding blessings and moments of gratitude has slowed them down and often led them to a renewed appreciation of the natural world. In some cases they have traded in fast-track ambitions for a better quality of life and a renewed commitment to private pleasures—whether family time, hobby, sport, craft, or volunteering. They have come to see that the "We" is about self-care as well as care for others. Only by taking care of and giving to ourselves will we continue to have the strength and resilience to provide for others.

What then are concrete steps that couples can take to perpetuate We-ness and to allow it to expand beyond themselves? Clearly, **building "We-events"** into the structure of family life is one valuable step. These We-events can range from pizza and movie nights to family vacations to worshipping together to a shared community service activity in which all family members participate. One family we knew made sure to take one day during the winter vacation to volunteer at a soup kitchen together; another couple brings their children on a yearly service trip to the Dominican Republic. Some couples have reengaged in the political process and put their We-ness to work making phone calls for candidates and canvassing door-to-door.

On a more conceptual level, we have already alluded to the exercise of writing a relationship vision. Let us return to this and put this activity clearly in the context of connecting the "We" to a larger shared purpose. Once the couple is comfortable thinking in "We" terms and demonstrating this thought process in the various spheres of the relationship (e.g., domestic tasks, finances, time allocation, child-rearing, intimacy), then we can ask them to consider **What is your "We" for?** These answers are often inspiring and help to concretize the importance of the union they have built in their lives. Victor and Inez wrote the following response in response to this question:

> Now that we are working together, we see ourselves working toward making the last years of our parents' lives better. Before we saw our in-laws as our partner's "concern" and maybe in our worse moments, as the other person's "problem." Now we are committed to taking a different approach—how can we help each other and share in the relationship with our parents, especially as they need us more. As we ask more questions about each other's family histories—we are learning more about each other's *raíces*.

A third method of "giving the 'We' away" is sharing our We-Stories with others. In the next section of the chapter, we elaborate on this approach in much greater detail. It is at the heart of our conviction that the most powerful way to cultivate "We" is to find our positive stories and then to share them with each other and with others in our lives.

Not too long ago, I (KS) was leading a premarital workshop designed to provide couples with basic relationship education, an opportunity to interact with other couples at the same transition point and to learn how to flag areas of concern in their current relationship. During a break, a young woman approached me with the following astute observation and question:

> It seems to us that there are plenty of places to get help when you're just starting out and there's a whole wedding industry

163

dedicated to our every question. But I already feel like once we're married, we're gonna drop into a hole and we won't know we're in trouble till it's too late. I asked my mother about that and she just said: "Oh, you guys will figure it out." I wish she'd tell us how she and Dad got through the tough times. How did they stay positive, stay in love? How come no one ever seems to talk about that?

Surely her mother's comment was intended to provide support but it left her daughter hanging and reflects a broader issue worth addressing. The imagery surrounding marriage/permanent commitment are so negative (e.g., "ball and chain," bachelor/bachelorette parties symbolizing the "end to freedom," etc.), it is a wonder anyone signs on. The feeling she expressed is understandable; after the initial blast of negativity, there *is* a black hole. Young adults are frequently left to piece together the Couple Stories of their parents and grandparents, an incomplete and unsubstantiated process at best. It seems to be more common that when adult parents do share stories with offspring, they tend to be their individual stories ("I loved to visit Gramma's farm," "I did well in Math and Science but hated English"). What they seldom tell are the We-Stories—the how we got from "here to there" tales that are both revealing and connecting.

Contrast the negative symbols and black hole to a lovely ritual created by a therapist colleague of mine. Several years ago when her stepson became engaged, instead of hosting the traditional wedding shower, she invited her future daughter-in-law to a "Sprinkle." Surrounded by an intimate group of family members, she told stories of what the Jones family was like over the years—funny stories, sad stories, and everything in between. She shared her We-Story and encouraged others to share what they thought it might be like to marry into and become a part of the Jones family. Almost two years later, her now daughter-in-law still tears up when she describes the "Sprinkle."

We have said that if the We-Story is to move toward increasing complexity in its depiction of the couple's relational vision, it must increasingly reach out to and include others. This expansion requires two things. The first is to cultivate an awareness of the multitude of ways others' stories have influenced our own and being willing to tell those stories. Next, it requires an appreciation and belief that our story is worthy enough to tell—a valued subplot within the larger story of family, extended family, and the larger community. With that in place, it is easier to realize that there is always something we can say and do to effect a positive difference in how others live their lives (Randall & McKim, 2008).

We often recommend a variation on Gottman's (2011) famous "5 positives for every negative" rule. We suggest that every 5 days or so, parents share a brief We-Story about their relationship with their children. Details should be altered to be age-appropriate and to respect adult privacy. Some stories, felt to be particularly meaningful, can be retold over time and become part of the family story legacy. The following are some examples couples have identified and then shared with their children.

A couple's (in their mid-40s) story as told to their middle-school-aged children:

I know you guys can see how busy our family is, with everyone always going in different directions. Your dad and I started to pay attention to how that busyness was affecting us.

Yeah, Mom helped me understand that she gets crabby when we don't spend enough time together, we lose track of what we love about each other.

Yeah, so we talked about it together and decided that we're gonna take Max for a walk together alone every night before bed so we can catch up with each other's days and find out where we can help each other. We feel really good about this and in case you haven't noticed— we've been doing that for the past couple of weeks already!

Another couple in their mid-50s talking to their adult children:

You know the past few months or so your dad and I have been going through a real bad patch. We've been arguing a lot about Grandma, that I'm the one stuck with her care more than he is, that she really needs more help than we can give her.

It was getting pretty nasty with each of us blaming and criticizing the other. I knew we were feeling pretty bad about the way we were acting but we couldn't seem to get out of our rut.

I feel bad to say that Grandma overheard us bickering one day, started to cry, and offered to go into a home. That was a wake-up call.

We realized we were both letting stress get the better of us and were forgetting how much we love each other and love Grandma.

We worked out a system of who does what each week, but even better, we reached an agreement for how to tell each other when we need a break. Now we're back on track and are a team again. I think even Grandma can feel the difference.

Another couple in their late 50s talking to adult children:

Your stepdad and I have had some real problems trying to get our finances straight. We didn't know how to do it.

I wanted everything separate.

I thought that wasn't really fair to you guys.

We talked to financial planners and it seemed like everyone had different ideas.

We started saying things like, "I think my idea is better." When you start talking like that, you're in trouble. We want to take an "our idea" approach. Our conversations were getting to be more about me and less about us.

What the process sort of got us to do was talk through what we wanted to share and how—both with you guys and with Sam and Holly and their families.

We worked out a system that we feel reflects who we are, what's important to us, and our priorities that we want to pass on.

Yeah, we feel good about this. Want to hear about what we decided?

Finally, a couple in their late 60s, talking with their adult children:

Heaven only knows what things will be like for you guys when you get to this point . . . maybe no one will retire! But we went back and forth for the longest time. What should we do?

Yeah, we thought there was one answer.

Then we realized we'd spent 8 years looking for and talking about "the answer"—maybe this is the answer!

Yeah, make it up as we go along!

We thought about our health and how much cash we think we'll need and realized neither of us felt wedded to our jobs.

If one of us wants to retire next year, then work at Home Depot part-time, that's good. Or maybe we'll both do that.

We like keeping it loose; we like living according to what's important to us—time with each other and time with the grandkids.

We've always been such planners . . . this is so nice to have the grand design be no grand design—just a work in progress!

Each of these We-Stories contains similar elements: a description of a challenge faced, a shift in consciousness from the "I" to the "We," a positive outcome, and a description of the impact for the relationship, including how each felt about the process. The stories exemplify the importance of ongoing communication about more than who takes out the garbage. They relay the critical message that successful relationships are always ongoing dialogues. They impart the "how tos," not with the intent that their children should or even will do it the same way. Rather, they reflect the spirit of sharing and open a window for intergenerational connection. We can't help but think the workshop attendee would find any one of those stories more helpful than, "You guys will figure it out."

While working in therapy with adult children and their parents, I (KS) have often worked to have the generations share one another's stories to maximize the positive potentials. For example, 38-year-old Alex and 36-year-old Reva initiated couple therapy around an impasse that had been triggered by Reva's desire to move her web design business to another city. Alex wanted to support her ambitions but was afraid of the implications attached to the commuter lifestyle and assumed this would further delay their decision to have a child. Reva had grown disillusioned with the marriage and wanted the stimulation and challenge that a new city and new job would bring. Although hard-working, Alex admitted he didn't have the drive or ambition Reva did and frequently worried that she had grown bored with him. He hounded her with requests that she be satisfied with what she had, and not "always want something more." Reva resentfully recalled her parents having said the same thing to her when she was growing up, and she couldn't see the problem with wanting to "better yourself." Alex wanted her to "kick it back," and she wanted him to "rev it up." They titled their Couple Story: "Idling Engines." Midway through our work, Reva's parents came to town for a visit and she extended an invitation for them to join us.

An attractive, articulate couple in their early 70s, Helen and Ben easily engaged with others, expressed devotion to Reva, and displayed a genuine desire to see them work through this impasse.

Alex and Reva sat up and took notice when her parents spontaneously offered the story of their "separation and near divorce" when they were in their 50s, and Reva had just moved out. They too had been embroiled in an impasse—this one over Ben's opposition to Helen's desire to return to school for a teaching degree. They "fought and fought" until Helen moved out to live with her sister for a few months. Reva was stunned—saying that she'd not only never heard the story, but struggled to imagine her parents ever being apart. Helen responded that that was the turning point for them—being apart and realizing how much worse they felt, while appreciating how much they loved one another. Ben said: "Your mother and I realized we were both trying to have our way—be right. When you're trying to be right, you're not in a relationship, you're just trying to be right." They talked about learning how to put the marriage ahead of their "separate agendas" and encouraged Alex and Reva to try to do the same.

The family session proved to be pivotal in our work together. Having felt so validated, understood, and inspired by Helen and Ben and deeply touched by their willingness to share their story, Alex and Reva rededicated themselves to negotiating their own impasse. Over a period of months, they explored a variety of creative options, all under the fuel of their new Couple Story: "One Engine in Gear Together."

The empathetic compassion and deeper bonding experienced by the couples of both generations instilled a profound appreciation for the complex web of history and the nests of stories into which all had been born. Through sharing their respective stories, both of impasse and breakthrough, the couples had crafted a truly expanded and expansive "We." In linking their stories to a time before themselves, Alex and Reva were able to assimilate into their family history an unknown and untold story and then recraft their own story to take them more effectively into the future. A genuine "Back to the Future" tale.

Telling We-Stories to our family members is a powerful way to enrich our own We-Story and build bridges that foster true connections. Another frequently neglected audience for our stories are friends, neighbors, and our wider community. Mark and Jenn, the couple we met in Chapter 4, did this in a particularly active and significant way.

Several months after we had completed our work, I (KS) received a call from Jenn asking if they could come in for a "booster" session. They arrived looking tired, but intent on impressing me that they were doing well overall. Adam had had several medical setbacks, which frightened them both, but ironically was linked to the issue they wanted to "run past me." During one of their lengthier medical visits, they had struck up a conversation with another couple whose son was being seen by another physician in the practice. Mark commented on how unusual it was to see a couple attend a visit together, and he noticed the ways in which the other Dad gravitated to him. All four began an animated discussion focused on parenting a child with special needs. Mark and Jenn commented that they found themselves sharing their own story—not the "parent story that we usually tell but the one about us . . . how close we came to losing each other and just how hard it's been on our marriage." Mark added, "We even told them about the sunshine part and they seemed so grateful that we were willing to share." The foursome exchanged numbers, promising to stay in touch. On the car ride home, Mark and Jenn reflected on how energized the experience of sharing was—"like spreading our light around"—and they came up with the idea on which they wanted my input. The idea they wanted to explore in that session has now, two years later, evolved into the following: Once every other month, couples who are parenting children with CP meet over a light meal to share resources, lend support, and generally "spread sunshine to one another." The group organized two 5K run/walks to raise funds for the National Center for Birth Defects and is continuing to expand its outreach. Jenn put it well:

> Every time we meet with our group, Mark and I feel like this has been such a terrific way to nourish our "We"—it reminds us of our very first vision statement. We've taken all the pain we all face every day and transformed it into something positive and way bigger than ourselves. And we literally feel like when we make a difference for those other couples, we're all solar powered . . . our group motto now is "Share your light."

In addition to verbally sharing We-Stories, we can symbolically share them through the practice of ritual. To qualify as a ritual, a practice simply needs to have meaning to both partners. Rituals are all about communication and connection and are powerful ways to capture one another's attention. They are as unique and varied as each couple and can be a permanent fixture on the couple landscape or be tweaked, modified, and updated as stories change.

One young adult commented that she always knew her parents placed a priority on their relationship because every night while she was growing up, they shared a cup of tea together before bed to talk over the day and plan for the next. "They didn't have to say anything—that habit said it all." Family therapist Bill Doherty tells the great and comical story of a ritual created by a couple he knew. In an effort to change the all-too-common routine of a spouse coming home to an eager dog, welcoming children, and a spouse in a different part of the house, they came up with the ritual called "Top the Dog." Since their dog unfailingly greeted them with exuberance, unconditional love, and excitement, they decided to try out a human version on one another. Each time they reunited, they "shook, panted, yipped" in every crazy, funny way they could think of to top the dog in expressing their excitement upon seeing one another again.

Humor is often such a neglected life-giving part of ritual. Another couple, both self-proclaimed "intense, serious, hard-working professionals," realized that their relationship could benefit from a lighter touch. Titling their Couple Story, "Lighten Up," they instituted a "joke-a-day" ritual. Their first laugh was in response to how hard it was for both of them to come up with a joke. That evolved into leaving written jokes around the house—in the suitcase of the one who was traveling, tucked in a bathrobe pocket, in the cat litter bag, and so on. That led to compiling monthly logs of jokes and humorous anecdotes that they could pull from when either "needed a laugh." Rituals like this can be wonderful companions to We-Stories and regular reminders of the essence and purpose of the relationship.

Writing is certainly another vehicle to give our stories away and a powerful avenue to record couple wisdom for future generations. One couple wrote out favorite We-Stories as a gift to each child as they married. Another couple wrote out their We-Story from the time of the birth of each child and gifted that adult child with the story when they became a parent. Other couples pass on the stories as a part of compiling keepsake DVDs of their children at various points in their lives. Mark and Jenn, our solar-powered couple, wrote up the We-Story that inspired the formation of the sunshine group to pass along to their children. With social media now prominent in our everyday lives, there are multiple platforms for sharing couple's stories, touchstone metaphors, and acquired wisdom—blogs, websites, YouTube, Twitter, Vines—any of these media can be a means of communicating and giving stories away.

One other strategy that is increasingly endorsed by couple therapists is to create networks of couples that share a common commitment to We-ness and a more holistic view of society (Madigan, 2011; Sheras & Koch-Sheras, 2006). Sheras and Koch-Sheras in their "Couple Power" approach advocate that couples that are committed to a more We-oriented vision create "communities of peers" that embrace this common perspective and support and promote it among each other. This support can take the shape of group meetings, retreats, and shared vision statements. Narrative therapists, like Madigan, have long endorsed the bonding of individuals, families, and couples in "leagues" that advocate for and reinforce their triumphs over socially imposed problems, such as body image concerns, domestic violence, and addiction. This is certainly similar to the spontaneous group that Mark and Jenn generated. Each of these perspectives encourages couples to take the "We" a step further by making their connection to the "third entity in the room" a conduit to an even larger sense of interlocking relationships. Soon couples are able to see not just the Hibiscus beyond themselves, but the entire garden of growing partnerships that both ask for and give back nurturance. The marital house that they have built together becomes a neighborhood of homes—a block party that has bonded to support a community of couples.

In promoting We-consciousness in our couples with all of the strategies we have just described, we believe that we are bucking the trend in psychotherapy toward increasing atomistic and disease entity explanations of psychological distress. With an emphasis on genetic roots of disorders, psychopharmacological interventions, and manualized treatment, psychiatry and psychology have embraced a rather mechanistic and reductionist vision of what causes suffering and how to ameliorate it. Increasingly, practitioners locate disease in the brain, positioning it in the interior of the person, and characterizing etiology in terms of defective parts (see Greenberg, 2013, for a scathing critique of this tendency). If we subscribe to this vision of illness, then we are likely to prescribe technical solutions to fix and fine-tune the workings of the individual. We become auto mechanics for the soul and seek only to get the person back on the road again and do not ask about the direction they are heading or the destination they hope to achieve.

On the other hand, a positive couple therapy approach that emphasizes We-ness in each partner knitted together through story takes us immediately out of the individual and into a relational dynamic that involves interaction and communication with others. It looks for connection rather than dissection and seeks integrative narratives and metaphors rather than disease agents and single causes. Although we certainly acknowledge distress and toxic elements in relationships, our emphasis is on strengths rather than deficits and on possibilities rather than obstacles. Rather than label individuals with disorders, we ask about the stories of resilience—what might be a vision for the future that expresses hope rather than dysfunction?

The Jewish mystical writer, Abraham Heschel (2001, p. 266), emphasized that the relationship between God and human beings involved a mutual commitment. He described this relationship in the following way.

Box 7.1 Living and Giving the "We"

1. Creating We-events
2. Writing up a Vision of What the "We" Is For
3. Telling the We-Stories to Others
4. Creating Networks of "We"

God has instructed angels to lower ladders for human beings to climb to Heaven. The ladders can only go so low and human beings can only leap so high. So angels reach down and human beings reach up and the effort to close what seems an insurmountable gap is where faith, hope, and trust reside. We-Stories are similar tales of the efforts of two very human beings (rather than angels and humans) to find connection across the gap of individual concerns and societal pressures that characterize our contemporary lives. The stories of moments when the gap is bridged by love are vital communications to our children and our larger communities. They give us, and those around us, reassurance and hope for a better life and a better world in the present and the future.

References

Gottman, J.M. (2011). *The science of trust: Emotional attunement for couples.* New York, NY: W.W. Norton & Co.

Greenberg, G. (2013). *The book of woe.* New York, NY: Blue Rider Press.

Heschel, A.J. (2001). *Moral and spiritual audacity: Essays edited by Susannah Heschel.* New York, NY: Farrar, Straus, & Giroux.

Kennedy, R.F. (1968, March 18). *Remarks delivered at the University of Kansas.* Retrieved from www.jfklibrary.org/Research/Research-Aids/Ready-Reference/RFK-Speeches/Remarks-of-Robert-F-Kennedy-at-the-University-of-Kansas-March-18-1968.aspx

Madigan, S. (2011). *Narrative therapy.* Washington, DC: American Psychological Association.

Obama, B. (2006). *The audacity of hope: Reclaiming the American dream.* New York, NY: Crown.

Putnam, R.D. (2013, August 4). *An essay from "The Great Divide," a series on inequality.* Retrieved from www.nytimes.com/opinionator

Randall, W.L., & McKim, A.E. (2008). *Reading our lives: The poetics of growing old.* New York, NY: Oxford University Press.

Romney, M. (2012, August 30). *Acceptance Speech, Republican National Convention.* Retrieved from www.npr.org/2012/08/30/160357612/transcript-mitt-romneys-acceptance-speech

Sheras, P.L., & Koch-Sheras, P.R. (2006). *Couple power therapy: Building commitment, cooperation, communication, and community in relationships.* Washington, DC: American Psychological Association.

AUTHOR INDEX

SUBJECT INDEX

Please note: Page numbers in *italics* followed by a *b* indicate boxes and by an *f* indicate figures.